"A Portion of His Life"

William Blake's Miltonic Vision of Woman

EUGENIE R. FREED

Lewisburg: Bucknell University Press
London and Toronto: Associated University Presses

Associated University Presses
440 Forsgate Drive
Cranbury, NJ 08512

Associated University Presses
25 Sicilian Avenue
London WC1A 2QH, England

Associated University Presses
P.O. Box 338, Port Credit
Mississauga, Ontario
Canada L5G 4L8

The paper used in this publication meets the requirements of the American National Standard for Permanence of Paper for Printed Library Materials Z39.48-1984.

Library of Congress Cataloging-in-Publication Data

Freed, Eugenie R., 1935–
  "A portion of his life" : William Blake's Miltonic vision of woman / Eugenie R. Freed.
      p.   cm.
  Includes bibliographical references and index.
  ISBN 0-8387-5265-9 (alk. paper)
  1. Blake, William, 1757–1827—Characters—Women.   2. Women and literature—England—History—18th century.   3. Milton, John, 1608–1674—Characters—Women.   4. Influence (Literary, artistic, etc.)   5. Milton, John, 1608–1674—Influence.   6. Women in literature.   I. Title.
PR4148.W6F74   1994
821'.7—dc20   92-56604
                                                                        CIP

PRINTED IN THE UNITED STATES OF AMERICA

"A Portion of His Life"

To Ellie, the "onlie begetter."

Discord began, & yells & cries shook the wide firmament.
Beside his anvil stood Urthona dark . . .
. . . the sweat chill'd on his mighty limbs.
He drop'd his hammer: dividing from his aking bosom fled
A portion of his life; shrieking upon the wind she fled. . . .
—William Blake, *The Four Zoas:* Night the First, lines 516–24

Contents

Acknowledgments

Most of chapter 2, "Thel," originally appeared as part of an article entitled "'Sun-clad Chastity' and Blake's 'Maiden Queens': *Comus, Thel* and 'The Angel'" in *Blake/An Illustrated Quarterly* 25 (1991–92), and is reprinted by kind permission of the editors of that journal.

For permission to reproduce photographs, I thank my son David Amoils (Toronto) and the following institutions: the Auckland Public Library (Auckland, New Zealand), the British Library and British Museum (London), the Fitzwilliam Museum (Cambridge, England), the William Hayes Fogg Museum and Houghton Library of Harvard University (Cambridge, MA), the Huntington Library and Art Collections (San Marino, CA), the Library of Congress (Washington, DC), the Museum of Fine Arts, Boston (Boston, MA), Oxford University Press, the Pierpont Morgan Library (New York, NY), the Tate Gallery (London), the Whitworth Art Gallery (Manchester), and the Yale Center for British Art (New Haven, CT). An artist's rendering of a "gryphon," originally from Beryl Rowland's *Blind Beasts: Chaucer's Animal World,* is reproduced in Chapter 1 by permission of Kent State University Press (Kent, OH).

The University of the Witwatersrand, Johannesburg, supported my research by means of a period of study leave in 1990, and thereafter through grants. In particular I am grateful to Professor Anthony G. Woodward, Head of the Department of English until the end of 1992, for his personal interest and encouragement. My thanks are due as well to Professor Brian Cheadle, currently Head of the English Department, who over many years shared with me not only his extensive knowledge of Romantic poetry and art, but also research material in the form of hundreds of slides of Blake's work.

Research for the project was carried out in the British Library in London and the John P. Robarts Research Library of the University of Toronto. I thank these institutions and their staffs for their assistance and for the privilege of using their resources.

Drafts of individual chapters were read by Professors Joseph Anthony Wittreich (City University of New York) and Sheila A. Spector (Kennesaw State College, Marietta, GA). To both these scholars, my sincere gratitude for responding promptly, helpfully, and with generosity, in the best traditions of international scholarship, to an unknown petitioner from a distant land wanting to draw on their specialized expertize. The writings of Professor Wittreich have influenced my own thinking about the "severe contentions" of the "friendship" between Blake and Milton, while those of Professor Spector encouraged me to pursue the line of thought developed in Chapters 5 and 6 of this book. The whole manuscript was read by Ms. Joan Bellis, of the University of the Witwatersrand, for whose acute and informed critique I am most grateful.

My family has been my best and surest resource. In London my brother Neville Freed did everything possible to facilitate my acquisition of research material and photographs from British sources. My son Joel Amoils, who made himself responsible for the technical production of the manuscript in all its drafts, has been unstintingly helpful. My step-daughter Michèle Isserow took pains to track down hard-to-find books for me on esoteric topics. I am deeply grateful to each of them. Nevertheless, my greatest debt, for his loving and sensitive support and continuing involvement, must be expressed in the dedication of this book to my husband, Ellie Isserow.

A Note on the Illustrations

*I*N THE CITATION OF BLAKE'S ILLUMINATED books, the title page date is given as part of the title. (Thus, the title page date of both *Milton* and *Jerusalem* is given as 1804, even though the former was not printed until 1808 or later, and the latter was in progress until about 1820–21.) Where the order of the plates varies in different copies, or a significant detail peculiar to one version of the book is discussed in my text (as in *The Book of Urizen*), I have in the captions identified the copy from which the illustration is taken according to the Keynes-Wolf census of extant copies of Blake's books.

A Note on the Texts

BLAKE'S WRITINGS ARE CITED FROM WILLIAM, Blake, *Complete Writings,* ed. Geoffrey Keynes (London: Oxford University Press, 1972). Page numbers refer to this edition.

Where whole-page illustrations are referred to, the plates of all Blake's illuminated books are cited in the order adopted in *The Illuminated Blake,* annotated by David V. Erdman (London: Oxford University Press, 1975). An exception is the discussion of illustrations to Blake's *Milton* in Chapters 5 and 6, where I use the ordering and numbering of Copy B. See my note preceding the endnotes to Chapter 5.

The poetry of John Milton is cited from John Milton, *Poems,* ed. John Carey and Alistair Fowler (London: Longmans, Green, 1968), to which page numbers refer.

Quotations from Spenser's *The Faerie Queene* refer to Edmund Spenser, *The Faerie Queene,* ed. A. C. Hamilton (London: Longman Group, 1977), whose page numbers are cited.

Shakespeare's works are cited from William Shakespeare, *The Complete Works,* ed. Peter Alexander (London: Collins, 1951), to which page numbers refer.

"A Portion of His Life"

1
Blake's Miltonic Vision

Then Quid & Suction were left alone. Then said Quid, "I think that Homer is bombast, & Shakespeare is too wild, & Milton has no feelings: they might easily be outdone. . . ." "Hang Philosophy! [said Suction] I would not give a farthing for it! Do all by your feelings, and never think about it. . . ."

—William Blake[1]

BLAKE'S RELATIONSHIP WITH THE WORKS OF John Milton began at the beginning of his creative life. Something of its tenor lies hidden beneath exuberant dismissiveness in the private exchange between the young artist-philosophers Quid and Suction (William and Robert Blake) in this early fragment.[2] Blake did indeed, in his maturity, continue to react against Milton's "Philosophy" and its orthodox Christian assertion of the supremacy of rationality over "feelings"—the emotions of the heart, and, most significantly, the workings of the imagination. Nevertheless, the youthful impudence of Quid is ironically undercut by his probable indebtedness to Milton's *L'Allegro* for the tongue-in-cheek opinion that "Shakespeare is too wild."[3] Blake later confided to his friend John Flaxman that Milton, his first guide in the "Heavens" of creative inspiration, "lov'd me in childhood & shew'd me his face."[4] Blake's writings contain innumerable echoes of, quotations from, and references to Milton's poetry, and throughout his life he sketched and painted Miltonic subjects. The earliest extant treatments of scenes from *Paradise Lost* date from about 1780, when Blake was twenty-three. The figures of Satan and Death in Blake's series of illustra-

tions to *Paradise Lost* done in 1807 and 1808 were based partly on these early sketches.[5] The very *last* commission Blake is known to have executed, working in his sickbed in the last days of his life in August 1827, was the coloring of a print of the frontispiece of *Europe*—the emblem now known as "The Ancient of Days," partly inspired by *Paradise Lost,* book 7, lines 225–31.[6] Miltonic themes appear in the *Notebook* inherited from his brother Robert, which William Blake used from about 1790 onward for both poems and sketches.[7] Blake's design "The House of Death," inspired by *Paradise Lost,* book 11, lines 479–93, was published in about 1795. Between about 1801 and 1821 Blake undertook, as commissions for patrons, successive series of illustrations in pen and watercolor of Milton's *Comus, Paradise Lost, On the Morning of Christ's Nativity, L'Allegro* and *Il Pensoroso,* and *Paradise Regained.*[8] These paintings, vivid and powerful readings of Milton, represent the appropriation and the virtual reworking of Milton's poems.[9]

Like Spenser in relation to Chaucer, Blake seriously regarded himself as Milton's peer and natural poetic successor. Spenser's invocation of the spirit of Chaucer in book 4 of *The Faerie Queene*—

17

*William Blake, "Satan Approaching the Court of Chaos,"
ca. 1780. (By permission of the Yale Center for British
Art, Paul Mellon Collection.)*

. . . through infusion sweete
Of thine own spirit, which doth in me survive,
I follow here the footing of thy feete. . . .[10]

—may indeed have inspired the pivotal event in
Blake's epic *Milton:* the poet's reception of the "infusion" of Milton's spirit, which "on my left foot falling on the tarsus, enter'd there."[11]

Blake's commissioned Milton illustrations are affirmations of a long established and continuing debt, since Milton's poetry, and some of his prose writings

as well, had inspired Blake's work from the time he first began painting and composing poetry. "Blake's deepest roots," says J. A. Wittreich, Jr.,

> are in the epic tradition that by Spenser and Milton was tied to the tradition of prophecy. This is the tradition . . . continually invoked by Blake, that stands behind his poetry from *Poetical Sketches* to *Jerusalem* and that provides the best guide to understanding it.[12]

Arguing that Milton's works are "the most important

context for reading Blake," Wittreich adds, in a later and longer study:

> Milton was not only an heir to the biblical tradition but, from Blake's point of view, its best knower, its most distinguished purveyor. Indeed, what may strike us as two discrete traditions are, in Blake's mind, one tradition—a Milton tradition, which is also a tradition of revolution.[13]

My own readings of Milton and Blake as well as of Spenser persuade me to agree with this view.[14] I would, however, extend the conclusion of this distinguished Miltonist that Blake's is "a poetry of contexts with Milton's poems serving as a backdrop for his own."[15] As I see the relationship, Milton's poetry is not "backdrop" alone, but *also* provides much of the raw material of Blake's. Spenser offers the best analogy, in his "Chamber of Phantastes" in the tower of the Castle of Alma—an allegory of the brain in relation to the human body—in book 2 of *The Faerie Queene:*

> His chamber was dispainted all within
> > With sundry colours, in the which were writ
> > Infinite shapes of things dispersed thin;
> > Some such as in the world were neuer yit,
> > Ne can deuized be of mortall wit;
> > Some daily seene, and knowen by their names,
> > Such as in idle fantasies doe flit:
> > Infernall Hags, *Centaurs,* feendes, *Hippodames,*

Apes, Lions, Egles, Owles, fooles, louers, children, Dames.[16]

Here, images of the beings of this world, as well as "some such as in the world were neuer yit," are "dispersed thin," attenuated to their elemental components, and reassembled in different modes. For instance, elements of the eagle and lion go to form the "gryphon," which has an eagle's head and wings and a lion's body; this creature later attacks Alma's castle, in alliance with "fowle misshapen wights, of which some were / Headed like Owles, with beckes vncomely bent."[17] Such unnatural dissociations and recombinations are brought about by the "quicke preiudize . . . sharpe foresight, and working wit" of Phantastes, a figure resembling the Arthurian magician Merlin (another of Blake's embodiments of the human imagination), to whom Spenser gives the slightly sinister status of a magus or prophet.[18] Phantastes is an aspect of the imaginative force Blake called Los (later giving to the "regenerated" Los the name "Urthona"), and his powers are those attributed by Coleridge to the "secondary" imagination, which "dissolves, diffuses, dissipates, in order to recreate."[19] The Renaissance view of the imagination combined a reluctant acceptance of that faculty with a deep distrust of its powers, on moral grounds.[20] This reservation is evident in Spenser: for instance, late in book 2 of *The Faerie Queene* monsters of the

A "gryphon." Artist's design in a chapter-heading from Blind Beasts: Chaucer's Animal World, *by Beryl Rowland. (By permission of the Kent State University Press.)*

Helen Martins (1898–1976), untitled, figure with rooster's head and the body of a man, in cement with colored glass (after 1958). From the yard of the "Owl House" at Nieu Bethesda, eastern Cape Province, South Africa. (Photograph by David Amoils, Toronto.)

same "dispersed" kind as those seen in the Chamber of Phantastes hinder Sir Guyon in his mission to destroy the Bower of Bliss, and have to be driven off by the "vertuous staffe" of the holy Palmer.[21] Blake's conviction that the imagination offers true "Vision" and his identification of it with the "divine body of the Saviour" put his view on a totally different plane to those of either Spenser or Milton.[22] Indeed, to Blake, Spenser's was a "fundamental misconception of the imagination."[23]

Milton's poetry was more than a context to Blake: it provided the living stuff his imagination could work upon, "disperse," recombine and re-form in countless new ways. Blake rejected altogether the principle of moral parameters within which Milton *consciously* confined the operation of his imaginary forces. The unfettered poetic genius, operating—as Blake believed—"at liberty" when Milton wrote of "Devils & Hell," freed that great Christian poet from such strictures. Blake therefore read Milton, as he claims in *The Marriage of Heaven and Hell* to read the Bible, in the "infernal or diabolical sense."[24] Such breaking down and "re-formation" was an essential element in Blake's employment of Milton's poetry as source material. Blake set his own personage "Milton" to work at the "re-formation" of his own corpus of writing in just this sense in the epic *Milton*.

Blake's figure of Los was a smith, laboring at the forge and using the element of fire to smelt down his raw material and form it afresh into new shapes. Blake's inspiration for the concept of Los probably came in the first place from Milton's poetic account of Mulciber, who fell

> . . . from noon to dewy eve,
> A summer's day; *and with the setting sun*
> *Dropped from the zenith like a falling star* . . .[25]

The spirit of Milton in Blake's poem *Milton* is first seen by the poet "in the Zenith as a falling star / Descending . . ."[26] In a subsequent passage Los descends, as

> . . . a terrible flaming Sun, just close
> Behind my back. I turned in terror, and behold!
> Los stood in that fierce glowing fire . . .
> And I became One Man with him arising in my
> strength.[27]

Both Blakean evocations of the moment of inspiration emanate from the same passage of *Paradise Lost.*[28] The name "Los" is an anagram of "Sol," the sun.[29] Mulciber is an alternative Latin name for Vulcan (Hephaistos in the Greek tradition), the smith-god of Roman and Greek mythology, who is an important aspect of Blake's Los/Urthona.[30] Mulciber means

"the softener"—the name was chosen deliberately by Milton to emphasize the role of the pagan god as artist and artificer, subduing an intractable medium to the form of his vision. Milton refers to the "fabled" account of how Vulcan/Mulciber, flung from heaven by an angry Jupiter, landed on the shores of "Lemnos the Aegean isle"; the legend goes that he was crippled ever after by the impact of this fall. Urthona's fall in Blake's *The Four Zoas*—the "fabled" plunge from heaven that Milton describes—brings him down "upon the shores / With dislocated Limbs," so that he appears "limping from his fall" at the end of the work.[31] Milton makes Mulciber the fabricator of "many a towered structure high" in heaven before his fall (in *Paradise Lost* he is one of the rebel angels who fell with Satan), as well as appointing him architect of the magnificence of Pandaemonium.[32] The spellbinding depiction in *Paradise Lost* of the works of this *faber* undoubtedly influenced Blake when he chose for Los, the prophet and artist who was his own alter ego, the profession of the smith.[33]

Always a "maker," always creative (even when plagued in later years by the "Spectre" of self-doubt), Los/Blake wrought upon materials consisting, usually, of the work of other writers and artists, whose treatments of their subject matter inspired the major part of Blake's vast body of extant engravings and paintings. Blake illustrated books on an amazing diversity of topics—scientific and mathematical subjects, aesthetics, mythology, contemporary and ancient history. The literary works he illustrated included those of Virgil, Dante, Chaucer, Spenser, Shakespeare, and John Bunyan, as well as the writings of Milton and a number of eighteenth-century poets. Throughout his life Blake also painted and engraved scenes and texts from the Bible, which inspired some of his finest works.[34] He read with minute attention every work he illustrated. His designs are meticulously faithful to the texts, though always extending imaginatively beyond them. Frequently in the course of his commercial work Blake engraved from designs created by other artists—not only paintings and drawings, but also works in other media, such as ceramics and sculpture.[35] In Blake's poetic workshop, the raw material being wrought upon the anvil of the imagination was often—perhaps more often than not—derived from the poetry of Milton. It becomes increasingly obvious as one studies Blake's work that he knew Milton's poetry, as he did certain parts of the Bible, so thoroughly that the texts had in effect sunk verbatim into his subconscious mind, becoming a rich lode in the matrix of creativity, to be smelted and fused at the forge of Los.

In the 1790s Blake, assisted by his wife Catherine,

William Blake, Milton, 1804, plate 21 (Copy "B," RB 54041): "And Los behind me stood, a terrible flaming Sun. . . ." (By permission of The Huntington Library, San Marino, California.)

worked as a printer and engraver in his own print-shop in Lambeth in South London. Part of his industry during this incredibly productive period was devoted to the composition, illumination, etching, and printing of a series of works (known as "the Lambeth books") in which he outlined his own version of the Fall of Man. The relationship of Blake's myth to the accounts given in the biblical *Genesis* and Milton's *Paradise Lost* is complicated and indirect, but undeniable. *The Marriage of Heaven and Hell,* composed and engraved in Lambeth between 1790 and 1793, concludes with a "Memorable Fancy" at the end of which an Angel, consumed in a flame of fire, arises as the prophet Elijah. Blake then adds:

> Note: This Angel, who is now become a Devil, is my particular friend; we often read the Bible together in its infernal or diabolical sense, which the world shall have if they behave well.
> I have also The Bible of Hell, which the world shall have whether they will or no.[36]

The First Book of Urizen is the "Genesis" of Blake's "Bible of Hell."[37] It describes in words and pictorial images the rebellion of Urizen, the figure who came to represent man's Reason (as Los the Imagination) in Blake's largest and most consistent mythic structure.[38] An immediate and highly significant consequence of Urizen's insurrection in Blake's "Genesis" is the emergence as a separate being of Blake's primary female figure, the "first woman," Enitharmon, in a parallel to the creation of both the biblical and the Miltonic Eve.

Milton's account of the creation of Eve in book 8 of *Paradise Lost* was illustrated by Blake in three versions, closely similar to one another.[39] All three show Eve as a slender and delicate figure, floating upright above the body of Adam, with her hands held between her breasts in an attitude of prayer, and a crescent moon in the sky over her head. The moon symbolizes "Beulah's moony shades," where Blake places "the weak & weary / Like Women & Children. . . ."[40] Blake had in mind as well Jakob Boehme's partly alchemical explanation of the function of Luna, the moon:

> Luna takes all into her body, for she is mother, and receives the seed of all the planets into her menstruum, and hatches it; Jupiter gives power therinto, and Sol is king therein. . . .
> [Luna] is as a wife of all the other forms [of nature]; for the other forms do all cast their desire through Sol into Luna; for in Sol they are spiritual, and in Luna corporeal: Therefore the moon assumes to it the sunshine, and shines from the sun. . . .[41]

Blake's working out of the relationship of Los/Sol and Enitharmon suggests Boehme's presentation of the relationship of Sol and Luna.[42] Blake's placement of the Creator, Adam, and Eve in his versions of the "Creation of Eve" in the *Paradise Lost* series also suggests Boehme's Jupiter-Sol-Luna triad in the first of these passages from *The Signature of All Things*.[43] All three of Blake's versions of the newly created Eve possess the serene and joyous radiance evoked by Milton's lines describing the effect of this vision upon the dreaming Adam:

> . . . so lovely fair
> That what seemed fair in all the world, seemed now
> Mean, or in her summed up, in her contained . . .[44]

In Milton's version, the Creator caused a sleep to fall upon Adam as he prepared to create Eve, but in a kind of dream Adam saw, through the "internal sight" of "the cell / Of fancy" in his mind (Spenser's "Chamber of Phantastes"), how Eve came into being:

> Mine eyes he closed, but open left the cell
> Of fancy my internal sight, by which
> *Abstract as in a trance* methought I saw . . .
> . . . the shape
> Still glorious before whom awake I stood,
> Who stooping opened my left side, and took
> From thence a rib, with cordial spirits warm,
> And life-blood streaming fresh . . .
> The rib he formed and fashioned with his hands;
> Under his forming hands a creature grew,
> Man-like, but different sex. . . .[45]

The event was observed only by the open "eye" of Adam's imagination, since he was asleep. The summing up, in Eve's person, of the beauty of the world in its primal state that Adam observes and records is reflected and confirmed in Satan's response to Eve's loveliness, when he comes upon her alone:

> . . . her heavenly form
> Angelic, but more soft and feminine,
> Her graceful innocence, her every air
> Of gesture or least action overawed
> His malice, and with rapine sweet bereaved
> His fierceness of the fierce intent it brought:
> *That space the evil one abstracted stood*
> *From his own evil,* and for the time remained
> Stupidly good, of enmity disarmed,
> Of guile, of hate, of envy, of revenge. . . .[46]

For a brief moment—"that space"—Satan's experience here parallels Adam's at the moment of the creation of Eve. In each situation, the observer is momentarily separated—"abstracted"—from his conscious self. "Abstract as in a trance," Adam had observed the fashioning of Eve's beauty from his own flesh by the divine Creator with the "internal

William Blake, "The Creation of Eve." From the Butts series of illustrations to Milton's Paradise Lost *(1808). (Gift by Subscription. Courtesy of the Museum of Fine Arts, Boston.)*

sight" of his "fancy" while his body lay asleep. Through his imagination he had foreseen that which the Divine presence had promised him he would have, "your wish exactly to your heart's desire."[47] The God-given pledge had ensured that the imagined "heart's desire" would become the reality when Adam awoke; but, in a certain sense, Adam's imagination—and his desire—had *participated* in the creation of Eve from his own substance. Satan, cast out from Heaven as the declared enemy of God, having by subterfuge broken out of his prison in Hell and by deception found his way into Paradise, spies like a malevolent voyeur upon the glory of woman in her primal perfection. Through the arousal of his desire for Eve, Milton implies, Satan is involuntarily transported by *his* imagination into a region of fanciful wish fulfillment—in his case, a vain "Paradise of Fools"—in which he, like Adam, may not only enjoy the "terrestrial heaven" in the possession of which he so envies Man, but may even, beyond that, in his utmost fantasy enjoy Eve, Adam's very own private Paradise within Paradise.[48] For just a moment, *through the workings of the imagination,* the beauty of Eve actually overcomes the evil intentions of Satan, annuls the warring of the forces of good against evil, virtue against vice, Heaven against Hell, that forms the central conflict in the drama of Milton's epic. At that instant, unthinkingly, Satan lets fall his weapons of malice and becomes "stupidly good, of enmity disarmed": the war of Satan against God is totally, albeit momentarily, suspended.

As *The Book of Urizen* opens, Urizen has torn himself apart from "the Eternals," the collective name Blake gives to the totality of Man's mental faculties in his immortal unfallen condition of humanity.[49] In Satanic hubris and a desire for dominion over his fellow "Eternals," Urizen has hidden himself in an "abominable void."[50] Blake describes this in images conflated from Milton's descriptions of the fiery wastes of Hell in books 1 and 2 of *Paradise Lost,* of the abyss of Chaos in books 2 and 7, and of the creation of the earth in book 7. An instance is this passage from Urizen's own account of his action:

> First I fought with fire, consum'd
> Inwards into a deep world within:
> A void immense, wild, dark and deep,
> Where nothing was: Nature's wide womb;
> And self balanc'd, stretch'd o'er the void. . . .[51]

This passage draws on Milton's "fiery deluge, fed / With ever-burning sulphur unconsum'd . . .," part of the description of Hell.[52] It glances at two views of the gulf of Chaos: the "vast immeasurable abyss /

Outrageous as a sea, dark, wasteful, wild . . ." and "this wild abyss, / The womb of nature . . ."[53] The first of these shows Chaos as it appears to God the Son as he comes to tame its wild disorder and create the universe; the second is the view of Satan, helpless at the mercy of its raging forces. Another element is the line "earth self balanced on her centre hung," which occurs in the account given by the archangel Raphael of the Creation.[54] Blake's lines are not merely echoes or quotations of Milton's; they are phrases and images "dispersed" (in Spenser's sense) and creatively re-formed. Their re-disposition sets Urizen's speech at variance with the Miltonic contexts there evoked, displaying the "unorganiz'd" Urizen as simultaneously a destructive Satanic rebel and, from his own confused perspective, a Creator.[55] By this paradoxical conflation, Blake collapses Milton's universe into one of his own, which he has fabricated by the fusion of apparently conflicting Miltonic elements. Blake's cosmos/chaos lies, as it were, in a plane created by the forceful *approximation* of the powers vertically polarized by Milton, of good and evil, respectively imposing order and perpetuating disorder. The reorganization suggests a serious application of the solution playfully postulated by Marvell for the eternally frustrated lovers, poles apart, who can meet only if by some cataclysm the globe of the world is punningly "cramp'd" (both "crowded" and "firmly attached by a clamp") "into a Planisphere."[56] This same remarkable effect, the creation of a new horizontal plane by the collapsing of polarities, is achieved especially in Blake's account of the emergence of Enitharmon. In a significant measure it is inspired by the poet's complex assimilation of that moment of ambivalence experienced by Milton's Satan when, overcome by his involuntary response to the beauty of woman, his desire is awakened and his imagination stimulated, as Adam's had been, to the fulfillment of his "wish exactly to [his] heart's desire"—and, at that moment, he ceases to be evil.

Los, the "Eternal Prophet," has contained as best possible the "wrenching apart" of the realm of the Eternals brought about by Urizen's separation from them, in his bid to compel them to submit to the tyrannical rule of Reason.[57] Los has turned to his furnace and anvil:

> The Eternal Prophet heav'd the dark bellows,
> And turn'd restless the tongs, and the hammer
> Incessant beat, forging chains new & new,
> Numb'ring with links hours, days and years.[58]

In desperate defiance of the threat of "formless, unmeasurable death" posed by Urizen's "activity un-

known and horrible," Los has created the iron chains of Time with which he has bound the "hurtling bones" of the rebel to form a mortal body of bone and flesh, severely restricting its senses.[59] In *The Four Zoas* Blake expands this very scene:

> Pale terror siezed the Eyes of Los as he beat round
> The hurtling demon; terrified at the shapes
> Enslav'd humanity put on, he became what he
>   beheld:
> He became what he was doing: he was himself
>   transform'd.[60]

Appalled at what he has done to a part of his own being, Los "suffer'd his fires to decay" and wept as he beheld Urizen, "deadly black / In his chains bound."[61] In an agony of compassion, Los "became

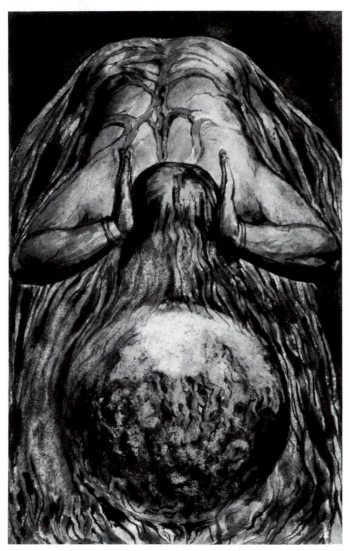

William Blake, The Book of Urizen, *1794, plate 17 (Copy "G"): Los exudes "the globe of life blood trembling." (The Lessing J. Rosenwald Collection of the Library of Congress, Washington, D.C.)*

what he beheld": and what he beheld was a divided soul. Thus, Blake says, "Pity began, / In anguish dividing & dividing, / For pity divides the soul. . . ."[62] The division inspired by Pity "left a round globe of blood / Trembling upon the Void."[63] A full-page illustration near or facing this point in Blake's text shows the figure of Los bending forward, hands pressed in anguish to either side of his head, as a great red "globe of life blood," draining from the whole of his body, emerges from the forepart of the head, blood pouring in fiery rivulets about it.[64] The emergence from this part of the head of the "globe of life blood," which is to become Enitharmon, reinforces the point Blake makes here, that this "female form" emanates from the Imagination. Spenser, following traditional teachings concerning the disposition of the higher faculties of the mind within the brain, places the chamber of Phantastes "in the forepart" of the tower of Alma's castle, which represents the brain.[65] In Blake's design "The House of Death" (1795) the head and crouching body of Adam can be seen in the lower right of two versions of the print.[66] His head is held between his hands in the same posture as Los in *Urizen,* plate 17, as he visualizes the horror of mankind in its decay, in the "Lazar-House" described in *Paradise Lost,* book 11, which is the principal subject of the design.[67] Since he is deliberately covering his eyes, Adam can "see" this tableau only with the "open . . . cell / Of fancy [his] internal sight"; his imagination "creates" as it "perceives" the scene described by the archangel Michael (who is giving Adam a preview of the collective lifespan of the human race in the fallen world).[68] Adam too is to become what he beholds.

From the "globe of life blood," "in tears and cries imbodied" there emanates "a female form, trembling and pale":

> 9. All Eternity shudder'd at sight
> Of the first female now separate,
> Pale as a cloud of snow
> Waving before the face of Los.
>
> 10. Wonder, awe, fear, astonishment
> Petrify the eternal myriads
> At the first female form now separate.
> They call'd her Pity, and fled.[69]

The upper third of the plate bearing the final line of the passage just quoted is devoted to Blake's earliest visual evocation of the creation of Woman.[70] Los, his body seen in profile at the viewer's right, kneels doubled up in agony, hands clasping his bent head. Enitharmon, standing in front of him at the viewer's left, sways her body away from him, leaning over to

William Blake, "The House of Death," 1795. (By permission of the Tate Gallery, London.)

the left. Her left arm is raised to cover her body and curve around her face, which—like the posture of her body—expresses distress and pain. She stands at the root of a tongue of flame, billowing to the left of the picture; the figure of Los is set against a background of dark cloud or smoke. Erdman points out that the form of Enitharmon actually arises from the word "Pity" in the first line of text on this plate, "They call'd her Pity, and fled."[71] Like Adam in "The House of Death," Los is wrenched by his compassion; indeed, he is depicted as being physically torn apart by it. The pity of Los—his fellow feeling—for the deterioration of Urizen, who was rent from his own being, gives rise, in every sense, to the further extended division of his wholeness that brings about the separate existence of this female form. Blake suggests in *Urizen,* as he does in "The House of Death,"

that the imagination "creates" as it "perceives" the separate form of the female. The imaginatively projected sympathy that Los, who is the human imagination itself, felt for the fallen and timebound Urizen, "abstracted, / Brooding, secret . . . Rifted with direful changes," overwhelmed him and reduced him to the same condition as Urizen. "Abstracted . . . rifted," divided—"for pity divides the soul"—he brings forth in a "globe of life-blood" his "Emanation," Enitharmon, the "first female form now separate."[72]

The ambience of the scene in which Enitharmon first appears is exactly opposite to the universal rejoicing in nature with which the creation of Eve and her union in marriage with Adam are celebrated in *Paradise Lost.*[73] In setting this scene in an aura of woe, Blake may well have had in mind—at Milton's sug-

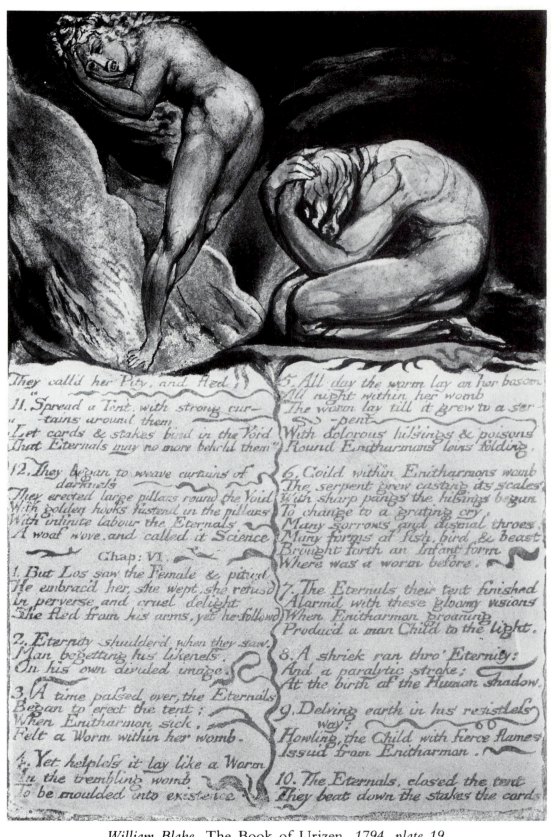

They call'd her Pity, and fled.

11. Spread a Tent, with strong cur-
       tains around them
Let cords & stakes bind in the Void
That Eternals may no more behold them

12. They began to weave curtains of
              darkness
They erected large pillars round the Void
With golden hooks fasten'd in the pillars
With infinite labour the Eternals
A woof wove, and called it Science

          Chap: VI.

1. But Los saw the Female & pitied
He embrac'd her, she wept, she refus'd
In perverse and cruel delight
She fled from his arms, yet he follow'd

2. Eternity shudder'd when they saw,
Man begetting his likeness,
On his own divided image.

3. A time pass'd over, the Eternals
Began to erect the tent;
When Enitharmon sick,
Felt a Worm within her womb.

4. Yet helpless it lay like a Worm
In the trembling womb
To be moulded into existence

5. All day the worm lay on her bosom
All night within her womb
The worm lay till it grew to a ser
-pent
With dolorous hissings & poisons
Round Enitharmons loins folding

6. Coild within Enitharmons womb
The serpent grew casting its scales
With sharp pangs the hissings began
To change to a grating cry,
Many sorrows and dismal throes,
Many forms of fish, bird & beast,
Brought forth an Infant form
Where was a worm before.

7. The Eternals their tent finished
Alarm'd with these gloomy visions
When Enitharmon groaning
Produc'd a man Child to the light.

8. A shriek ran thro' Eternity:
And a paralytic stroke;
At the birth of the Human shadow.

9. Delving earth in his resistless
              way;
Howling, the Child with fierce flames
Issu'd from Enitharmon.

10. The Eternals, closed the tent
They beat down the stakes the cords

William Blake, The Book of Urizen, *1794, plate 19
(Copy "G"): "the first female now separate. . . ." (The
Lessing J. Rosenwald Collection of the Library of Con-
gress, Washington, D.C.)*

gestion—Hesiod's story of Pandora, molded from clay by Hephaistos (the Roman Vulcan, Blake's model for Los) at the command of Zeus, who used her to set free upon mankind all the troubles of man's earthly existence, in revenge for Prometheus's theft of fire from Heaven.[74] When Eve is guided by an angel to Adam, Milton compares her to Pandora, who

> . . . ensnared
> Mankind with her fair looks, to be avenged
> On him who had stole Jove's authentic fire.[75]

Blake's Enitharmon is born "in pangs" and is "in tears and cries imbodied." She is "trembling and pale . . . pale as a cloud of snow"—a description that links her to Milton's personification of fallen nature, "hid-[ing] her guilty front with innocent snow," in the *Hymn on the Nativity of Christ*.[76] At the sight of her, "all Eternity shudder'd."[77] The "shuddering" response is repeated when Los forcibly overpowers and rapes Enitharmon, begetting their son Orc.[78] The distress of the "Eternals" corresponds to the "pangs" and tears of Earth and Nature in *Paradise Lost* at the eating of the forbidden fruit, first by Eve and then by Adam.[79]

For Enitharmon's emergence Blake draws on Milton's depiction of the birth of Sin from the head of Satan. Sin herself in *Paradise Lost* reminds Satan how, as he conspired with his followers against God,

> All on a sudden miserable pain
> Surprised thee, dim thine eyes, and dizzy swum
> In darkness, while thy head flames thick and fast
> Threw forth, till on the left side opening wide . . .
> Out of thy head I sprung: amazement seized
> All the host of heaven; back they recoiled afraid
> At first and called me Sin. . . .[80]

Blake's pictorial representation on page 19 of *The First Book of Urizen* was clearly inspired by this passage. The subsequent account of the union of Los and Enitharmon continues:

> *Chap: VI*
> 1. But Los saw the Female & pitied;
> He embrac'd her; she wept and refus'd;
> In perverse and cruel delight
> She fled from his arms, yet he follow'd.
>
> 2. Eternity shudder'd when they saw
> Man begetting his likeness
> On his own divided image.[81]

Blake's narrative conflates Milton's account of the incestuous unions of Sin, first with Satan, her father and "author," and then with her own monstrous off-spring Death. The impulse of Los to embrace his own "Emanation," Enitharmon, arises from that same treacherous "Pity," the imaginative sympathy that divided the soul of Los when he witnessed the torments of Urizen in bondage. Enitharmon's response is to reject him and flee "in perverse and cruel delight." Los's pursuit of Enitharmon then has a shadowy Miltonic parallel in Death's "perverse and cruel" pursuit of his mother Sin, with the difference that Blake attributes the perversity to the female. Milton's Sin recounts how

> . . . he, my inbred enemy
> Forth issued, brandishing his fatal dart
> Made to destroy: I fled, and cried out Death . . .
> I fled, but he pursued . . . .
> And in embraces forcible and foul
> Ingendering with me, of that rape begot
> These yelling monsters that with ceaseless cry
> Surround me . . .[82]

The fleeing of the "Eternals" at the sight of Enitharmon, and of Enitharmon from her "author" and progenitor Los, reenact the recoil of Milton's "host of heaven" and the flight of Sin from Death; but Milton's Eve was also briefly reluctant to espouse Adam, whom she too called her "author."[83] The outcome in Blake's myth is the conception and birth of Orc, son of Los and Enitharmon. Orc's birth resembles the unnatural nativity of Death, Satan's son, in *Paradise Lost*, through which the body of his mother Sin is contorted below the waist into "many a scaly fold / Voluminous and vast, a serpent armed / With mortal sting. . . ."[84] Sin describes how, when she gave birth, her

> . . . odious offspring, breaking violent way
> Tore through my entrails, that with fear and pain
> Distorted, all my nether shape thus grew
> Transform'd. . . .[85]

The child in Enitharmon's womb is a "worm," which

> . . . lay till it grew to a serpent,
> With dolorous hissings & poisons
> Round Enitharmon's loins folding.[86]

Shedding its scales, the worm assumes the form of an infant, and is finally born in the same baptism of fire as that in which Sin came forth from the head of Satan, and Enitharmon (in *Urizen*, plate 19) from the head of Los:

> Howling, the Child with fierce flames
> Issu'd from Enitharmon.[87]

Once again, Blake's manipulation of Miltonic ma-

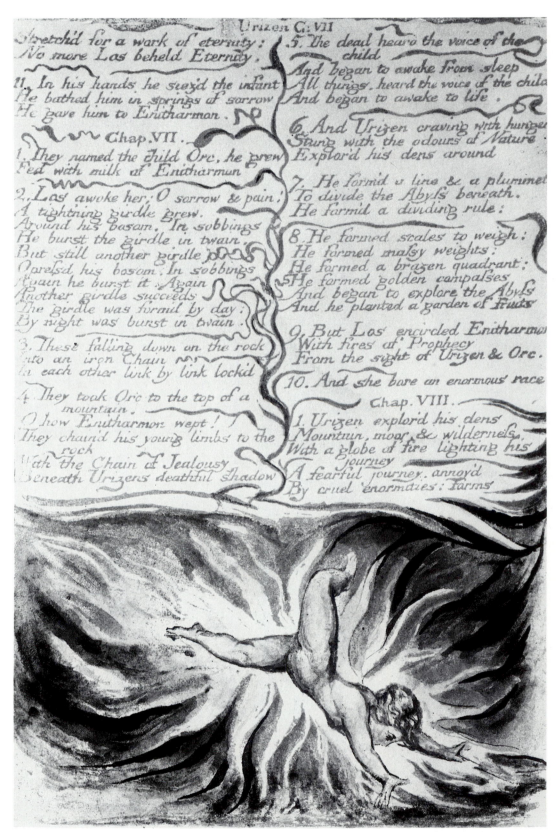

Stretch'd for a work of eternity:
No more Los beheld Eternity.

21. In his hands he seiz'd the infant
He bathed him in springs of sorrow
He gave him to Enitharmon.

Chap. VII.

1. They named the child Orc, he grew
Fed with milk of Enitharmon

2. Los awoke her; O sorrow & pain!
A tight'ning girdle grew.
Around his bosom. In sobbings
He burst the girdle in twain.
But still another girdle
Oppress'd his bosom. In sobbings
Again he burst it. Again
Another girdle succeeds
The girdle was form'd by day:
By night was burst in twain.

3. These falling down on the rock
Into an iron Chain
In each other link by link lock'd

4. They took Orc to the top of a
mountain.
O how Enitharmon wept!
They chain'd his young limbs to the
rock
With the Chain of Jealousy
Beneath Urizens deathful shadow

5. The dead heard the voice of the
child
And began to awake from sleep
All things, heard the voice of the child
And began to awake to life.

6. And Urizen craving with hunger
Stung with the odours of Nature
Explor'd his dens around

7. He formd a line & a plummet
To divide the Abyss beneath.
He formd a dividing rule:

8. He formed scales to weigh:
He formed massy weights:
He formed a brazen quadrant:
He formed golden compasses
And began to explore the Abyss
And he planted a garden of Fruits

9. But Los encircled Enitharmon
With fires of Prophecy
From the sight of Urizen & Orc.

10. And she bore an enormous race

Chap. VIII.

1. Urizen explord his dens
Mountain, moor, & wilderness,
With a globe of fire lighting his
journey
A fearful journey, annoy'd
By cruel enormities: Forms

William Blake, The Book of Urizen, 1795, plate 20
(Copy "G"): "Howling, the Child with fierce flames /
Issu'd from Enitharmon." (The Lessing J. Rosenwald
Collection of the Library of Congress, Washington, D.C.)

terial has paradoxically superimposed an act of anti-creation upon one of procreation. Los is not Satan, but by continuous suggestion and association the emergence of Enitharmon from his head is bound to recall to the reader familiar with Milton the unnatural birth of Sin from Satan's head—or of Athena from the head of Zeus, when Hephaistos/Vulcan smote the forehead of Zeus with his hammer.[88] Neither is Los Adam, but the reader (continually encouraged by Blake's pictorial "illuminations") perceives him as fully human, and almost unthinkingly relates the "female form now separate" to Eve, who is Adam's flesh. Enitharmon is neither Sin nor Eve, nor is she Nature: though Milton himself makes Adam briefly suggest a parallel with Sin that *includes* Nature when he declares to Eve

> . . . if death
> Consort with thee, death is to me as life;
> So forcible within my heart I feel
> The bond of nature draw me to my own,
> My own in thee. . . .[89]

Nor, for that matter, is Enitharmon Athena, goddess of Wisdom—although both the pagan Athena and the Christian Gnostic "emanation" Sophia, "Divine Wisdom," partly inspired Blake's creation of her.[90] Blake's lifelong insistence that "the Poetic Genius . . . is the Lord" and that the Imagination, from which Enitharmon "emanated," is "the Divine Body in Every Man" reinforce the analogy with Sophia, but the paradox remains.[91] Like Eve, Sin, and also Sophia, Enitharmon is an essential part of her "author" and must unite with him in order that *he* may be wholly functional. Milton on the one hand dwells upon Adam's relation to Eve (who is "[his] likeness, [his] fit help, [his] other self"), and on the other implies Satan's need of the monstrous hermaphroditic Sin/Death—"for Death from Sin no power can separate"—in the execution of his mission:

> . . . Sin and Death amain
> Following his track, such was the will of heaven
> Paved after him a broad and beaten way
> Over the dark abyss. . . .[92]

In his pictorial interpretations of the scenes from *Paradise Lost* Blake displays a coupled Sin and Death hovering like a hungry vulture over Adam, Eve, and Christ in "So Judged he Man"; and he shows Sin and Death flung down, lifeless but still coupled, around the foot of the Cross in his three versions of "Michael Foretelling the Crucifixion." At the same time, in the latter paintings, Eve is seen lying asleep, naked, before the Cross in a presentation that relates her to the figure of fallen nature, veiled by snow, in Blake's *Nativity Hymn* illustrations. Bette Charlotte Werner perceptively identifies the unveiled figure beneath the cross as "Nature redeemed by Christ's sacrifice."[93] Eve's position there also echoes that of the sleeping Adam in "The Creation of Eve" in the *Paradise Lost* series. Eve in the "Michael Foretelling . . ." plate bears the same relationship to the body of the crucified Jesus, Son of Man, as did *her* figure to the supine body of Adam from which it arose in the "Creation."[94] Thus Blake signals the interdependence, in the wholeness of the "Divine Humanity," of the male and the "female form."

Enitharmon's union with Los evokes the same horror as that of Sin with Death—unlike the marriage rites of Adam and Eve, it is not the cause of rejoicing. But the child Orc—whose name, derived from a Latin word for "hell," is that of an infernal deity supposed to punish perjury—though suggesting in his origins and birth the monstrosity of Satan's offspring Death, becomes a force that consumes and destroys in order to recreate.[95] The role of Orc in Blake's myth as it develops after *The First Book of Urizen* is that of the fiery spirit of political revolution, seen in idealization as consuming the old order so as to renew the vitality of a human society.[96]

Once again, in depicting the "birth" of Enitharmon, Blake is collapsing together the Miltonic poles of evil and good, Hell and Heaven, in composing his "Bible of Hell." The result of this process is that Blake's myth operates in the psychological planes of the emotional and the imaginative, in which acts and events are *neither* good nor evil. There is no divisive morality, there are only "feelings." "Hang Philosophy! . . . Do all by your feelings, and never think about it . . . !" Blake certainly gave intense and searching thought to whatever he did as an artist, but Suction was, in a sense, putting his callow finger on a crucial point: "feelings" are neither right nor wrong. Blake's understanding of his own creative powers convinced him that the creative imagination operates in a realm apart from the polarized moral "Philosophy" artificially imposed by the Reason. Hence his conviction that because Milton was "a true Poet," he was "of the Devil's party without knowing it."[97] Hence too Blake's attempt in his own epic *Milton* to redeem this great poet from the destructive consequences of his error in perpetuating this polarization—which involves the acknowledgment of Blake's personage Milton that the "female portion" is an essential part of his spiritual being.

Drawing on his original, continuously con-

William Blake, "So Judged He Man." From the Butts series of illustrations to Milton's Paradise Lost *(1808). (By permission of the Houghton Library, Harvard University.)*

William Blake, "Michael Foretelling the Crucifixion to Adam." From the Butts series of illustrations to Milton's Paradise Lost (1808). (Gift by Subscription. Courtesy of the Museum of Fine Arts, Boston.)

William Blake, "The Descent of Peace." From the Thomas series of illustrations to Milton's Hymn on the Nativity of Christ *(1809). (By permission of the Whitworth Art Gallery, University of Manchester.)*

structed, ceaselessly elaborated, and sometimes contradictory myth woven about the interaction of the faculties of the human mind, Blake produced a series of works that provide unparalleled insights into the imaginative and intellectual aspects of creativity as well as the actual processes through which artistic creation takes place. In the following chapters I wish to look in particular at the significant part played in Blake's representations by some of the principal *female* personages he created in his unfolding of this myth over many years—Thel, Enitharmon, Ololon the "Emanation" of Blake's character "Milton" in his epic by that name, and Jerusalem. In the creation of each of these figures, Blake drew in complex and fundamental ways not only on Milton's characterizations of his female personages—especially Eve, Sin, Nature, and the Lady of *Comus*—but even more on the *substance* of Milton's works, the transmitted words, phrases, images and ideas that had embedded themselves in the matrix of Blake's own imagination.

2
Thel

. . . To him that dares
Arm his profane tongue with contemptuous words
Against the sun-clad power of chastity;
Fain would I something say, yet to what end?

—John Milton[1]

THE "MASQUE PRESENTED AT LUDLOW CASTLE" *(Comus)* in which Milton defended the "sun-clad power of chastity" was the subject of the earliest of Blake's commissioned series of Milton illustrations. Blake executed them for the Reverend Joseph Thomas around 1801; but he had long reflected on the theme of Milton's masque, with wit and subtlety arming his "profane [read: "iconoclastic"] tongue with contemptuous words" against it, years before he made *Comus* the subject of a series of paintings.[2] In the ethos of his declaration in *The Marriage of Heaven and Hell* that "Opposition is true Friendship," and among the "severe contentions" that marked the lifelong "Friendship" Blake enjoyed with the spirit of Milton, Blake found abundant inspiration in Milton's *Comus* while vigorously opposing the principles of the "sage / And serious doctrine of virginity" Milton espoused in it.[3] Such is the relationship between *Comus* and Blake's *Book of Thel*.[4]

The virgin Thel, whose name means "wish" or "will" (from the Greek verb meaning "to desire"), is the only one of Blake's personages who is given the option of accepting or rejecting the fallen condition of mortality. Thel avails herself of this privilege, choosing, when she has previewed this "land of sorrows & of tears," to flee "back . . . into the vales of Har."[5] The poem makes it clear that the "daughter of beauty" will indeed, as she foresees, "fade away."[6] As Spenser put it in a passage that Blake certainly had in mind, "that faire flowre of beauty fades away, / As doth the lilly fresh before the sunny ray."[7] She will leave behind no trace or useful legacy of her existence—"And all shall say, 'Without a use this shining woman liv'd. . . .'"—because she refuses to commit herself to earthly generation, fearing the pains of Experience that inevitably accompany sexuality in the fallen world.[8] *The Book of Thel* affirms that sexuality, and the giving of oneself in love to procreation, is good, and a necessary commitment to life on earth. For the most part it does so within a gentle, almost childlike ambience that sets this poem apart from the intensity of the *Songs of Experience* and the later prophecies, and places it between "Innocence" and "Experience," into which latter condition Thel enters only hesitantly, fearfully, and briefly.[9]

The Book of Thel shares its pastoral setting with both *Comus* and the *Songs of Innocence*.[10] "The secret air" Thel seeks out "down by the river of Adona" was inspired by the "regions mild of calm and serene air" from which the Attendant Spirit descends, the

William Blake, The Book of Thel, *1789, plate ii. (By permission of the Trustees of the British Museum.)*

William Blake, The Book of Thel, *1789, plate 2. (By permission of the Trustees of the British Museum.)*

"broad fields of the sky" to which he returns again in the closing lines of *Comus.*[11] Here Adonis appears:

> Iris there with humid bow,
> Waters the odorous banks that blow
> Flowers of more mingled hue
> Than her purfled scarf can shew,
> And drenches with Elysian dew . . .
> Beds of hyacinth and roses,
> Where young Adonis oft reposes,
> Waxing well of his deep wound
> In slumber soft, and on the ground
> Sadly sits the Assyrian queen. . . .[12]

Milton's rainbow "drenches" and nourishes "beds of hyacinth and roses," symbolic of regeneration and love, where the youth Adonis, beloved of "the Assyrian queen" Venus, lies recovering from the wound given him by a boar. Milton's passage—and the opening lines of *The Book of Thel* as well—stems at least partially from Spenser's account of Venus lovingly sustaining Adonis in the "Garden of Adonis" in *The Faerie Queene.*[13] Both Spenser and Milton as-

sociate Adonis with fertility in the fallen world—the combating of death and decay by means of earthly generation.[14] Time, in Spenser's Garden, "beats down both leaves and buds without regard."[15] Though Venus weeps for their loss, she has no remedy, for "All things decay in time and to their end do draw."[16] Adonis embodies the principle of plenitude, which continually redresses the ravages of Time:

> All be he subiect to mortalitie
> Yet is eterne in mutabilitie
> And by succession made perpetuall. . . .[17]

Thel, lamenting by the river of Adona, compares herself to a "wat'ry bow"—Milton's "humid bow."[18] Through a series of parallel similes ("shadows in the water," "a smile upon an infant's face," "transient day"), Thel emphasizes the *evanescence* of the rainbow, where Milton's passage stresses its functional *continuity* within the cycle of regeneration.[19]

Thel encounters four symbolic figures. The first, the "Lilly of the valley," is a "gentle maid of silent valleys and of modest brooks" who retires after speaking with Thel to a "silver shrine."[20] Blake's "Lilly" is primarily Spenser's "faire flowre of beauty [that] fades away," but this appealing little "wat'ry weed" is also related—through the "twisted braids of lilies" knitted into the "loose train of [her] amber-dropping hair"—to Milton's Sabrina, "a gentle nymph . . . that with moist curb sways the smooth Severn stream."[21] Sabrina, sitting "under the glassy cool translucent wave," is "Goddess of the silver lake" and a patron of maidenhood.[22] She is invoked by the Attendant Spirit to free the Lady held fast by Comus's magic spell. Blake's "Lilly," a self-effacing "little virgin of the peaceful valley," contrasts with the regal Sabrina, whose narcissistic adorning of herself suggests an immature self-involvement rather like Thel's own.[23] The life of the "Lilly" is one of self-sacrifice and selfless caring for other living creatures; she gives of her own material being to "nourish the innocent lamb" and "revive the milked cow," scatters her perfume "on every little blade of grass" and goes, after speaking with Thel, "to mind her numerous charge among the verdant grass."[24]

Thel's second dialogue is with a Cloud, which "shew[s] his golden head . . . / Hovering and glittering on the air. . . ."[25] Blake's Cloud takes his "bright form" from the "hovering angel girt with golden wings" who accompanies Faith, Hope, and Chastity in the Lady's soliloquy in *Comus* (and is there perhaps to be identified with Hope).[26] He also resembles the "glistering guardian" whom the Lady trusts to keep her "life and honour unassailed" (and whose semblance Blake was to borrow for the equivocal guardian of maidenhood in "The Angel" of the *Songs of Experience*).[27] The Cloud declares to Thel:

O virgin, know'st thou not our steeds drink of the
    golden springs
Where Luvah doth renew his horses?[28]

"Our steeds," air-currents upon which clouds are mounted in moving about the sky, "renew" their vitality at the same source as the "horses of Luvah," here virtually identified with the fiery horses of the classical sun-god Phoebus Apollo.[29] Luvah is a symbol of sexuality, wherever he appears in Blake's later work, and the Cloud is likewise portrayed, both visually and in the text, as a figure of young and virile sexuality.[30] Blake may have associated the "golden springs / Where Luvah doth renew his horses" with the "orient liquor" which Comus, descendant of the Sun, offers to weary travelers "to quench the drought of Phoebus."[31] That magic potion "flames, and dances in his crystal bounds" as Comus presses it

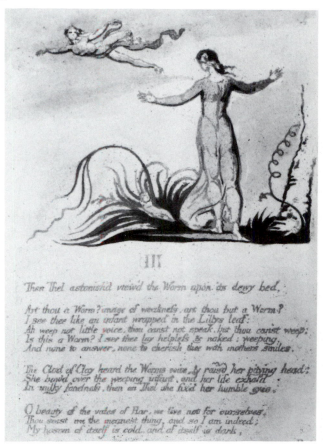

William Blake, The Book of Thel, *1789, plate 4. (By permission of the Trustees of the British Museum.)*

upon the obdurate Lady, urging

". . . see, here be all the pleasures
That fancy can beget on youthful thoughts,
When the fresh blood grows lively, and returns
Brisk as the April buds in primrose season. . . ."
                                                    (667–70)

These images of the fires of lust, of spring, morning, and regeneration are tinged in the Miltonic context with the evil of Comus's nature, but Blake was obviously determined that the devil should not have the best tunes or the finest poetry. Blake chose to associate Milton's phrase from *Comus,* "the sun-clad power of chastity," with the lines from *Paradise Lost* describing the "apostate" Satan "exalted as a god . . . in his sun-bright chariot . . . Idol of majesty divine."[32] In Blake's reading of *Comus,* Chastity is the "apostate," the "idol of majesty divine," for the divinity Blake delineates in the *Book of Thel* is one who blesses earthly plenitude and sustains and encourages its increase: and *he* is embodied in the sun.[33] The Lady in *Comus* is transfixed by magic to Comus's enchanted chair, "as Daphne was / Root-bound, that fled Apollo."[34] Blake was sufficiently struck by this

William Blake, "The Little Black Boy" (1). From Songs of Innocence and of Experience, *1794. (By permission of the Trustees of the British Museum.)*

image to illustrate it in an emblem in his *Notebook,* inscribing beneath it "As Daphne was root-bound."[35] Thel may be seen as an insubstantial analogue of the "Vegetated body" of Daphne, for she too has "fled Apollo."[36] In the opening lines of the poem she shuns the company of sisters who "led round their *sunny* flocks."[37] Instead she has "sought the secret air, / To fade away like morning beauty from her mortal day . . . ," becoming "like a faint cloud kindled at the rising sun."[38] The Cloud, with his "golden head and . . . bright form" is indeed "kindled at the rising sun"—in common with all living beings—but he has *followed,* not fled, its beams. He rejoices not only in his materialization, "glitter[ing] in the morning sky," but also in his dissolution, "scatter[ing] [his] bright beauty thro' the humid air."[39] In his vaporous state he returns to water his "steeds" at the "golden springs / Where Luvah doth renew his horses," a generative

source where his life is renewed and he comes again into visible being.[40]

Like the "humid bow" of Milton's Iris, the Cloud is a vital link in the cycle of earthly generation. Comus describes to the Lady his first sight of her two young brothers as

> . . . a faery vision,
> Of some gay creatures of the element
> That in the colours of the rainbow live
> And play i' the plighted clouds. . . .[41]

Blake's Cloud is, like those of Milton in this passage, "plighted"—but with a shift of semantic emphasis.[42] The Cloud of the *Book of Thel* is "plighted" in being betrothed to his "partner in the vale," whom he goes to join when he takes leave of Thel.[43] The Cloud's "partner" is "the fair-eyed dew," who "kneels before the risen sun," surrendering herself—like Spenser's "Morning dew" Chrysogone—to that divine source of life just as obviously as Thel hides away from it when she seeks out "the *secret* air" (my emphasis).[44] The "plighted" couple are "link'd in a golden band and never part, / But walk united bearing food to all our tender flowers."[45] Like the "Lilly of the valley," they give selflessly of themselves, both to one another and to others in the fulfillment of social responsibilities.

The Cloud brings to Thel the Worm, one of the "numerous charge" of the "Lilly."[46] The visual image of the Worm on plate 4 of the *Book of Thel* confirms that Blake either had in mind, or had already sketched, "What is Man!," the emblem design he chose to place first in *The Gates of Paradise.*[47] Blake's introduction of the Worm confirms an association stemming from the caption he wrote in the *Notebook* beneath his rough sketch of the emblem—the passage from the Book of Job from which he took its title,

> What is Man that thou shouldst
> magnify him & that thou shouldst set
> thine heart upon him[48]

Three of Thel's four visitants—the Cloud, the Worm, and the Clod of Clay—emerge from the context of this verse of Job:

> My flesh is clothed with worms and clods of dust. . . .
> As the cloud is consumed and vanisheth away; so he
> that goeth down to the grave shall come up no more.[49]

Thel knows that she too will be "consumed," to become "at death the food of worms."[50] The Cloud offers Thel the wise counsel of acceptance. Though he will "vanish and [be] seen no more" he assures her that when he passes away he goes "to tenfold life." If worms should consume her flesh, the Cloud ex-

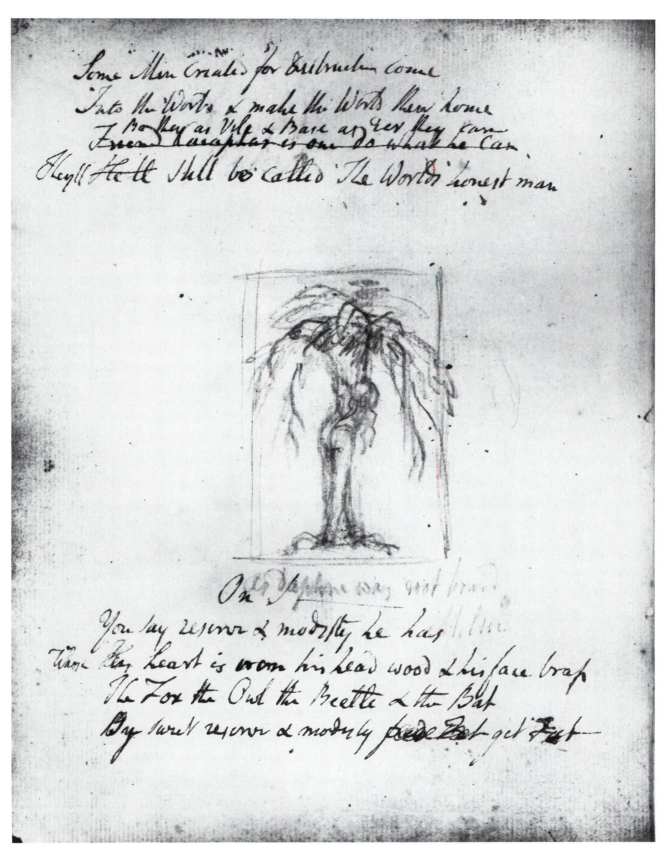

William Blake, draft sketch of emblem, "As Daphne was root-bound." From the Notebook of William Blake, p. 36. (By permission of the British Library).

William Blake, "Comus with his Revellers," ca. 1801. From the Thomas series of illustrations to Milton's Comus. (By permission of the Huntington Library and Art Gallery, San Marino, California.)

Frontispiece

O What is Man!

Published by W Blake 17 May 1793

William Blake, "What is Man!" Frontispiece of For Children: The Gates of Paradise, 1793. (By permission of the Trustees of the British Museum.)

claims, "How great thy use, how great thy blessing!"[51] For, he tells her, "Every thing that lives / Lives not alone nor for itself."[52] The emblem "What is Man!" shows two worms: one realistic, crawling in an arc down an oak leaf, the other with the face of a sleeping child, lying face upward on an adjoining leaf, chrysalis-like in swaddling bands. In the *Book of Thel* the helpless Worm appears to Thel "like an infant wrapped in the Lilly's leaf," and is shown in just this way on plate 4.[53] It cannot speak, but cries like a baby. Thel expresses compassion at its helplessness— "[There is] none to cherish thee with mother's smiles"—and indeed the cries of the infant do raise the "pitying head" of the motherly Clod of Clay.[54]

The Clod of Clay "bow'd over the weeping infant and her life exhal'd / In milky fondness. . . ."[55] This last personage of the poem attains the ultimate degree of selflessness, willingly giving her life as well as her substance for the Worm.[56] She echoes the Cloud's teaching: "O beauty of the vales of Har! we live not for ourselves."[57] In response to Thel's "pitying tears" the "matron Clay" invites Thel to survey her subterraneous "house," assuring her "'Tis given thee to enter / And to return: fear nothing. . . ."[58] And Thel accepts the invitation.

What does she find in the underground realm of Clay? "Couches of the dead"; tombs such as the grand monuments Blake had sketched fifteen years earlier, as a young apprentice, in Westminster Abbey.[59] In this "land of sorrows & of tears" Thel sees "Vegetated bodies" like that of Daphne, for there "the fibrous roots / Of every heart on earth infixes deep its restless twists."[60] Like the Lady in *Comus,* who finds no shelter "from the chill dew, amongst rude burs and thistles," Thel strays, unprotected and unguided, about the thorny undergrowth of the fallen world.[61] She enters a region (described by the Elder Brother in *Comus*) where "thick and gloomy shadows damp" are "oft seen in charnel-vaults, and sepulchres / Lingering, and sitting by a new-made grave, / As loth to leave the body that it loved. . . ."[62] Blake depicts Thel wandering

. . . in the land of clouds thro' valleys dark, list'ning
Dolours and lamentations; waiting oft beside a dewy grave
She stood in silence, list'ning to the voices of the ground. . . .[63]

At last she comes to her own grave plot, where a "voice of sorrow breathed from the hollow pit."[64] The voice Thel hears is potentially her own, moaning from the depths of the grave after the ending of a

The Last Judgment is not Fable or Allegory but Vision Fable or Allegory are a totally distinct & inferior kind of Poetry. Vision or Imagination is a Representation of what Eternally Exists. Really & Unchangeably. Fable or Allegory is Formd by the daughters of Memory. Imagination is Surrounded by the daughters of Inspiration who in the aggregate are called Jerusalem

The Hebrew Bible & the Gospel of Jesus are not Allegory but Eternal Vision or Imagination of All that Exists. The Last Judgment is one of these. Stupendous Visions I have represented it as I saw it to different People it appears differently as

William Blake, draft sketch of emblem, "What is Man. . . ." From the Notebook of William Blake, *p. 68. (By permission of the British Library.)*

William Blake, The Book of Thel, *1789, plate 5. (By permission of the Trustees of the British Museum.)*

life-in-possibility to which the maiden has not yet committed herself. This potential self laments the painful intensity of the experiences of each of the senses in earthly life:

> Why are Eyelids stor'd with arrows ready drawn,
> Where a thousand fighting men in ambush lie? . . .
> Why a Tongue impress'd with honey from every wind?
> Why an Ear, a whirlpool fierce to draw creations in?
> Why a Nostril wide inhaling terror, trembling, & affright?[65]

At its climax the agonized murmur articulates the anguish of the sexual sense of touch: the pangs of desire frustrated, the greater torment of desire satisfied—the agony of self-realization in earthly life that awaits the virgin whose name means "desire":

> Why a tender curb upon the youthful burning boy?
> Why a little curtain of flesh on the bed of our desire?[66]

At this, Thel rushes "with a shriek" back to the "vales of Har." She flees the precepts of teachers who affirm that commitment to earthly life demands a continual sacrifice of selfhood. Experiential existence in the fallen world is a course to inevitable destruction, marked by the fierce suffering and terror her own disembodied voice describes. Rather than face that, Thel—who prayed that she might live in "gentleness"—chooses not to enter into it at all.[67]

Thel's "Motto," in most copies a kind of postscript to the poem, suggests that Thel might have learned more from her brief sojourn in the "house of Clay" than she allowed herself to do:

> Does the Eagle know what is in the pit?
> Or wilt thou go ask the Mole?
> Can Wisdom be put in a silver rod?
> Or Love in a golden bowl?[68]

The Mole, the earth dweller, knows "what is in the pit," and may also be a symbol of the regenerative potential within experience.[69] The Eagle, inhabiting the sky and aspiring always in Blake's work to the visionary condition, knows nothing of the realm of Clay. The "rod" and "bowl" may at one level be reminders of the charming–rod and the cup of Comus; a rod may be a symbol of authority or of the phallus, a bowl may represent the Holy Grail or be a symbol of the womb. Blake obviously intends no simple answers to the four rhetorical questions in "Thel's Motto." All Thel can do is look in the direction these questions point. They direct her (and the reader) to the indisputable value of such experience of the skies and the earth as may be gained respectively by the Eagle and the Mole from their diametrically opposed perspectives and "contrary" ways of life. And they question the *validity* of a distinction between Love and Wisdom:

> . . . love indeed is Esse and wisdom is Existere for love has nothing except in wisdom, nor has wisdom anything except from love. Therefore when love is in wisdom, then it *exists.*[70]

Blake commented on this passage of Swedenborg's *Divine Love and Wisdom:* "Thought without affection makes a distinction between Love & Wisdom, as it does between body & Spirit."[71] His annotation indicates that he regards the division between Love and Wisdom in the same light as he does that "between body & Spirit"—as a notion "to be expunged."[72]

The illumination with which Blake concludes the *Book of Thel* depicts Thel's choice quite clearly, and incidentally suggests the source of his inspiration in Milton's work. Plate 6 shows three children—a girl

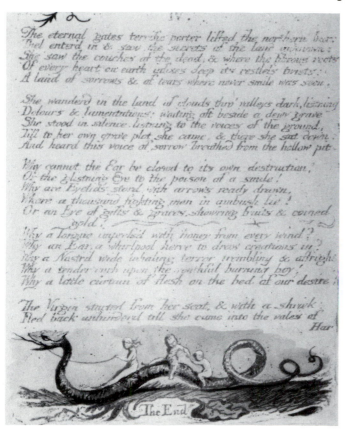

William Blake, The Book of Thel, *1789, plate 6. (By permission of the Trustees of the British Museum.)*

and two younger boys—riding a dragon-headed serpent who coils across the width of the page over the legend "The End." They cannot be identified from the text of *Thel* (or from that of *America,* where Blake was to use the same motif again); and indeed, in their first appearance, on the final plate of *The Book of Thel,* they may represent the Lady and the Elder and Younger Brothers of Milton's *Comus,* shown almost in babyhood. Perhaps, in one of the several possible meanings of the configuration, these figures embody the desire of both Thel and Milton's Lady to retreat toward the security of infancy—reversing the natural process of growth through adolescent sexuality into maturity. With the girl astride and holding the reins, the three children ride the seemingly tractable serpent—symbol of man's fall—without fear.[73] Back they gallop, in a leftward or "sinister" direction, to "the vales of Har," where the phallic serpent has no *visible* sting, in a paradise *apparently* not yet lost—but only apparently, for the pastoral landscape of that country is a false Paradise of arrested development. As Blake clearly shows, the consequences of the fall of man are ineluctable.

Thel is the unrealized "wish" whose fulfillment was promised by Milton's God to Adam when he was about to create Eve, in a pristine Paradise before Time began.[74] In a fallen Paradise continually laid waste by the depredations of Time, Thel laments that she and every form of living beauty about her must yield to this "Great enimy."[75] She longs to hear "the voice / Of him that walketh in the garden in the evening time," not in wrath, but "gentl[y]."[76] The "Lilly of the valley," herself a "gentle maid," assures Thel that, little and weak and ephemeral though she is,

"Yet am I visited from heaven, and he that smiles
   on all
"Walks in the valley and each morn over me spreads
   his hand. . . ."[77]

When her brief life in time is over the "Lilly" is blessed with the certainty that she will "flourish in eternal vales." The Cloud directly addresses Thel's fear that "like a faint cloud kindled at the rising sun / I vanish from my pearly throne. . . ."[78] Although, he says, "I vanish and am seen no more," yet "when I pass away / It is to tenfold life, to love, to peace and raptures holy. . . ."[79] Thel knows that the Worm is loved by God, and that whoever injures it will be punished; but more than that, she learns, the Worm is "cherish'd . . . with milk and oil"—for, as Blake repeatedly declares, "every thing that lives is Holy."[80] And the "matron Clay" assures Thel that though she herself is "the meanest thing," and though her bosom is cold and dark, "he, that loves the lowly, pours his oil upon my head, / And kisses me, and binds his nuptial bands around my breast. . . ."[81] The divine visitant who "spreads his hand" in benediction over the humble "Lilly" and "binds his nuptial bands" about the breast of the "matron Clay" is also the force who charges with life the "golden springs" where the Cloud's existence is renewed. Blake typically makes the female personages passive and acquiescent, and the male personage, the Cloud, an active agent—an inseminator, while the "Lilly" and the "matron Clay" are receptacles for seed. Yet all are vehicles for the divine force of life emanating from "[him] that smiles on all" and "loves the lowly," who has linked them all, together with the Worm, in a "golden band" of earthly generation. Thel, inspired by Blake's complex response to Milton's treatment of what appeared to Blake as obdurate chastity in *Comus,* deplores the loss of Paradise. And she rejects the only alternative offered to man: coming to terms with experience, which includes procreation and generation, in the fallen world. Thel is Blake's first embodiment of the "Female Will" that withholds or frustrates the "heart's desire," and Milton's *Comus* is one of his primary sources for that concept.[82]

3
Enitharmon

Toward the end of *THE FOUR ZOAS,* BLAKE'S "Eternal Men" gather at a "golden feast" which heralds the Last Judgment in "Night the Ninth" of this unfinished epic.[1] The regenerated company celebrates the recognition that "not for ourselves, but for the Eternal family we live. / Man liveth not by Self alone. . . ."[2] They reject the fallen state of mankind, "in his selfish cold repose / Forsaking Brotherhood & Universal love. . . ."[3] Especially they condemn as degenerate their own former condition of divided sexuality:

> And Many Eternal Men sat at the golden feast to
> see
> The female form now separate. They shudder'd at
> the horrible thing
> Not born for the sport and amusement of Man,
> but born to drink up all his powers.
> [And *del.*] They wept to see their shadows; they
> said to one another: "This is Sin. . . ."[4]

Michael Ackland has noted that Mary Wollstonecraft's vision of liberated female potential in *A Vindication of the Rights of Woman* (1792) greatly influenced the "redemptive role that Blake attributes to the emanation."[5] Wollstonecraft's constant emphasis, Ackland says,

> is on the need to emancipate woman from a constricting sexual role: *to have her recognized as an intellectual and, in the widest sense, a human creature.* As she explains, the female "was not created merely to be the solace of man, and *the sexual should not destroy the human character."*[6]

This enlightened recognition of woman as an essential part of Man's *humanity* plays a part in the horrified response of the "Eternal Men" to the separated "female form" they call "Sin." The annulment that Blake insists upon of the division between the sexes is one of the most significant features of the final recovery of Man and his inner world from the death-like "fallen" condition of self-involvement, of his attainment of a full humanity, and of the restoration to Urthona—the "Zoa" of man's imagination in its regenerated state—of "all his ancient strength" so that, "no longer now / Divided from Enitharmon," he may "form the golden armour of science / For intellectual War."[7]

The division of Urthona into Los and Enitharmon, beings of different sexes, is one of the first effects of the disastrous rebellion of Urizen, the Zoa representing man's Reason. In the *Book of Urizen* (1794), Urizen makes a claim to godhead which is repudiated by the other "Eternals." They banish Urizen, and he then proceeds, in his isolated state, to create his own empire. As Los attempts to restore unity and coherence within this rifted universe, he himself is divided, Enitharmon emerging from him as a separate being. In *The Four Zoas,* which Blake may have begun within a year of the date etched on the *Urizen* title page, this event is extensively elaborated.[8] There it follows an attempted conspiracy (like that of Milton's Satan in *Paradise Lost*) proposed by Urizen to Luvah—Zoa of the passions—which results in a battle between them for supremacy.[9] Blake depicts a complex "psychomachia," a conflict between the human reason, Urizen, and the passions, personified by Luvah. Urizen himself describes his rebellion as his own wrongful act of withholding his presence and his

"Steeds of Light"—Man's intellectual powers—from "the lord of day."[10] This supreme being, a development of the life-giving deity associated with the rising sun in *The Book of Thel* and "The Little Black Boy," was to become Blake's "Divine Humanity," Man in his ideal wholeness and perfection.[11] Urizen failed to respond to the "mild & holy voice" that bade him "Go forth & guide my Son who wanders on the ocean" (the "Son" being the sun in the heavens as representative of human consciousness, the "ocean" the "wat'ry world" of matter over which Tharmas, the Zoa of the five senses, presides). Instead, Urizen confesses "I hid myself in black clouds of my wrath."[12] Moreover, Urizen had also agreed to an irresponsible bargain initiated by Luvah. In a furtive transaction he had allowed himself to be persuaded by Luvah to give over to him the control of those "Steeds" of the enlightening intellect in exchange for "the wine of the Almighty"—Man's capacity for passionate emotion—which was in Luvah's charge.[13] In the resultant fall from his "throne sublime," Urizen had dragged Urthona and Luvah down with him.[14] Tharmas meanwhile had made his own claim to godhead, attempting also to gain supremacy over the other three.[15] Of the Four Zoas, only Urthona, the human imagination who is their guardian in Eternity, had stood apart from this contest for power, for, as Wilkie and Johnson put it, "Blake's regenerated artist is the servant and not the lord of humanity."[16]

In each of these conflicts the division, when Man falls, of a female "Emanation" from her male counterpart—who is then reduced to the condition of a "Spectre"—features consistently, appearing in every mutation of Blake's myth. It is a notable and deeply painful event in the history of each of the "Four Mighty Ones . . . in every Man," as Blake calls the Four Zoas."[17] Tharmas, as the human senses, is the "Parent power" or origin of the other Zoas.[18] He is parted at the beginning of the first "Night" of *The Four Zoas* from his "Emanation" Enion.[19] Tharmas alternately laments her departure and rages against her throughout the remainder of the work. Urizen is separated from his "Emanation" Ahania and, despite his initial anguish, viciously repulses her once he has asserted his tyranny over the Eternal Man.[20] By contrast, the separation from his "Emanation," Vala, of Luvah, Zoa of the Passions and embodiment of the Eternal Man's "capacity for love and joy," transforms Vala into a powerfully destructive force and Luvah into a suffering martyr in *The Four Zoas, Milton,* and *Jerusalem*.[21] But the division of Urthona, Zoa of the Imagination, into Los and Enitharmon was the *first* such event that Blake conceived in the inception

of his myth. The interaction of this couple, and the influence of Enitharmon, whether positive or negative, supports the myth in all its dynamic proliferations of meaning in the course of Blake's dramatic allegorization of the workings of human creativity.

Enitharmon's name may have come from the Greek "anarithmon" ("numberless").[22] It may also, and at the same time, be a partial anagram of "Catherine." Catherine was the name not only of Blake's wife, his devoted assistant in all his mature creative work, but also of his mother, and of the sister who was evidently the sibling closest to him after the death of his brother Robert.[23] It seems reasonable that Blake should associate a version of this name with his "Eternal Female," and that "Cathedron" should be the name he gives to the place where Enitharmon sets up "Looms" in which to weave material "Bodies

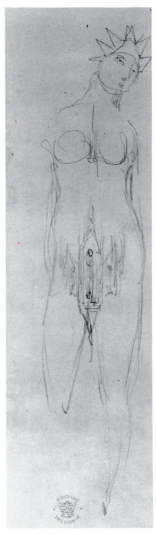

William Blake, The Four Zoas, *British Museum Add. MS 39764. Detail of folio 22 verso. (By permission of the British Library.)*

of Vegetation" for fallen humanity.[24] Blake sketched into the manuscript of *The Four Zoas* a female figure with an ornate Gothic shrine between her thighs—a *"sanctum sanctorum"* whose form suggests the implied personal association of Catherine/cathedral/"Cathedron" with the female sexual organs and the generative function.[25] The sanctuary between the lady's thighs takes the form of a hinged Gothic triptych. This implies that the "holy image" at its heart can be closed up (in "hypocrite modesty") by the two wings designed to fold over and obscure it—probably a comment on the "woman's secrecy" Enitharmon in *Europe* rebukes Oothoon for giving up.[26]

Blake's patron William Hayley, observing William and Catherine Blake working together at Felpham, remarked that though married by then for almost twenty years they were as happy as if still on their honeymoon, and that "He and his excellent wife (a true helpmate!) pass the plates through a rolling press in their own cottage together."[27] Yet Blake's obsession with marriage as a socially approved and imposed form of *bondage,* expressed in poems written into his *Notebook* during the earlier part of the Lambeth period, suggests that his own feelings about his marriage may not always have been what Hayley's idealizing comments would indicate.[28] Like any other long-term relationship, that of William and Catherine Blake had its rough passages; but despite their lifelong poverty, despite even the extraordinary demands of Blake's temperament and his work, there is no doubt that they enjoyed periods of great happiness. However, George Cumberland, himself an artist and a patron of Blake over many years, expressed a commonly held view of both the Blakes when in about 1815 he wrote to his son concerning them "he is a little Cracked, but very honest—as to his wife she is the maddest of the Two."[29] Both Hayley's observations and Cumberland's seem to be implicitly corroborated by Henry Crabb Robinson's recollection of his first visits to Blake and his wife at Fountain Court in The Strand in December 1825.[30] Robinson commented that Catherine Blake

> seemed to be the very woman to make [her husband] happy[.] She had been formed by him. Indeed, otherwise she could not have lived with him; . . . she had that virtue of virtues in a wife[,] an implicit reverence of her husband[.] It is quite certain that she believed in all his visions . . . In a word—She was formed on the Miltonic model—And like the first Wife Eve worshipped God in her Husband—He being to her what God was to him.[31]

Blake himself, in *Jerusalem,* pointedly distinguishes Enitharmon from the other three "Emanations" (whom he calls "evanescent shades"), asserting that "Enitharmon is a vegetated mortal Wife of Los, / His Emanation, yet his Wife till the sleep of Death is past."[32] Nevertheless, it would be naïve, and actually misleading in many contexts, literally or even allegorically to identify Enitharmon with Catherine Blake. However, Enitharmon, who was unquestionably "formed by [Blake]," was distinctly "formed on the Miltonic model." The model was not exclusively that of the perfect wife. In some passages Enitharmon does indeed approximate to the Eve who "worshipped God in her Husband," declaring in *The Four Zoas*

> "O [lovely *del.*] Lovely terrible Los, wonder of
> Eternity, O Los, my defence & guide,
> Thy works are all my joy & in thy fires my soul
> delights . . ."[33]

—lovingly supporting and actively contributing to the creative labors of Los:

> . . . springing up aloft
> Into the heavens of Enitharmon in a mighty
> circle . . .
> . . . he drew a line upon the walls of shining
> heaven,
> And Enitharmon tinctur'd it with beams of
> blushing love . . .[34]

But elsewhere Enitharmon seems to be animated by other Miltonic conceptions of the female. Blake recognized the innuendo of the declaration Adam makes, all unconsciously, when he accepts the forbidden fruit from the eagerly proffering hand of Milton's Eve:

> . . . if death
> Consort with thee, death is to me as life;
> So forcible within my heart I feel
> The bond of nature draw me to my own.[35]

Here Eve, linked by "the bond of nature" to Adam, has become the shadow of Sin, who "consorts with" Death. Indeed, Blake (who usually identified with Los in the role of the creative artist) referred to *himself* by the nickname "Death" in the bitter autobiographically based satirical fragment "And his legs carried it like a long fork . . ." (written in about 1808), implying a parallel for the association of his wife Catherine—often identified with Enitharmon—with Sin, consort of Death.[36]

It is, in fact, as an analogue of Milton's Sin that Enitharmon first appears in Blake's work, emerging from the forepart of the head of Los in *The Book of Urizen,* as Milton's Sin does from the head of Satan.

The "globe of life blood" that is to become "the first female now separate" emanates from the traditional location in the brain of the imaginative faculty of man's mind. In the relevant plate in *The First Book of Urizen* the blood that forms the "globe" appears to drain not only from the head but also from the trunk and loins of Los. "Head, heart and reins" contribute to the formation of the first "Emanation."[37]

Four other accounts of Enitharmon's origin as a separate individual are given in *The Four Zoas*. In the earliest draft of "Night the First," Enion, the Emanation of Tharmas, gives birth to Los and Enitharmon as twins, fathered by the "Spectre" of Tharmas. In a late addition to "Night the First," Enitharmon flees from the "aking bosom" of Urthona when Urizen and Luvah, disputing the question of supremacy among the Eternals, create universal discord; Tharmas gives her refuge, whereupon she is slain and then internalized by the jealous Enion.[38] "Night the Fourth" offers a version in which Tharmas forcibly rends Enitharmon from the "left side" of Los. Blake's account here leaves no doubt that Los and Enitharmon were connected by a fleshly "bond of nature," for both suffer bleeding wounds when they are torn apart.[39] In consequence of this forcible separation Los falls "on the rocks"; simultaneously the "Dark Spectre" of Urthona falls "upon the shores / With dislocated Limbs. . . ."[40] Arising "in pain" as "a shadow blue, obscure & dismal," the Spectre of Urthona gives yet another version of the emanation of Enitharmon, in which she "divid[ed] from [his] *loins, a weak & piteous / Soft cloud of snow, a female pale & weak. . . .*"[41]

Each of these five accounts of the origin of Enitharmon has its own implications. Her manifestation from the head of Los in *The Book of Urizen* (discussed in Chapter 1) associates her with Milton's account of the birth of Sin from the head of Satan, and with the classical account of the emanation of Athene (the Roman Minerva), goddess of Wisdom, from the head of Zeus.[42] However, her birth as the twin of Los in "Night the First" of *The Four Zoas* carries somewhat different connotations.

The birth of Enitharmon (together with Los) from Enion is in effect the outcome of a furious quarrel between Enion and the "Spectre of Tharmas." This "Spectre"—the first such being to appear in Blake's myth—combines with the qualities of Milton's Satan the vainglorious longings that the Serpent's false flattery (couched in the hyperbolic terms of praise to a courtly love mistress) suggests to Milton's Eve when he is tempting her. A dazzling and narcissistic creature, the "Spectre of Tharmas" is "exalted in ter-

rific pride" and "repin[es] . . . That nought but Enion could be found to praise, adore & love."[43] He angrily condemns Enion as a "sinful Woman," declaring "In my jealous wings / I evermore will hold thee . . . 'Tis thou hast darken'd all My World, O Woman, lovely bane."[44] At the climax of their altercation he rapes and abandons her.[45] "Wandering desolate," Enion gives birth, in the "fierce pain . . . sorrow & woe" visited upon Eve as penalty for her part in Man's Fall, to Los and Enitharmon, infants weeping "upon the desolate wind," and afflicted from birth with the "shame & fear" of the postlapsarian condition.[46]

Blake evidently had in mind the twin birth of Apollo, god of the sun and of the arts (especially poetry), and Diana, goddess of the moon and of chastity—"Latona's twin-born progeny, / Which after held the sun and moon in fee."[47] The parallel is reinforced by his consistent linking of Los and Enitharmon with the Sol and Luna of alchemy.[48] "Scorn &

William Blake, Illustrations for the Book of Job, *the Butts Set: "When the Morning Stars Sang Together" (1805–6). (By permission of the Pierpont Morgan Library, New York.)*

Jealousy" are the "embryon passions" that fill Enitharmon's young breast.[49] Her "scorn" is a legacy of
Milton's *Comus*: she is associated not only with Diana, goddess of chastity, whose "stern frown" was
feared by "gods and men," but also with the "wise
Minerva" (Athena) whose "rigid looks of chaste aus-
terity" are commended by the Elder Brother of the
Lady of *Comus*.[50] The emotions attributed to the
young Enitharmon are certainly a forewarning of her
potential for exercising the coldly malicious "Female
Will."[51] Her qualities, partly those of "the huntress
Dian . . . queen of the woods," whose chill lunar
radiance also governs the tides of the sea, are distinguished significantly from those of Los.[52] He, by contrast, is moved by "Alternate Love & Hate," a
development of the "warlike fires & raging desires"
with which Blake crowns his own vision of Apollo,
the Sun of creative inspiration:

> His head beam'd light & in his vigorous voice was
>   prophecy.
> He could controll the times & seasons & the days &
>   years;
> She could controll the spaces, regions, desart, flood
>   & forest,
> But had no power to weave a Veil of covering for
>   her sins.[53]

Los is associated with Time, Enitharmon with Space.
Blake later wrote "Time and Space are Real Beings,
a Male and a Female. Time is a Man, Space is a
Woman, & her Masculine Portion is Death."[54] In
identifying the male Los and the female Enitharmon
with Time and Space respectively, Blake implies the
association of Enitharmon with Milton's Sin, whose
"Masculine Portion is Death." The "Veil of covering
for her sins," which Enitharmon is unable to weave,
obliquely relates this conception of her to the description of the newly created "first female now separate, /
Pale as a cloud of snow / Waving before the face of
Los" in *The Book of Urizen,* and also to that "weak
& piteous / Soft cloud of snow," the Enitharmon who
emerges from the loins of the "Spectre of Urthona"
in "Night the Fourth" of *The Four Zoas*.[55] Their principal common source is Milton's description of postlapsarian Nature in his *Hymn on the Morning of
Christ's Nativity:*

> Nature in awe to him
> Had doffed her gaudy trim,
>   With her great master so to sympathize:
> It was no season then for her
> To wanton with the sun her lusty paramour.
> Only with speeches fair
> She woos the gentle air

*William Blake, "The Sun at the Eastern Gate." From a
series of illustrations to Milton's L'Allegro, ca. 1816–20.
(By permission of the Pierpont Morgan Library, New
York. Purchased with the assistance of the Fellows, with
the special support of Mrs. Landon K. Thorne and Mrs.
Paul Mellon. 1949.4:3.)*

> To hide her guilty front with innocent snow,
> And on her naked shame,
> Pollute with sinful blame,
>   The saintly veil of maiden white to throw,
> Confounded that her maker's eyes
> Should look so near upon her foul deformities.[56]

Milton's fallen "Nature," conventionally defiled with
the "sinful blame" of Mankind's lapsed condition,
does need to "hide her guilty front" with a "saintly
veil" of snow in the presence of her maker, much as
Eve and Adam feel obliged to conceal their loins with
fig leaves, veiling themselves from each other and
from the sight of God, when they become ashamed
of their nakedness after they have transgressed.
Herein lies the crux of the distinction between
Blake's Enitharmon, on the one hand, and Milton's
meticulously orthodox Protestant characterizations
of Nature, Eve, and Sin on the other. Blake rejects
the judgmental moral criteria by which Milton's concepts were consciously influenced. In the Miltonic

context the dalliance between Nature, veiled in snow, and the Sun, her "lusty paramour," is implicitly condemned by the verb "to wanton."[57] Shakespeare's Imogen, another exemplar of frigidity Blake had in mind, was said by her husband to be "as chaste as unsunn'd snow," a phrase that assumes the association Blake had implied in *The Book of Thel* between the Sun—a creative source which is life-giving and life-sustaining—and fertile sexuality.[58] Enitharmon has "*no* power to weave a Veil of covering for her sins" and would have no *need* for covering if not for the imposition by Urizen of his "deceitful religion," which had induced him to label his own "parted soul," his "Emanation" Ahania, with the name "Sin" and to hide her "in darkness, in silence. . . ."[59] The "Spectre of Urthona" also identifies his "Emanation" as Sin, crying out to Los "Where is my lovely Enitharmon? . . . where is my Great Sin? She is also thine."[60] (Significantly, it is not Los but the degenerate "Spectre" who calls Enitharmon "Sin"; Los the artist eschews the "fallen" moral stance implied in the term.) The "Spectre of Tharmas" denounces his "Emanation" Enion, as "Thou sinful Woman . . .," while Vala, the "Emanation" of Luvah, derives her very name and nature from the concept of the "Veil of covering for her sins." The "veil" is symbolic of "Mystery," which was to Blake the principal curse of Man's Fall, and which he hated and rejected in both the sexual and the metaphysical senses.[61]

Enitharmon's link with *fallen* Nature is analogous to the visual parallel of the figure of "sinful" Nature in "The Descent of Peace" (the first illustration in the series of Milton's *Hymn on the Morning of Christ's Nativity*) with that of Eve in Blake's illustration to *Paradise Lost*, "Michael Foretells the Crucifixion."[62] (See Chapter 1.) In all Blake's versions of both these scenes the figure of personified Nature lying before the stable where Christ was born in the *Nativity* paintings is closely similar in position and appearance to the recumbent Eve lying in a trance before the Cross in the *Paradise Lost* illustrations. Symbolically, Nature has her eyes open and hands clasped in prayer, her body turned *away* from the viewer, and her loins strategically "veiled" with snow. Eve's eyes are closed; her body is turned *toward* the viewer and is entirely naked. As Bette Charlotte Werner notes,

> Eve, mother of all living, is also a figure for the procreative earth. . . . The unveiled figure beneath the cross represents Nature redeemed by Christ's sacrifice.[63]

In confirmation of Enitharmon's association in her separate existence with *fallen* Nature as well as Sin, Los declares that she will perpetually be restricted to Tharmas's "wat'ry" realm of material being, unable to participate in the spiritual and intellectual life of Man:

> Tho' this bright world of all our joy is in the Human Brain
> Where Urizen & all his Hosts hang their immortal lamps,
> Thou ne'er shalt leave this cold expanse where wat'ry Tharmas mourns.[64]

But Enitharmon, pitting her will against that of Los, defies him, and calls upon Urizen to "descend with horse & chariots" predicting the destruction of "Human Nature" and the replacement of "Human acts" with "War & Princedom, & Victory & Blood."[65] By inciting Urizen to impose his lordship upon Los, she will actually *induce* Man's fall. In this way she intends to wreak her spite on the "visionary" who has relegated her to the realm of the senses; and Blake's *Europe* shows her exacting this terrible revenge.[66]

The biblical account of the creation of Eve from a rib in Adam's side is played upon, "with difference discreet," in two further versions of Enitharmon's origin.[67] A late addition to "Night the First" has her "dividing from [Urthona's] aking breast"—his heart rather than his rib—as he stands transfixed at his anvil, appalled at the "yells & cries" emanating from the power struggle of Urizen and Luvah, to which Urthona is a horrified spectator. "Shrieking upon the wind," Enitharmon flees the conflict to take refuge with Tharmas.[68] In "Night the Fourth," Tharmas becomes, for the moment, the "doubting Thomas" who could not be convinced of the resurrection of Jesus until he had thrust his hand into the wound in Jesus' side.[69] Blake's doubting Tharmas actually *creates* the wound as he effects a violent and bloody separation, rending Enitharmon from the left side of Los "in griding pain" in response to Los's insulting defiance of his authority.[70] In both these passages Blake emphasizes the pain and suffering experienced by Urthona/Los as well as Enitharmon when they are forcibly separated, their "bond of nature" torn apart. In each account Enitharmon goes over to, or is reclaimed by, the possessive "Parent power" Tharmas, so that she *is*, in effect, relegated to his realm of the senses. The fall of Los "on the rocks" after the forcible separation of "Night the Fourth" is linked with the simultaneous fall of the "Spectre of Urthona," who is dashed "upon the shores," sustaining "dislocated Limbs."[71] Tharmas lays down a condition on which this "dolorous shadow" will be permitted to live and be healed. The "Spectre of Urthona" must take Enitharmon back to "the Eternal Prophet" Los

Then the Divine hand found the Two Limits, Satan and Adam,
In Albions bosom: for in every Human bosom those Limits stand.
And the Divine voice came from the Furnaces, as multitudes without
Number! the voices of the innumerable multitudes of Eternity.
And the appearance of a Man was seen in the Furnaces:
Saving those who have sinned from the punishment of the Law,
(In pity of the punisher whose state is eternal death,)
And keeping them from Sin by the mild counsels of his love.

Albion goes to Eternal Death: In Me all Eternity.
Must pass thro' condemnation, and awake beyond the Grave:
No individual can keep these Laws, for they are death
To every energy of man, and forbid the springs of life;
Albion hath enterd the State Satan! Be permanent O State!
And be thou for ever accursed! that Albion may arise again:
And be thou created into a State! I go forth to Create
States: to deliver Individuals evermore! Amen.

So spoke the voice from the Furnaces, descending into Non-Entity

William Blake, Jerusalem, *1804, plate 31 (Copy "A").*
(By permission of the Trustees of the British Museum.)

and "build her a bower in the midst of all my dashing waves; / Make first a resting place for Los & Enitharmon, then / Thou shalt have rest."[72] Both Los and Enitharmon are constrained to remain in the material world under the rule of Tharmas, "rough Demon of the waters" (his name is also a pun on the River Thames), the skeptical materialist whom Los contemptuously, but also with precision, had called "father of worms & clay."[73]

The "Spectre of Urthona" is Blake's genius, the spectral shadow—both in the sense of "reflection" and as "the darkened side"—of the Platonic ideal of the human imagination. It is he who by his labors must support Los and Enitharmon, embodied in the temporal forms of William and Catherine Blake, in this "vegetative" world. At one level, the allegory here is clearly a coming-to-terms, albeit reluctantly, with the real conditions with which the Blakes had to contend in order to survive, however precariously, in time and space, around the end of the eighteenth century in England, and principally in the London milieu. Patronage was the artist's lifeline.[74] Much as Blake disliked and resented the climate of art and the values prevailing in the class-ridden and war-obsessed society of the time, he had to earn his bread as an engraver and painter.[75] Consequently he was obliged to make certain unwilling concessions for the sake of obtaining patronage:

> Therefore Los stands in London building Golgonooza,
> Compelling his Spectre to labours mighty; trembling in fear
> The Spectre weeps, but Los unmoved by tears or threats remains.[76]

The first account given in "Night the Fourth" clearly indicated that Enitharmon had been joined to the left side of Los, but the "Spectre of Urthona" declares some forty lines later that Enitharmon emanated from his loins.[77] The "Spectre" recalls the event thus:

> "... I saw
> My loins begin to break forth into veiny pipes & writhe
> Before me in the wind englobing, trembling with strong vibrations,
> The bloody mass began to animate. I, bending over,
> Wept bitter tears incessant. Still beholding how the piteous form
> Dividing & dividing from my loins, a weak & piteous
> Soft cloud of snow, a female pale & weak, I soft embrac'd

> My counter part & call'd it Love. I nam'd her Enitharmon,
> But found myself & her issuing down the tide ...
> ... breaking forth,
> A shadow blue, obscure & dismal, from the breathing Nostrils
> Of Enion I issued into the air, divided from Enitharmon.
> I howl'd in sorrow. ...."[78]

This account describes the "englobing" of a "bloody mass," which emanates from the loins, the seat of sexuality, instead of from the head, the seat of the intellect, although in fact in the illuminations of *The Book of Urizen* blood for the "globe of life blood" drains from the whole of Los's body, *including* the loins, to emerge from Los's head.[79] That Blake intended to make use of his earlier poetic narrative is clear from his insertion into the latter part of "Night the Fourth" of four lines adapted from *The Book of Urizen:*

> In terrors Los shrank from his task; his great hammer
> Fell from his hand, his fires hid their strong limbs in smoke;
> For [in *del.*] with noises ruinous, hurtlings & clashes & groans,
> The immortal endur'd, tho bound in a deadly sleep.[80]

Los, attempting desperately to bind together and reorganize the fragmenting Urizen (who is surrounded by the conditions Milton describes in the abyss of Chaos), begins himself to fall apart:

> Pale terror siezed the Eyes of Los as he beat round
> The hurtling demon; terrified at the shapes
> Enslaved humanity put on, he became what he beheld:
> He became what he was doing: he was himself transform'd.[81]

At this point in the manuscript of *The Four Zoas* Blake inserted a note to himself: "Bring in here the Globe of Blood as in the B. of Urizen."[82] The emergence of the "Globe of Blood" which becomes Enitharmon leaves Los weak and terrified, and in the continuation of the narrative in "Night the Fifth," Los and Enitharmon have "shrunk into fixed space."[83] Enitharmon shortly afterward gives birth to Orc, the "new born King," hailed (in a parody of the "loud and solemn quire" of angels in Milton's *Hymn on the Nativity* ...) by a howling chorus of "Enormous Demons ... Crying, 'Luvah, King of Love, thou art the King of rage & death.'"[84] At the end of "Night the Fifth" Urizen fearfully recalls a prophecy that Luvah would "burst his way from Enitharmon."[85] It has been fulfilled, for the firstborn of Enitharmon and Los does indeed prove to be a monstrous mutation of Luvah, "hid . . . in that Outrageous form of Orc."[86] The fiery Orc personifies the wrathful and destructive form taken by passions and sexuality repressed under the social and political conditions of degenerate Europe in the last decade of the eighteenth century:

> Raging furious, the flames of desire
> Ran thro' heaven & earth, living flames
> Intelligent, organiz'd, arm'd
> With destruction & plagues.[87]

The conflict between these differing accounts of the origin of Enitharmon is symptomatic of the

movement back toward chaos that characterizes the Fall of Man, especially as Urizen recalls it. Luvah persuaded Urizen to hand over to him the control of the fiery "Steeds of Light," symbolic of the illuminating brilliance of the human intellect, in exchange for "the wine of the Almighty"—a draught that, like the "cordial julep" of Milton's Comus (one of Blake's likely sources for the image), inflames passion and has the "power to stir up joy."[88] Urizen describes the moment when *he* fell, causing Urthona and Luvah to fall with him:

> "We fell. I siez'd thee, dark Urthona. In my left
>   hand falling
> I siez'd thee, beauteous Luvah. . . ."[89]

Blake had shown the triple fall just as described in

William Blake, "Fallen Angels," ca. 1793. (Courtesy of the Fogg Art Museum, Harvard University. Bequest of Grenville L. Winthrop.)

William Blake, The Book of Urizen, *1794, plate 6 (Copy "G"): Urizen falls, with Los and Luvah. (The Lessing J. Rosenwald Collection of the Library of Congress, Washington, D.C.)*

William Blake, "Satan Watching the Endearments of Adam and Eve." From the Butts series of illustrations to Milton's Paradise Lost (1808). (By permission of the Huntington Library and Art Collections, San Marino, California.)

these lines in a watercolor of about 1793, and had elaborated it on plate 7 (in Copy G) of *The Book of Urizen*.[90] A still-youthful Urizen, arms flung outward, falls through fire at the center of the *Urizen* design. Luvah and the dark Los/Urthona fall on either side of him, each clutching his hands to his head. All three are entwined in serpents, linking the concept with Milton's account of the transformation of the fallen hosts of Satan, after Satan has caused Man to fall, into serpentine forms in book 10 of *Paradise Lost*.[91] But whereas the serpents twisted about the trunks of Los/Urthona and Luvah wrap themselves around only one leg of each figure, leaving the other leg free, the figure of Urizen is bound by the spiralling body of a serpent from the armpits downward. Like Milton's Satan, he is unable to part his legs: "his legs entwin[ed] / Each other, till supplanted down he fell. . . ."[92] Obviously Urizen is more firmly restrained—and more repressed sexually—than either of the two Zoas he has dragged down with him. The head and neck of the serpent, curving around and virtually encircling the head of the plummeting Urizen, seems to imply a circumscription of the fallen intellect greater than that of either the imagination or the passions in their fallen conditions.

Urizen laments the fallen condition of Luvah, comparing it with the beauty and unblemished purity of his previous state:

When thou didst bear the golden cup at the
    immortal tables . . .
Thy pure feet step'd on the steps divine, too pure
    for other feet,
. . . thy fair locks shadow'd thine eyes from the
    divine effulgence,
Then thou didst keep with Strong Urthona the
    living gates of heaven,
But now thou art bound down with him, even to
    the gates of hell.

Because thou gavest Urizen the wine of the
    Almighty
For Steeds of Light, that they might run in thy
    golden chariot of pride,
I gave to thee the Steeds, I pour'd the stolen wine
And drunken with the immortal draught fell from
    my throne sublime.[93]

The passage as a whole has fascinating implications, Luvah before his fall resembles the "stripling youths rich-clad, of fairer hue / Than Ganymede . . ." who appear offering "wine / That fragrant smell diffused" at the banquet arrayed by Satan to tempt Christ fasting in the wilderness in Milton's *Paradise Regained*.[94] He shares with the classical cupbearer of Zeus his

beauty and his effeminate sexuality.[95] He persuades Urizen to give over to him the "Steeds of Light," "that they might run in [his] golden chariot of pride"—which suggests that the passions Luvah personifies become, in the postlapsarian perspective, the bestial embodiments of the Deadly Vices that pull the golden chariot of Spenser's Lucifera, personification of sinful pride.[96] Blake repeatedly asserted, in works of the 1790s, that such passions are not *inherently* vicious, that their "sinfulness" depends on their being thus perceived:

"O Times remote!
When Love & Joy were adoration,
And none impure were deem'd:
Not Eyeless Covet,
Nor Thin-lip'd Envy,
Nor Bristled Wrath,
Nor Curled Wantonness. . . ."[97]

In his unfallen state, together with "Strong Urthona," Luvah had kept "the living gates of heaven."[98] Now that they have both fallen they are "bound down . . . even to the gates of hell." Luvah and Urthona momentarily, as keepers of the gates of Hell, pass into analogy with Milton's Sin and Death respectively. The parallel has a twofold implication. In the fallen condition of Mankind the free expression of sexuality and of passion is condemned as sinful: thus Luvah, suggestively embodying both the sexes in his Ganymede-like "eternal" state when he kept the gates of Heaven, becomes in his fall the deformed and dangerous Sin, female, but part phallic serpent, who has charge of the key to the gates of Hell and can open them to abysmal Chaos. The conditions of the degenerate world are hostile, even deadly, to creativity: thus Urthona, who in his "Eternal" state is the strong guardian of the gates of Heaven, in his fallen state becomes Death. Blake, who usually identified in his work with Los/Urthona, ironically referred to himself as "Death" at a time when he felt that he was being so intolerably persecuted, exploited, and betrayed by those who claimed to be his friends and supporters, that he believed not only his livelihood, but even his creativity to have been seriously impaired.[99]

To Blake, creative processes involve the whole human being. Creativity is bound up inseparably with emotional states and with the expression and the experience of sexuality. When Urizen, the rational intellect, falls, he drags Luvah as well as Urthona down with him. Restricted in his fallen condition to a "dungeon horrible," Urizen is no longer able to drive the "Steeds of Light" through the infinite heavens of the human mind, as it was in its unbounded "eternal" state.[100] As the fallen Urizen rises to explore his "dens" or "caverns"—the hellish confines to which the human mind is reduced when subjected to the unrestrained tyranny of the Reason—he utters a gnomic sentence: "When Thought is clos'd in Caves Then love shall shew its root in deepest Hell."[101] Thus Urizen sums up Blake's allegory of the "Four Mighty Ones . . . in every Man" in their postlapsarian state. The line encapsulates the paradox of the creative and destructive potentialities of human energies. For both of these Blake's symbol is the flame: the incandescence of the shaping and transforming fire of inspiration, "the burning fire of thought" in a Heaven of creativity, where desire is enacted and fulfilled, and also its negation—the conflagration in Milton's Hell of searing moral condemnation and frustrated sexual longing.[102]

The flames in which Milton's Sin is born, depicted visually by Blake in *The Book of Urizen* in relation to the birth of Enitharmon, are associated both in its text and its illuminations with the birth of Orc, first son of Enitharmon and Los.[103] Fire is the element Los employs in his blacksmith's forge of creativity. The flames from which Enitharmon and Orc arise ultimately become not only the shaping force but also the *medium* used by Los in the creative process in which Enitharmon participates:

> . . . Los, his hands divine inspir'd, began . . .
> To modulate his fires; studious the loud roaring flames
> He vanquish'd with the strength of Art, bending their iron points
> And drawing them forth delighted upon the winds of Golgonooza
> From out the ranks of Urizen's war & from the fiery lake
> Of Orc, bending down as the binder of sheaves follows
> The reaper, in both arms embracing the furious raging flames.[104]

Here Blake draws on Milton's description of Satan rising from the "burning lake" in *Paradise Lost,* book 1, lines 221–24:

> Forthwith upright he rears from off the pool
> His mighty stature; on each hand the flames
> Driven backward slope their pointing spires, and rolled
> In billows leave i' the midst a horrid vale.

Blake had illustrated this subject with precision in an emblem in his *Notebook,* emphasizing especially the sloping parting of the pointed flames. Milton's description embodies the breakdown of normal associative imagery that characterizes his concept of Hell in a universe based upon the rational causation of divine logic: it suggests that the flames of Hell are both solid ("slope their pointing spires") and liquid ("rolled / In billows").[105] Blake's development of Milton's fire imagery in this particular passage from "Night the Seventh" shows Los as an artisan, "his hands divine inspir'd," "vanquish[ing]" and "bending [the] iron points" of the flames of the infernal lake "with the strength of Art," mastering through his skill the "stubborn structure" of his medium.[106] "As the binder of sheaves follows / The reaper," delightedly he gathers a rich harvest of Miltonic forms and images. Joyously grasping Milton's text in its "infernal or diabolical sense," Los/Blake prepares to redeploy these infernal images in the creating spirit of his own individual genius, "upon the winds of Golgonooza," and "from out the ranks of Urizen's war," waged among "the great Wars of Eternity, in fury of Poetic Inspiration. . . ."[107]

In the next phase of creation, Enitharmon joins her forces with those of Los:

> Los drew them forth out of the deeps, planting his right foot firm
> Upon the Iron crag of Urizen, thence springing up aloft
> Into the heavens of Enitharmon in a mighty circle.
>
> And first he drew a line upon the walls of shining heaven,
> And Enitharmon tinctur'd it with beams of blushing love.
> It remain'd permanent, a lovely form, inspir'd, divinely human.
> Dividing into just proportions, Los unwearied labour'd
> The immortal lines upon the heavens, till with sighs of love,
> Sweet Enitharmon mild, Entranc'd breath'd forth upon the wind
> The spectrous dead. . . .[108]

Having gathered up the "raging flames," Los plants "his right foot firm / Upon the Iron crag of Urizen," making the rational intellect his steppingstone "Into the heavens of Enitharmon."[109] Los rearranges the images and forms he has harvested at will, in his own style, just as Milton himself, with inspired artistic logic, broke up the conventional causal sequence in order to depict a Hell. But unlike Milton, Los finds indispensable the collaboration of his female "counter part," Enitharmon.[110] She provides the matrix, "the walls of shining heaven," upon which Los lays down his "immortal lines," and it is she who "tinctur[es]"

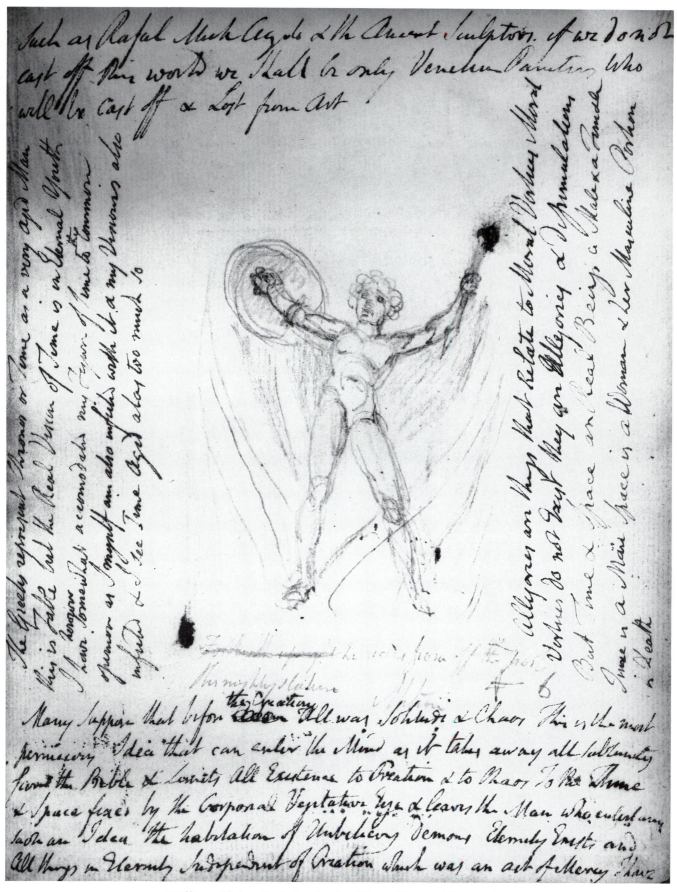

William Blake, draft sketch of emblem, "Forthwith upright he rears from off the pool / His mighty stature. . . ." From the Notebook of William Blake, *p. 91. (By permission of the British Library.)*

5   Fire.
     Pub⁰ by W Blake 17 May 1793

William Blake, "Fire," plate 5 of For Children: The Gates of Paradise, *1793. (By permission of the Trustees of the British Museum.)*

And yet, although at moments such as that just described she is an essential complement to Los, both inspirational and supportive, the emergence of Enitharmon as a separate being is greeted with anguish and dismay by the other "Eternals" as well as by Los himself. This is so not only in *The Book of Urizen* (1794), but also in *The Four Zoas* (in progress from about 1795 for perhaps over a decade). Each separation of a Zoa into an "Emanation" and a "Spectre" takes place in a similar atmosphere of distress. There is an obvious paradox within *The Four Zoas* between, on the one hand, the mourning response to the parturition first of Enitharmon and then of the fiery Orc, and, on the other, the "delighted" harvesting by Los (while Enitharmon breathes "sighs of love") of "furious raging flames" emanating "from the fiery lake of Orc," which—with Enitharmon's adoring aid—become under the hand of Los "a lovely form, inspir'd, divinely human."[114] Damrosch's observation that Blake "wants contraries, but not otherness" has some truth in it, but it is not the whole truth.[115] One of the necessary functions Enitharmon performs is to offer a kind of material matrix for the creative activity of Los.[116] In these terms Jakob Boehme explains the function of Luna, the moon, in its relation to Sol, the sun:

> . . . whatever the sun is, and makes in the spirit-life in itself, the same Luna is, and makes corporeal in itself. It is heavenly, and earthly, and rules the vegtative life; it has the menstrum, viz. the matrix of Venus in it; all whatever is corporeal does congeal [*Gloss:* thicken, curdle] in its property. . . .[117]

Enitharmon as "matrix of Venus" plays her most significant positive role in Blake's myth. The identification with Venus is strengthened by her designation as Los's "Emanation, yet his Wife," since Los is identified with the classical Vulcan, whose wife was Venus. As Venus, Enitharmon is associated with Love and with Beauty—both evident in her creative relationship with Los—and she is also the mother of a potential love-god. Enitharmon's firstborn son, the fiery Orc, is a form assumed by Luvah, Zoa of the passions. Orc might have been a Cupid or Eros, but in effect can never appear in such a role, given the moral rigors and the hypocrisies of the political and social conditions that Blake reacts against in his work. When suppressed, as we have seen, Orc becomes an angrily destructive force. Ironically greeted at birth (in *The Four Zoas*) as "King of Love," he proves himself to be "King of rage & death," the fiery embodiment of social and political revolution.[118]

If Enitharmon embodies in one of her aspects the

them, just as Catherine Blake applied the coloring to her husband's "illuminated books." "Entranc'd" like the dreaming Eve at the foot of the Cross in Blake's depictions of the archangel Michael foretelling to Adam the redemption of mankind, Enitharmon "breath[es] forth" "Spectres," and cradles and nurtures in her maternal arms "those forms, Embodied & Lovely" that Los delineates.[111] In *Paradise Lost* Milton uses the word "entranced" to describe the condition of Adam when the archangel Michael purges his eyes of the film caused by "that false fruit that promised clearer sight," so that he will be enabled to foresee the effects of his Fall in scenes from biblical history, shown to him while Eve lies asleep.[112] Los, like Adam in Milton's lines, is awoken to prophetic foresight—to Blake, synonomous with creative ability—just as Adam himself had been when Eve was created, an analogy Milton causes the archangel Michael to draw as well.[113] But Blake's Enitharmon, though "entranc'd," is not asleep: she participates actively and willingly in the creative process.

wisdom of Athena (or of the Gnostic Sophia), then she can impart it to Los only after he has endured and triumphed in a painful struggle to be reunited with her, a "Union . . . not to be Effected without Cares & Sorrows & Troubles / Of six thousand Years of self denial and . . . of bitter Contrition."[119] "Six thousand years" is traditionally the period of this world, from the Creation to the Day of Judgment.[120] In other words, the union of the sexes from which inspired creation arises takes place, not within historical time, but in a moment of eternity set apart from the stream of time:

> Every Time less than a pulsation of the artery
> Is equal in its period & value to Six Thousand
>   Years,
> For in this Period the Poet's Work is Done: and all
>   the Great
> Events of Time start forth & are conceiv'd in such
>   a Period. . . .[121]

The condition of which Blake spoke to the uncomprehending Crabb Robinson, "a Union of Sexes in Man as in God," cannot be realized in this temporal world.[122] The building of a "resting place for Los & Enitharmon" in the material realm where Tharmas, "rough Demon of the waters," rules, constitutes an implicit acknowledgment of this.[123] Such union is achieved only during those precious moments of inspiration when, in the full flux of creative power, the artist at work engages in "the great Wars of Eternity." Blake gave to this state of being the name "Eden," but described it in *Milton* as "too exceedingly unbounded" for female "Emanations" to endure for long. For them the moonlit "Temporal Habitation" of Beulah is created, "from Great Eternity a mild & pleasant Rest": but an "Emanation" who lingers in "Beulah" or withdraws permanently to it is defecting from her essential role in the artist's "great task," and indeed is undermining his working capability.[124]

In Blake's myth, the androgynous "Union of Sexes," in which human creativity raises and expands Man's consciousness to the limitless potential of his "Divine Humanity," is an ideal state. Its intensity makes it attainable, like the sexual ecstasy which for Blake was its closest parallel, only briefly. In its consummation, Enitharmon, as creative matrix, provides Los with the "shining heaven" upon which he may "fabricate forms *sublime*."[125] But the union may be violently ruptured: by the insurrection of the power-hungry Urizen (who in so doing separates himself from Ahania and rejects her); by the sly manipulation of Luvah (who thereby releases Vala to deceive and torment humanity); by the brute force of Tharmas (who casts out Enion, thus laying waste the earth); or—in a development rather different from those traced through the emanative processes of the other three Zoas—by Enitharmon's assertion of the "Female Will" when, like Eve insisting upon leaving Adam to work apart from him in Paradise, she defies Los and "divides" herself from him. Separated from either Los or the Spectre of Urthona, Enitharmon may then become an image of Milton's Sin, with all that that implies within the morally polarized Miltonic universe. As provider of a creative matrix, Enitharmon plays a positive and constructive role; but as Sin, the emanated Enitharmon is a living and actively destructive fragment of a tragically divided humanity. She becomes treacherously serpentine in nature; her sexuality, both threatening and disgusting, is employed in manipulative ways in order to dominate. (To a large extent Blake shifts this aspect of the separated female on to the characterization of Vala in *The Four Zoas* and *Jerusalem*.) In a parallel to the continual coupling of Sin with Death—"for Death from Sin no power can separate"—Enitharmon is linked in a reprehensibly hermaphroditic sense with her firstborn son. Voracious for power, she unites her forces with those of the terrible Orc and incites the activities of other, equally dangerous and more insidious, offspring.[126] Enitharmon divided from Los is—like Milton's Sin—literally a "key figure" because she holds and can use the key that gives admission into the state that Blake the artist regarded as far more dreadful and threatening than the fiery magnificence of Milton's Hell: the abyss of Chaos.

4
"The Winds of Enitharmon"

"Now comes the night of Enitharmon's joy!
"Who shall I call? Who shall I send,
"That Woman, lovely Woman, may have dominion?"
                                        —William Blake[1]

Northrop Frye observed that the fallen Enitharmon "is typically the mistress of chivalry, spiritually inviolate because wrapped up in herself in a way which makes devotion to her a teasing mockery of love, a frustration of life to be expressed in murder."[2] Blake's prophecy *Europe* (1794) gives to Enitharmon a role that demonstrates par excellence the accuracy of this insight of Frye's. Ruled by the malevolent Female Will, Enitharmon is impelled, in the desire to gain the "dominion" over the male implicit in her assuming the status of the courtly love "domina," to become the negation of, instead of the complement to, the creative force of Los.

Blake's context and inspiration for this work was especially the burgeoning Napoleonic wars in Europe of the 1790s. Warfare was perceived by Blake as "energy Enslav'd"—as the repression and consequent perversion of a huge collective resource of human spiritual energy, ambiguous in its nature, involving man's sexuality and his passions as well as his imagination and his reason.[3] In *Europe* Enitharmon commands the balance between the potentially creative and the actually destructive utilization of the energy of "Warriors" who, "drunk with unsatiated love, . . . rush again to War, for the Virgin has frown'd and refus'd."[4] The frowning "Virgin" whose refusal drives a rejected lover in frustration into battle is the goddess Diana as she appears in Milton's *Comus*.[5] In *Europe* Enitharmon takes on this aspect of the goddess of chastity, with whose birth hers is paralleled in *The Four Zoas*.[6]

Europe opens with the utterance of the "nameless shadowy female" whom Blake had identified in the "Preludium" to *America* as "the shadowy daughter of Urthona."[7] There, Blake had described an incestuous, elemental, encounter between this "dark virgin"—who has been identified with David Hume's "blind nature"—and the fiery firstborn son of Urthona/Los and Enitharmon, the imprisoned Orc, whom Los had bound down.[8] In the opening lines of *Europe* this female arises "from out the breast of Orc, / Her snaky hair brandishing in the winds of Enitharmon."[9] Whether she rises from her embrace with the "terrible boy," or emanates from his bosom as did Enitharmon from that of Urthona, remains unclear: perhaps Blake perceives both as the same thing.[10] This monstrous embodiment of Nature calls upon her mother Enitharmon in tones of loathing. She is presented in the throes of continual childbirth, imaged in a sky-enfolding placenta like an inverted tree:

My roots are brandish'd in the heavens, my fruits
  in earth beneath

Surge, foam and labour into life, first born & first
    consum'd!
Consumed and consuming!
Then why shouldst thou, accursed mother, bring
    me into life?
I wrap my turban of thick clouds around my
    lab'ring head . . .
And all the overflowing stars rain down prolific
    pains.
Unwilling I look up to heaven . . .
[I] bring forth howling terrors, all devouring fiery
    kings . . .
. . . Ah mother Enitharmon!
Stamp not with solid form this vig'rous progeny of
    fires.
I bring forth from my teeming bosom myriads of
    flames.
And thou dost stamp them with a signet; then they
    roam abroad
And leave me void as death. . . .[11]

By invoking Enitharmon during the labor of childbirth, the "daughter of Urthona" emphasizes the relationship of Enitharmon with Luna, the moon, for Lucina, patron of women in childbirth, was an aspect of Diana.[12] The Enitharmon of *Europe* shows all the negative characteristics of the dreaded and ruthless patroness of the Lady of *Comus.* The "snaky-haired" daughter herself is Milton's chilling emblem,

. . . that snaky-headed Gorgon shield
That wise Minerva wore, unconquered virgin,
Wherewith she freezed her foes to congealed
    stone. . . .[13]

"Unwilling," the daughter painfully gives birth through her "lab'ring head," as did Jupiter to that "unconquered virgin."[14] So Milton's Satan gave birth to Sin, and Los in *The Book of Urizen* to Enitharmon. The resentful daughter also brings forth offspring from her "teeming bosom," repeatedly the source from which Blake's "Emanations" emerge from male "Spectres." The "howling terrors" and "myriads of flames" to which she gives rise emerge from the intellectual and emotional sources from which usually, in Blake's mythmaking, female elemental beings emanate from males. This primal material is shaped and branded by Enitharmon herself—"stamp[ed] . . . with a signet."[15] At one level, what is happening is almost, though not quite, a kind of parthenogenesis, as suggested by the Miltonic parallel of the "shadowy female" with the virgin goddess Minerva in *Comus.* Enitharmon is, anomalously (as the inverted–tree image of the "Preludium" implies), the active creative force that molds the "vig'rous progeny of fires" continually brought forth by the daughter whom Orc

had inseminated.[16] The "Preludium" thus describes an essentially *female*—hence, to Blake's patriarchal view, an *unnatural*—process of creation, in which Enitharmon is the dominant "ruach," or creating spirit. Blake's phrase "the winds of Enitharmon" clearly indicates this, for "the winds of Golgonooza" blow when Los and Enitharmon harmoniously and fruitfully unite their labors, which invariably are initiated and guided by Los.[17]

An important parallel to the outcry of the "Preludium" is Satan's revelation to his followers, in book 6 of *Paradise Lost,* that the germinal matter of Hell lies hidden within the soil of Heaven. It contains materials from which, with diabolic ingenuity, the Satanic forces can manufacture deadly explosive devices for use against the hosts of heaven:

This continent of spacious heaven, adorned
With plant, fruit, flower ambrosial, gems and gold,
Whose eye so superficially surveys
These things, as not to mind from whence they
    grow

William Blake, Europe, a Prophecy, *1794, plate 1 (Copy "I"). (By courtesy of the George Grey Rare Books Collection, Auckland City Library, Auckland, New Zealand.)*

William Blake, Europe, a Prophecy, 1794, plate 2 (Copy "I"). (By courtesy of the George Grey Rare Books Collection, Auckland City Library, Auckland, New Zealand.)

> Deep under ground, materials dark and crude,
> Of spiritous and fiery spume, till touched
> With heaven's ray, and tempered they shoot forth
> So beauteous, opening to the ambient light.
> *These in their dark nativity the deep*
> *Shall yield us pregnant with infernal flame. . . .*[18]

To Blake, Milton's lines were a poetic inversion of a passage he annotated at the end of Swedenborg's *Divine Love and Wisdom:*

> It was further shown in the light of heaven, which shone brightly upon it, that the structure of this little brain, as to its arrangement and flux, was in the order and form of heaven, and that its outer structure was in direct opposition to that order and form.[19]

Blake commented on this passage, "Heaven & Hell are born together."[20] So it is with the flamelike progeny of the nameless daughter of Enitharmon in her incestuous union with "the horrent Demon" of ungoverned energy: rooted in Heaven—almost by definition the "heavens of Enitharmon," which pro-

vide Los with the receptive matrix from which to embody his creative inspiration in "divinely human" form—this female's "fruits on earth beneath" are brought forth as "howling terrors, all devouring fiery kings. . . ."[21] In a text surrounded with recognizable images of British political figures of the 1790s, spying upon and throttling one another, the nameless female describes the cataclysmic onset of the Napoleonic Wars in Europe.[22]

War is foreseen by Los, and then invoked by Enitharmon in thwarted spite, as an act of vengeance against her "visionary" male counterpart, in "Night the First" of *The Four Zoas.* Los there prophesies that Enitharmon will remain confined to Tharmas's realm of the senses, never to enter the "bright world" of the human intellect; whereupon, in "Scorn & Indignation," she calls upon Urizen to "descend with horse & chariots!" and to subjugate Los, replacing "Human Nature" and "Human Acts" with "War & Princedom. . . ."[23] The flames whose "burning power" is seized and transformed into "terrors" represent the threatened triumph of Urizen, in "Victory & Blood," in response to Enitharmon's call.

These consuming fires are potentially the same "furious raging flames" that Los the artist (in "Night the Seventh" of *The Four Zoas*) "vanquish'd with the strength of Art . . . drawing them forth delighted . . . From out the ranks of Urizen's war & from the fiery lake / Of Orc."[24] At Enitharmon's urging, and with her loving collaboration, Los with "sweet moderated fury" deployed "the ranks of Urizen's war"— a dynamic intellectual contest, a "Mental Fight"— and harnessed the fiery energy of Orc to "fabricate . . . forms *sublime.*"[25] But in *Europe* the flames of energy are transformed relentlessly into forces of destruction, "devouring & devoured."[26] The plea of Enitharmon's "nameless" daughter to her "accursed mother" *not* to cause these forces to materialize in this destructive form—"Stamp not with solid form this vig'rous progeny of fires"—goes unheard.[27]

The "nameless female" of the "Preludium" foresees the birth of a monstrous offspring, the product of *abused* human energies, when she cries

> "And who shall bind the infinite with an eternal band?
> To compass it with swaddling bands? . . ."[28]

The phrase "who shall bind / the Infinite" is inscribed in Blake's *Notebook* beside a sketch of what was to become the frontispiece of *Europe,* the so-called "Ancient of Days."[29] The finished plate has long been recognized as partly inspired by a passage that in its Miltonic context describes the action of God the son

Lines
Written on hearing the surrender of Copenhagen

The Glory of Albion is tarnishd with shame
And the pride of her might is the scorn of her fame
Her giant strength blesses the nations no more
And the race of the Sun of her honour is oer

Like an Eagle she soard in the youth of her pride
And her joy was the battle of Freedom to guide
As the fate bearing lightning she sped on the wind
And her young on the shade of her pinions reclind
Her haunt was the rock & she chased in dismay
The vulturous Wolf from her Eyrie away
And when the wild tempest howld over the war
Her delight was the wretch from its fury to save
But her giant strength blesses the nations no more
And the race of the Sun of her honour is oer
She hath tasted of blood & her anger hath hurld
The flames blast of war oer a desolate world

O England. when mercy soft murmurd her prayer
And bade the blood of the nations to spare
Thy soul was for war & thy haughty behest
Chasd the Seraph of Peace from thy merciless breast

William Blake, draft sketch, "Who shall bind the infinite. . . ." From the Notebook of William Blake, p. 96. (By permission of the British Library and Oxford University Press. Photograph by David Amoils, Toronto.)

William Blake, Europe, a Prophecy, *1794, plate i (Copy "I"). (By courtesy of the George Grey Rare Books Collection, Auckland City Library, Auckland, New Zealand.)*

as he begins to demarcate the universe and to separate it from original Chaos.[30] Blake's Creator, however, is not the Son, but an aged man with a long beard, the fallen Urizen, whom Enitharmon has called to aid her in her defiance of Los.[31] His beard and hair are blown sideways by the "winds of Enitharmon." The wind blows from the *left* side of Urizen, and he holds the compasses in his *left* hand: literally, in Blake's work, "sinister" signs of a descent into, or confinement within, the material universe, "this cold expanse where wat'ry Tharmas mourns."[32] The phrase "who shall bind the Infinite," and details of the visual image and its association with the "wat'ry Tharmas" of materialism, were suggested to Blake chiefly by two passages from the Book of Job, 26.11: "He hath compassed the waters with bounds . . .," and 38.5–11:

> . . . Who hath laid the measures thereof . . . who hath stretched the line upon it? . . . who shut up the sea with doors, when it brought forth, as if it had issued out of

the womb? When I made the cloud the garment thereof, and thick darkness a swaddling band for it . . . and said, Hitherto shalt thou come, but no further: and here shall thy proud waves be stayed?[33]

This "binder of the Infinite" is surrounded by heavy, threatening clouds and is enclosed within the confines of a circle of his own making. In this atmosphere of gathering darkness and growing oppression, the despairing cry of Blake's "nameless female" trails away, and the terrible progeny, swathed in a "swaddling band" of "thick darkness," enters the world in lines plainly recognizable as a pastiche of Milton's *On the Nativity of Christ.*

The relationship of this poem to Blake's *Europe* is summed up by Bette Charlotte Werner when she compares the optimism of Milton's *Hymn,* express-

William Blake, "The Human Abstract." From Songs of Innocence and of Experience, *1794. (By permission of the Trustees of the British Museum.)*

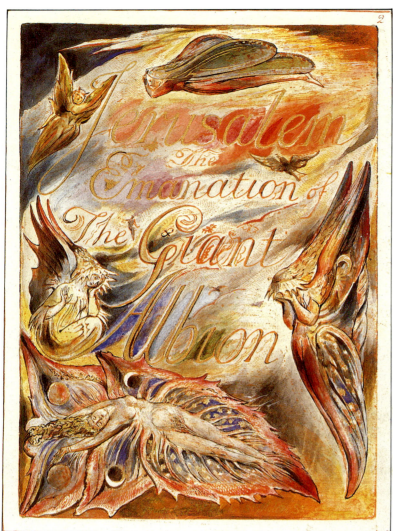

William Blake, Jerusalem, *1804, plate 2 (Copy "E").*
(By permission of the Yale Center for British Art, Paul
Mellon Collection.) See discussion in Chapter 7 of this
version of the title page in relation to Jerusalem, *plate*
85.22 to plate 86.32.

William Blake, "The Flight of Moloch." From the
Thomas series of illustrations to Milton's Hymn on the
Nativity of Christ *(1809). (By courtesy of the Whit-*
worth Art Gallery, University of Manchester.) Compare
the image of Moloch on this plate with the figure of Orc
in Europe, *plate 5 (see Chapter 4).*

William Blake, "The Archangel Raphael with Adam and Eve." From the Butts series of illustrations to Milton's Paradise Lost (1808). (Gift by Subscription. Courtesy of the Museum of Fine Arts, Boston.) See the parallel drawn in Chapter 7 between Milton's account of Raphael in book 5 of Paradise Lost, and Blake's description of Jerusalem in Jerusalem, plates 85 and 86.

ing "a rising note of expectation as [the Puritans] looked for the coming reign of Christ with his saints on earth" with the "reflective and ironic pessimism" of *Europe,* written "near the end of a revolution, at the violent culmination of the Jacobin years."[34] Blake's ironic parody of Milton's hymn to the "Paci-ferum . . . regem [King who brings peace]" sets its scene in a deliberate travesty of Milton's delicately structured stanza form:

> The deep of winter came
> What time the secret child
> Descended thro' the orient gates of the eternal day:
> War ceas'd, and all the troops fled like shadows to
> their abodes.[35]

Beside the etched text of these lines on Blake's plate, the fiery form of the "secret child" is confined—like that of the "binder of the Infinite"—within a circle, a version of the "globe of circular light" in which Milton's warlike cherubim and seraphim appear.[36] When Blake illustrated Milton's lines in 1809, he showed the heavenly warriors thus enclosed carrying

William Blake, Europe, a Prophecy, 1794, plate 3 (Copy "I"). (By courtesy of the George Grey Rare Books Collection, Auckland City Library, Auckland, New Zealand.)

William Blake, The Book of Urizen, 1794, plate 1 (Copy "B"). (By courtesy of the Pierpont Morgan Library, New York. PML 63139.)

William Blake, "The Annunciation to the Shepherds." From the Thomas series of illustrations to Milton's Hymn on the Nativity of Christ (1809). (By courtesy of the Whitworth Art Gallery, University of Manchester.)

the "swords & spears of futurity" foreseen in the vision of Los.[37] Blake's version of Milton's "dreaded infant" is to be "devoted," in his rephrasing of the account given by Milton's God of the dismal future of fallen Man, "to destruction from his mother's womb."[38]

In this pause in hostilities, an ironically "peaceful night" which mocks at that "wherein the Prince of Light / His reign of peace upon the earth began," Los and Enitharmon meet their children in "the crystal house," a fusion of the "crystalline sphere" and "crystal wall" of Milton's Heaven.[39] Los at that moment is "possessor of the moon," being in the harmonious creative relationship with Enitharmon for which Blake's analogue was the alchemical union of Sol and Luna.[40] The sons of Los "shook their bright fiery wings"—an image perceptively rendered by David Erdman as "the poet's works displayed their bright pages."[41] In his joy in the Heaven of creativity, united with Enitharmon, Los contemplates the fruits of their collaborative artistic labors, and is stimulated by his reflections to utter a further illuminated prophecy.

Los speaks of Urizen "unloos'd from chains," glowing "like a meteor in the distant north."[42] The "chains" from which Urizen has been released are those which in Milton's *Hymn* bound "the old dragon under ground / In straiter limits. . . ."[43] Newly liberated, Urizen rises in the place of "Lucifer," the morning star, in the *Hymn*. There Lucifer's warning that dawn was about to break went unheeded by the stars, whose "glimmering orbs did glow" as they, and time, stood still on the morning of Christ's nativity.[44] But Urizen's light is not that of a star rejoicing at the miraculous birth; the quarter from which it arises, glowering ominously "like a meteor," is not the east, from which the light of Milton's newborn Savior emanates, but "the distant north."[45] Urizen is aligned with the rebellious Satan, the *fallen* Lucifer, who in *Paradise Lost* established headquarters in "the limits of the north."[46]

Los commands his sons to "strike the elemental strings," but the sons of Urizen cry out in envy:

> "Sieze all the spirits of life, and bind
> Their warbling joys to our loud strings!"[47]

The birth of Blake's "secret child" arouses universal discord—a bitter inversion of Milton's "full consort" of harmony on the birth of Christ. If the "sons of Los" echo the "divinely-warbled voice" of Milton's angels "answering the stringed noise" of heavenly harmony, those of Urizen respond in carping envy.[48] Reflecting their mood, which in *The Four Zoas* she actually initiated, Enitharmon turns away from Los

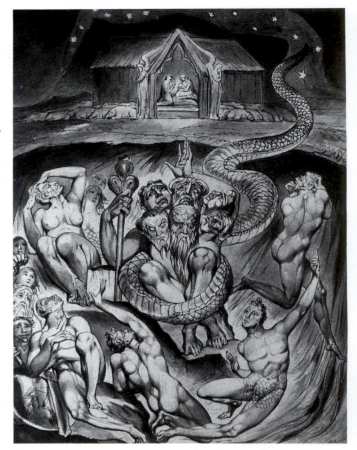

William Blake, "The Old Dragon." From the Thomas series of illustrations to Milton's Hymn on the Nativity of Christ *(1809). (By courtesy of the Whitworth Art Gallery, University of Manchester.)*

to defy him and to assert herself by calling up and thereby *releasing* Orc, whose binding by Los is as consistent a feature of Blake's myth as the separation of the "Emanation" from the "Spectre."[49]

Orc, rising in response to Enitharmon's summons, presents himself in a form derived from Swedenborg's account of the Lord surrounded by angelic hosts in *Heaven and Hell:*

> . . . an entire angelic society, when the Lord manifests Himself as present, appears as one in the human form. There was visible on high, towards the east, something like a cloud, from dazzling white becoming red, with little stars round about . . . as it descended it became brighter and at last was seen in a perfect human form.[50]

Orc's appearance is an inversion of this manifestation:

> The horrent Demon rose surrounded with red stars of fire
> Whirling about in furious circles round the immortal fiend.[51]

Enitharmon, descending to meet him, is engulfed in

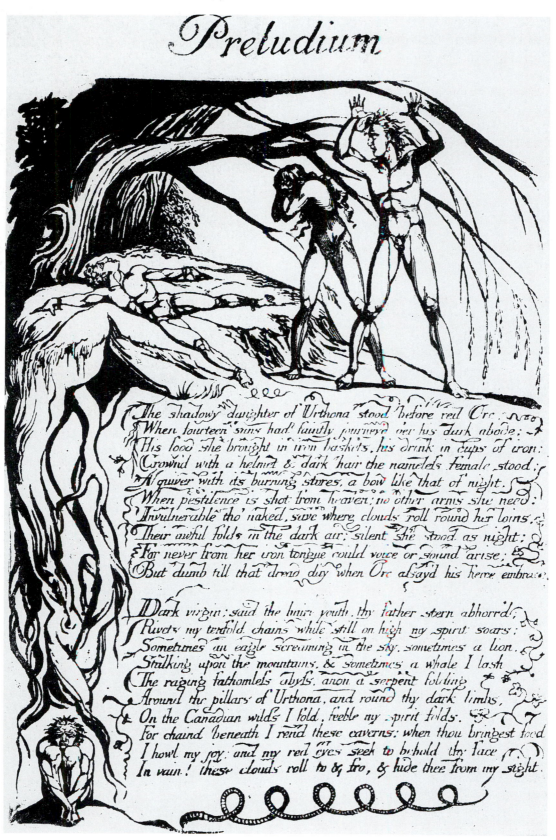

Preludium

The shadowy daughter of Urthona stood before red Orc.
When fourteen suns had faintly journey'd o'er his dark abode;
His food she brought in iron baskets, his drink in cups of iron;
Crown'd with a helmet & dark hair the nameless female stood;
A quiver with its burning stores, a bow like that of night.
When pestilence is shot from heaven; no other arms she need:
Invulnerable tho' naked, save where clouds roll round her loins,
Their awful folds in the dark air; silent she stood as night;
For never from her iron tongue could voice or sound arise;
But dumb till that dread day when Orc assay'd his fierce embrace.

Dark virgin; said the hairy youth, thy father stern abhorr'd;
Rivets my tenfold chains while still on high my spirit soars;
Sometimes an eagle screaming in the sky, sometimes a lion,
Stalking upon the mountains, & sometimes a whale I lash
The raging fathomless abyss, anon a serpent folding
Around the pillars of Urthona, and round thy dark limbs.
On the Canadian wilds I fold, feeble my spirit folds.
For chain'd beneath I rend these caverns; when thou bringest food
I howl my joy; and my red eyes seek to behold thy face
In vain! these clouds roll to & fro, & hide thee from my sight.

William Blake, *America, a Prophecy, 1793,* plate 1.
(By permission of the Trustees of the British Museum.)

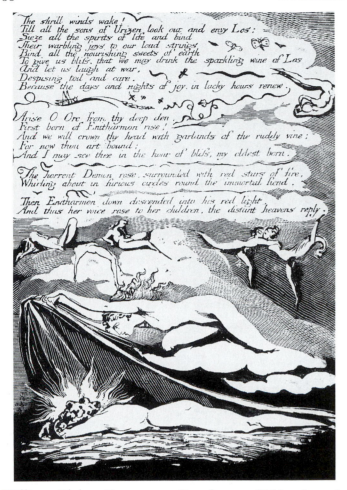

William Blake, Europe, a Prophecy, *1794, plate 4 (Copy "I"). (By courtesy of the George Grey Rare Books Collection, Auckland City Library, Auckland, New Zealand.)*

his "red light."[52] Milton's Satan had explained to his followers that the primary "materials dark and crude" beneath the soil of Heaven respond to the "ambient light" of the celestial atmosphere by "shoot[ing] forth" in forms of heavenly beauty.[53] Correspondingly, Enitharmon shows the influence of Orc's "red light," his wrath-filled ambience, in her declaration of gleeful spite, which resounds through the heavens:

> "Now comes the night of Enitharmon's joy!
> "Who shall I call? Who shall I send,
> "That Woman, lovely Woman, may have
>   dominion? . . ."[54]

Blake's satirical allusion to the well-known passage from Thomas Otway's *Venice Preserved*—

> Oh Woman! lovely Woman! Nature made thee
> To temper man: we had been brutes without you;
> Angels are painted fair, to look like you . . .

—finds its visual expression in the three figures he placed over the text of plate 5, although they also refer obliquely to Milton's *Hymn.*[55] The "horrent Demon," wearing a spiky crown, stands scowling in front of two winged females, fair-skinned and robed in pale gold, one on either side of his figure.[56] In contrast to their fair smoothness, he is dark, almost black, and rough, completely covered with black scales. His "sinister" hand grasps a sword, while his right is placed behind his back (perhaps concealing another weapon). Fear and consternation are expressed in the faces and gestures of the two angelic-seeming female forms flanking him. One, on his right, is light-haired, and folds her arms defensively over her breast; the other, with dark curls, clasps her hands as though in prayer. Both have their eyes fixed apprehensively upon the "brute" standing before them, and appear to be pleading with him.[57] The scale-covered male figure with its crown of spikes is markedly similar, *except in age,* to the figure of Moloch as depicted in both Blake's series of illustrations

William Blake, Europe, a Prophecy, *1794, plate 5 (Copy "I"). (By courtesy of the George Grey Rare Book Collection, Auckland Public Library, Auckland, New Zealand.)*

him "from the ranks of Urizen's war & from the fiery lake / Of Orc."[60] In the "heavens of Enitharmon," with Enitharmon's loving collaboration, and indeed, within a creative matrix she alone can provide—an image of the womb—the fiery harvest is transformed into "a lovely form, inspir'd, divinely human."[61] The "horrent Demon" of *Europe* is the source of the uncontrollable, wildfire spread of "flames of desire" suppressed by social and moral censure, "run[ning] thro' heaven & earth . . . arm'd / With destruction & plagues" and taking the appalling form of war amongst the nations.[62] The flames in both cases are Blake's symbol of passionate energy. In one context it is disciplined and creatively employed; in the other, distorted by repression and subjected to moral censure. Orc has the potential of being either a youthfully handsome love-god or a "horrent Demon," a young Moloch.

The form Orc will take is decided in large part by Enitharmon, now operating in rebellious indepen-

William Blake, Europe, a Prophecy, *1794, plate ii (Copy "I"). (By courtesy of the George Grey Rare Book Collection, Auckland Public Library, Auckland, New Zealand.)

to Milton's *Hymn on the Nativity of Christ* (ca. 1809 and ca. 1815): a "grisly king," an "idol all of blackest hue."[58] In fact the two appear to be the same personage, the figure in *Europe* having aged noticeably by the time he appears, fifteen years or so later, as the gloomy black idol covered with scaly armor in the earlier of the two *Nativity* series. Blake certainly followed Milton in perceiving in Moloch, the barbaric deity to whom children were sacrificed, the personification of War.[59] And Europe was still being ravaged by war when Blake executed his *Nativity Hymn* paintings, whether in 1809 or even 1815.

The scaly monster on plate 5 of *Europe* has a significantly different form from the Cupid-like figure, his head surrounded by a fiery aureole, whose coverlet Enitharmon is lifting on the facing page (plate 4). Nevertheless, *both are forms assumed by Orc.* The image of the godlike youth emanates from the "furious raging flames" of inspired creativity as mastered by Los "with the strength of Art," and gathered up by

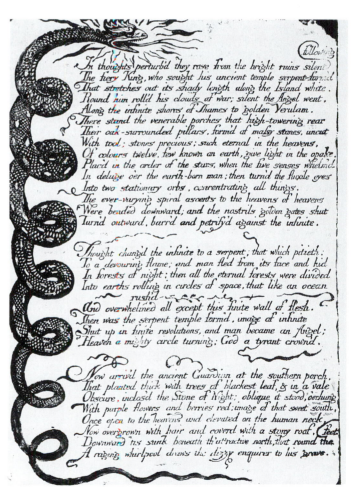

William Blake, Europe, a Prophecy, *1794, plate 10 (Copy "I"). (By courtesy of the George Grey Rare Book Collection, Auckland Public Library, Auckland, New Zealand.)

William Blake, Europe, a Prophecy, *1794, plate 14 (Copy "I"). (By courtesy of the George Grey Rare Book Collection, Auckland Public Library, Auckland, New Zealand.)*

dence of Los as the *negation* of his creativity. In this she becomes the embodiment of the evil and destructive "Female Will" that brings about the disaster. Her assertiveness, in Blake's view, is analogous to that of Eve in her insistence on working apart from Adam in *Paradise Lost,* which enabled the Serpent successfully to tempt her by flattering the "celestial beauty" of his "sovereign mistress" in the absurdly inflated terms of courtly love.[63] The serpents that adorn the title page and plates 10 and 14 of *Europe*—that on plate 10 is an "all devouring fiery king," crowned and spewing out fire—are partly reminders of that "event perverse," when, in Milton's terms, Eve "divided her labours" from those of Adam, and in Blake's, "the Feminine separates from the Masculine & both from Man . . . Life to Themselves assuming. . . ."[64]

Los in *Jerusalem* cries aloud in lamentation:

"O Albion, why wilt thou Create a Female Will?

"To hide the most evident God in a hidden covert, even

"In the shadows of a Woman & a secluded Holy Place. . . ."[65]

The "secluded Holy Place," from which the "Female Will" exercises its malignant domination, brings inevitably to mind Blake's representation of "Catherine/cathedral/Cathedron," the "lady with the 'sanctum sanctorum' between her thighs" in the manuscript of *The Four Zoas.*[66] The female icon secluded in its tryptych shrine in the "Holy Place" suggests the mock-religious climax of *Le Roman de la Rose,* when the ecstatic lover kneels in adoration before the "biau saintuaire" of his ultimate sexual goal—Blake's "rough basement" of English permitting a sardonic wordplay beyond the scope of the French poet's ingenious euphemisms.[67] Blake links the assertion of the "Female Will" with the promulgation by the female, out of false modesty, fear, and a desire to dominate, of the kind of courtly love mystique for her sexuality that is implied in Milton's account of the Serpent's flattery of Eve, perpetuated in Otway's idealizing lines, and satirized by Blake, using much the same imagery, in the "Song of Experience" entitled "The Angel."[68] And, according to Blake, cultural attitudes of this inhibitive kind toward sexuality result eventually in an explosion of man's forcibly repressed passions in naked aggression. Blake had certainly read, by the time he began composing *Europe,* Edmund Burke's *Reflections on the Revolution in France* (1790), in which Burke recalled a meeting with the ill-fated French queen Marie Antoinette:

> It is now sixteen or seventeen years since I saw the Queen of France, then the Dauphiness, at Versailles; and surely never lighted on this orb, which she hardly seemed to touch, a more delightful vision. I saw her just above the horizon, decorating and cheering the elevated sphere she just began to move in, glittering like the morning star, full of life, and splendour, and joy. . . . Little did I dream that I should have lived to see disasters fallen upon her in a nation of gallant men, in a nation of men of honour, and of cavaliers. I thought ten thousand swords must have leaped from their scabbards to avenge even a look that threatened her with insult.[69]

The "ten thousand shields and spears" with which the "maiden queen" in "The Angel" guards her chastity make the same connection between false female modesty and the response of armed aggression as in *Europe* and may well have been inspired by Burke's *Reflections.* The image of the beautiful and doomed queen of France (with whom David Erdman identifies one of the angelic females on plate 5), "just above the horizon, [in an] elevated sphere . . . glittering like the morning star, full of life, and splendour, and joy" must have linked itself in Blake's imagination with the glittering Lucifer of Milton's *Hymn on the Nativity of Christ,* whose light is transformed in *Europe* into the threatening glow of Urizen, about to bring disaster upon a whole continent.[70] The deceiving arts of the separated female, who absorbs the guile of the serpent, are a factor that accelerates and precipitates the imminent catastrophe. This characterization of femininity is encouraged or even created by the courtly love idealization of woman, the attitude assumed by both Burke and Otway. In this tradition she is seen as an angelic creature, apart from and raised *above* man, as Eve was elevated in the seductive speech of the serpent in *Paradise Lost*. In fact, as Blake perceived it, man is indeed maimed when separated from his feminine "counter part"—crippled, like Mulciber/Vulcan after his fall, and like the Spectre of Urthona when *he* falls, with Los, after Enitharmon is physically torn away from the left side of Los by Tharmas. Man without woman is disabled, but Los needs Enitharmon as the partner and helpmeet she was intended to be, according to the patriarchal tradition Blake took over from Milton and the Scriptures. When she assumes the role of a "domina" or courtly love mistress whose will is his law, Enitharmon can only be a pernicious influence on the male from whose being she arose.

The command sent out by Enitharmon to her sons Rintrah and Palamabron is the manifesto of the "Female Will":

> "Go! tell the Human race that Woman's love is Sin;
> That an Eternal life awaits the worms of sixty winters
> In an allegorical abode where existence has never come.
> Forbid all Joy, & from her childhood shall the little female
> Spread nets in every secret path."[71]

Here is the actualization of Urizen's utterance, "When Thought is clos'd in Caves Then love shall shew its root in deepest Hell."[72] Enitharmon as the "counter part" of the "Spectre of Urthona" is a "type" of Venus (as Urthona/Los of Vulcan) and was first called by him "Love."[73] Separated from Los, submitting to the influence of the "horrent Demon" who embodies passion perverted through repression into destructive rage, she firmly identifies herself with "Sin" and roots herself, like Milton's captive personification, "in deepest Hell."[74] By placing herself there she is upholding the morally polarized universe of *Paradise Lost,* in which, according to Blake,

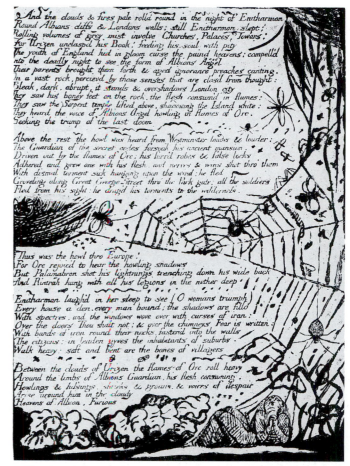

William Blake, Europe, a Prophecy, *1794, plate 12 (Copy "I"). (By courtesy of the George Grey Rare Book Collection, Auckland Public Library, Auckland, New Zealand.)*

Milton recorded the history of the restraint of desire.[75] The antitype of Hell in this universe is the "allegorical abode where existence hath never come." In the futile hope of attaining its false hypothesis of Heaven, the "worms of sixty winters" are constrained to observe Enitharmon's prohibition on "all Joy," and especially on the free and natural expression of sexuality.

To support this joyless social structure, Enitharmon decrees that

> ". . . from her childhood shall the little female
> Spread nets in every secret path."[76]

The coquette in training, this young female who "spread[s] nets in every secret path," is represented visually throughout Blake's illuminated text by images of spiders and their prey. The first spider appears on plate 1 between lines 3 and 4, just before the "nameless female" begins to utter her lament in the "Preludium."[77] Plate 12, whose text recounts the tentacular spread, during Enitharmon's long sleep, of

William Blake, Europe, a Prophecy, *1794, plate 13 (Copy "I"). (By courtesy of the George Grey Rare Book Collection, Auckland Public Library, Auckland, New Zealand.)*

the repressive system fostered by her decree, is covered with spiders and their webs.[78] At the bottom of this page is a human figure tightly bound in a spider's web. Another spider tightropes on its web on a prison wall between lines 8 and 9 on plate 13 of *Europe,* heralding Enitharmon's awakening from her slumber.[79] Several more are scattered, together with the flies they prey on, and other noxious creatures, over plate 14, on which Blake etched the text of Enitharmon's renewed encouragement to her children to continue the culture of sexual repression.[80]

Swedenborg had compared "infernal Love, with its Affections of Evil and of what is False" to

> a Spider and the Web which encompasseth it . . . the Love itself is the Spider . . . and the Delights of these concupisciences with deceitful Machinations are the more remote Threads, where Flies are caught, entangled and devoured.[81]

Blake had parodied this image in the fourth "Memo-

rable Fancy" of *The Marriage of Heaven and Hell,* in which the infernal sun is surrounded by "fiery tracks round which revolv'd vast spiders, crawling after their prey. . . ."[82] But the spiders of *Europe* seem to have a larger significance than those of *The Marriage,* which in any case vanish once the restraint of rationality is removed (the rational Angel climbs "up from his station into the mill") and flexibility of perspective becomes possible ("The man who never alters his opinion is like standing water, and breeds reptiles of the mind").[83] Blake identifies the symbol of the spider's web more expansively in the *Book of Urizen:*

> . . . where ever [Urizen] wander'd, in sorrows . . .
> A cold shadow follow'd behind him
> Like a spider's web, moist, cold & dim . . .
>
> Till a Web, dark & cold, throughout all
> The tormented element stretch'd . . .
> *And the Web is a Female in embrio.*
> None could break the Web, no wings of fire,
>
> So twisted the cords, & so knotted
> The meshes, twisted like to the human brain.
>
> *And all call'd it The Net of Religion.*[84]

Blake's use of the image of the spider in *Europe* may have been influenced by Spenser's enchanting account of the capture of a fly by a spider, and of the legend of Arachne's contest with Minerva, in *Muiopotmos: or, the Fate of the Butterflie* (from which Milton had borrowed details for his descriptions of the flight of Satan and of the Garden of Eden). Spenser's references to Arachne in *The Faerie Queene* may be addi-

William Blake, "The River of Life," ca. 1805. (By permission of the Tate Gallery, London.)

tional sources for Blake's association of the spider with the spiteful manipulation of sexuality in a repressive, morally polarized social system. The spider is an emblem of the sense of touch, with which sexual pleasure is traditionally identified (by Spenser and Milton as well as Blake).[85] Arachne, when outdone in her weaving by Minerva, did "inly fret and felly burn, / And all her blood to poisonous rancour turn" before the goddess transformed her to a spider.[86] Although not specifically identified as a weaver in *Europe*, Enitharmon and her "Daughters" are thus characterized in a positive sense in Blake's mythology, performing the essential function of "clothing the limbs" of "spectres" before they "plunge into the river of space:" that is, clothing spirits with flesh after their conception in the womb, before they are born into the material world.[87] In *The Faerie Queene* Spenser displays the "cunning web" of Arachne spread over the filthy lucre in the Cave of Mammon, *locus classicus* of corrupt and sterile materialism; he

William Blake, Europe, a Prophecy, *1794, plate 11 (Copy "I"). (By courtesy of the George Grey Rare Book Collection, Auckland Public Library, Auckland, New Zealand.)*

also associates Arachne with Acrasia, the female embodiment of destructive sexuality.[88] Both these latter usages, with their connotations of predatory greed, deception, and sexual entrapment, as well as the traditional association of the spider with "poisonous rancour," may have inspired Blake to use the spider as the visual symbol in *Europe* of Enitharmon, whose natural task in his mythic structure is the weaving of mortal bodies at the "Looms of Cathedron," when she leaves Los as Eve willfully left Adam, to "divide [their] labours."[89] In her separated condition, her creative capacity, distorted—as Blake perceives it—by the influence of Orc grown monstrous in his confinement, becomes purely destructive.

Enitharmon now calls upon her sons Rintrah and Palamabron. Rintrah, who is Wrath, hides his "jealous" bride Ocalythron "in desert shades," and here also symbolizes sexual jealousy.[90] Palamabron, a "horned priest," in this context represents the repressive Mosaic law (and may at one level of the allegory be the male figure depicted on plate 11, a pompous, bat-winged pope).[91] His "queen" Elynittria, "silent" and "silver bowed," appears (like Ethinthus later) as a type of frigid chastity derived from Milton's "huntress Dian" with her "dread bow, / Fair silver-shafted queen for ever chaste."[92] As Enitharmon calls for Rintrah's "brethren" she rejoices in the strength and fury of this "king of fire" among her sons, "second to none but Orc."[93] Then, with little warning, she falls asleep.

The sleep of Enitharmon, enduring for "eighteen hundred years," is occupied by her "female dream," the terrifying dream fulfillment of the malevolent "Female Will." It pervades history from the time of the birth of Christ (ironically recalled through the parody of Milton's *Hymn on the Nativity. . . .*) until the present moment of the poem's composition. Plate 9, on which Blake begins to recount the dream in the text, is adorned with one of his most striking images: two energetic flying figures blasting away at serpentine apocalyptic trumpets from which pour flecks of mildew, "destruction and plagues," upon ripening grain, the traditional sustenance of mankind.[94] In the course of this extended nightmare the Council House of England collapses, and its king goes to worship at the temple of Baconian materialism situated by Blake at Verulam (Francis Bacon, whose *Novum Organum* was a kind of gospel of materialistic science, was created Baron Verulam). Humanity shrinks into pitifully diminished forms, and the restrictive religious laws and social constraints of Urizen are enforced throughout the Western world. As Britain becomes engulfed in the flames of war, Orc rejoices to hear the

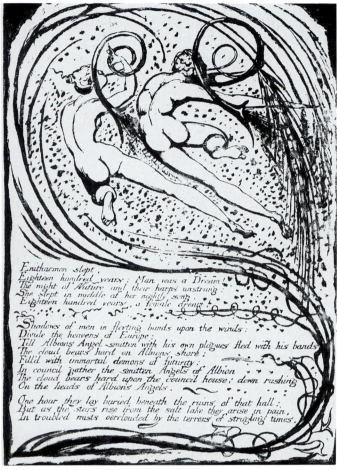

William Blake, Europe, a Prophecy, *1794, plate 9 (Copy "I"). (By courtesy of the George Grey Rare Book Collection, Auckland Public Library, Auckland, New Zealand.)*

"howling" of the "shadows" brought forth in pain by the "shadowy female" of the "Preludium" and stamped at birth by Enitharmon with the "signet" of destruction. Palamabron "[shoots] his lightnings" and the wrathful and jealous Rintrah, imitating the spitefully venomous spider, "[hangs] with all his legions in the nether deep," an image Blake had originally conjured up to depict the Reign of Terror in France in *The Marriage of Heaven and Hell:*

> ". . . a void boundless as a nether sky appear'd beneath us, & we held by the roots of trees and hung over this immensity . . . the nether deep grew black as a sea, & rolled with a terrible noise. . . ."[95]

At this evidence of her sons' loyal support, Enitharmon

> . . . laugh'd in her sleep to see (O woman's triumph!)
> Every house a den, every man bound . . .
> Over the doors "Thou shalt not," & over the chimneys "Fear" is written. . . .[96]

The flames of Orc eventually threaten to consume the flesh of "Albion's Guardian," King George III (whose features, caricatured into foolish vacancy, adorn Blake's bat-winged pope on plate 11). The ineffectual "Guardian" attempts to end the apocalyptic holocaust by blowing the Last Trump but is unable to do so; at last it is seized and blown by "a mighty Spirit . . . nam'd Newton."[97] Miltonic echoes put both Albion's blustering "Guardian" and Newton the rationalist into analogy with the fallen Satan.[98] As "myriads of Angelic hosts" fall through the sky (like Satan's fallen legions) at the sounding of the trumpet, Enitharmon wakes, as suddenly as she fell asleep, "nor knew that she had slept." She calls to her sons and daughters, and "thus her song proceeds."[99]

Enitharmon's roll call of her children enumerates them as "the progressive frustration of sex under the domination of the female."[100] Four couples are summoned: Ethinthus and Manathu-Vorcyon, Leutha and Antamon, Oothoon and Theotormon, Sotha and Thiralatha. Each couple represents one of the consequences of the spider web of false religion spun out by the rebellious "Female Will" that decrees "that Woman's love is Sin." Ethinthus symbolizes frigidity sanctified by religion, coupled—in Manathu-Vorcyon—with the viciously self-righteous punishment of natural sexual responses. Ethinthus is the companion of the "earth-worm" and brings with her a continual morbid awareness of man's mortality. The bleak and cold radiance of this Diana-like daughter of hers is "sweet as comforts" to the soul of Enitharmon. The waters of Ethinthus, like tides responding to changes of the moon, "warble round the feet of Enitharmon" like the "flowery brooks . . . that wash [the] hallowed feet" of Milton's Mount Sion—for Enitharmon has set herself up in her "Woman's Dominion" as Sion, the Temple Mount bearing the "secluded Holy Place" from which the "Female Will" exerts its destructive force.[101] Indeed, Ethinthus's warbling streams recall the "warbling charms" of Milton's Dalila, who, according to S. Foster Damon, embodies "the first thorough analysis" in literature of the "Female Will."[102] Manathu-Vorcyon—"Light of thy mother's soul!"—flames "in soft delusion" as the consort of Ethinthus.[103] His predatory familiars are "lovely eagles"—not in the common sense of "lovely" as "fair," but "arising from [so-called?] love."[104] They "rend their bleeding prey," the breast of the tormented and victimized Oothoon.[105] The "melancholy" Oothoon, and Theotormon, "robb'd of joy," are figures of sexual frustration whose painful history Blake had recounted in the *Visions of the Daughters of Albion.*[106] Oothoon had flown impetuously to unite herself with her lover Theotormon,

William Blake, Visions of the Daughters of Albion, *1793, plate iii. (By permission of the Trustees of the British Museum.)*

desiring to love him openly, without shame; before she could reach him she was raped by Bromion.[107] Rejected by Theotormon, Oothoon in her longing to be loved again by him had called upon eagles "to prey upon her flesh"; but still he could not forgive her.[108] Enitharmon's admonition to her, "Why wilt thou give up woman's secrecy . . . ?" emphasizes that sexual experience in the fallen world is inseparable from shame.[109] The rainbow-colored Leutha, "sweet smiling pestilence," is sexual pleasure condemned as sinful.[110] Blake drew the image from a poem written in his *Notebook* in response to the passage from Burke's *Reflections* quoted earlier. In Blake's poem the "beautiful Queen of France" commands

> "Let the Brothels of Paris be opened
> With many an alluring dance
> To awake the Pestilence thro the City. . . ."[111]

When the queen smiles, "the pestilence / From street

to street did fly."[112] On the same page of the *Notebook* Blake had written stanzas related to the coupled concepts embodied in the "soft deceit" of Leutha and her consort Antamon:

> What is it men in women do require
> The lineaments of Gratified Desire
> What is it women do in men require
> The lineaments of Gratified Desire.
>
> The look of love alarms
> Because tis filld with fire
> But the look of soft deceit
> Shall Win the lovers hire.[113]

Antamon is "Prince of the pearly dew . . . Floting upon the bosom'd air / With lineaments of gratified desire."[114] Probably intended to represent the "pearly dew" of male semen, he materializes tantalizingly only to vanish, like the Cloud (likewise a prince of the "fair-eyed dew" and a figure of virility, but in a positive sense) in the *Book of Thel*.[115] Leutha and Antamon together insinuate pestilence, deceit, and futile evanescence into the enjoyment of sexual experience. Sotha and Thiralatha, inhabitants of the "dreamful caves" of sexual fantasy, are urged by Eni-

William Blake, Visions of the Daughters of Albion, *1793, plate 3. (By permission of the Trustees of the British Museum.)*

tharmon to "arise and please the horrent fiend with your melodious songs."[116] They, more than the other three couples, arouse and pander to the consuming rage of "the horrent fiend." In this last symbolic couple the increasing intensity of sexual repression is brought to the critical point where the fantisizing of frustrated desire is transmuted into aggression.

All these aspects of repressed sexuality summoned by Enitharmon now

> . . . sport beneath the solemn moon,
> Waking the stars of Urizen with their immortal
>   songs,
> That nature felt thro' all her pores the enormous
>   revelry. . . .[117]

The adjective "enormous" is usually used by Blake to mean "monstrous." Nature is appalled at these hideous distortions, which defeat her most fundamental function, the transmission of life. The line describing Nature's response is appropriately remi-

William Blake, Songs of Innocence and of Experience, *1794, title page. (By permission of the Trustees of the British Museum.)*

William Blake, Europe, a Prophecy, *1794, plate 15 (Copy "I"). (By courtesy of the George Grey Book Collection, Auckland Public Library, Auckland, New Zealand.)*

niscent of Milton's description of the effect of the Fall of Eve upon the earth at large:

> Earth felt the wound, and nature from her seat
> Sighing through all her works gave signs of woe
> That all was lost. . . .[118]

So Enitharmon finds ultimately that, like Eve, in establishing her "dominion" she has brought about a "frustration of life to be expressed in murder" and has set into motion a train of events whose outcome appalls even her:

> But terrible Orc, when he beheld the morning in
>   the east
> Shot from the heights of Enitharmon . . .
> And in the vineyards of red France appear'd the
>   light of his fury.
> The sun glow'd fiery red!
> The furious terrors flew around
> On golden chariots raging with red wheels

dropping with blood! . . .
And Enitharmon groans & cries in anguish and
   dismay.[119]

Finally Los himself is dragged into the battle. As
when he had found himself unable to curb the chaotic
rebellion of Urizen, he is swept away helplessly by
the flood tide of events set into motion by Enitharmon's revolt: "He [becomes] what he [beholds] . . .
he [is] himself transformed."[120] So also with the cataclysmic forces set into motion by Enitharmon's revolt. Under the unnatural courtly love "dominion"
of "Woman, lovely Woman," Los is constrained,
"against his better knowledge," absurdly to bend his
creative forces to anticreation. The effects upon Los
are found to correspond with the earthshaking consequences of Adam's yielding, when "Earth trembled
from her entrails . . . nature gave a second groan"
and the poles of the earth "turned askance."[121] Like
the "nameless female" of the "Preludium," Los is
compelled to bring forth fire and bloody warfare in
the sinister blast of the "winds of Enitharmon." Arising in the same "snaky hair[ed]" form as the shadowy
and tragic creature with whose lament the prophecy
began,

> . . . his head he rear'd in snaky thunders clad;
> And with a cry that shook all nature to the utmost
>   pole,
> Call'd all his sons to the strife of blood.[122]

Yet in the final plate of *Europe* Blake still shows
Los saving mankind from the conflagration of the
Napoleonic wars. Man's "Divine Humanity" is represented by the child Los leads from the flames and
by the swooning woman whose senseless form he
carries on his right shoulder. Above the waves of fire
on the right the Bird of Paradise can be seen, rising
unharmed, symbolizing—as on the title page (etched
in the same year as *Europe*) of the combined *Songs of
Innocence and Experience*—the transcendence over the
flames of "Experience" of an artist's capacity for inspired creative work.

5
Ololon I

"Is this our Femin[in]e Portion, the Six-fold Miltonic Female?"
—William Blake[1]

IN THE EPIC *MILTON,* BLAKE TOOK ISSUE ONCE again with the "Miltonic Female" whom he had begun to confront in *The Book of Thel.*[2] It was while he was composing this great prophecy that for the first time he approached the problem overtly in pictorial terms—in the first set of *Comus* designs (1801), his earliest complete series of Miltonic illustrations. In *Milton,* Blake speculates that John Milton's representations of the "Female" and her relationship with her male partner may have been influenced by difficulties he must himself have experienced during his lifetime, in reconciling his own needs—artistic and intellectual, spiritual, emotional, and physical—with the demands and the conflicts of the women about him.[3] Blake too, while working and living at Felpham, had to cope with such pressures, amongst his many other problems. He implies as much in a poem included in a letter to Thomas Butts written late in 1802 which refers to antagonism between his wife and his younger sister, toward whom Blake's attitude was evidently protective, if not somewhat paternal.[4] Taking up suggestions from the biographical account written by his patron William Hayley, Blake must to some extent have identified himself with Milton in that respect as in others.[5] As Blake perceived it, one of the long-term effects of the smoldering domestic insurrection in John Milton's household was that a "feminine principle" essential to creativity was distorted or inadequately represented in Milton's cre-

ative life, as perhaps it had been in Blake's at a critical period.

The historical John Milton (1608–74) married three times.[6] His first wife, Mary Powell, was the daughter of a Royalist family whose political convictions totally opposed those of Milton. Perhaps it was a coincidence that her father Richard Powell owed a large sum of money to Milton's father. Mary, who was only seventeen at the time of the marriage (Milton was twice her age), went back to her family home within two weeks of the marriage in 1642, evidently at her mother's urging. After three years (by which time Milton was seriously considering divorcing her), Mary was persuaded to return to her husband. In what Hayley described as "an occurrence, which has the air of an incident in romance," the truant young spouse suddenly and dramatically reappeared in Milton's house, "repentant . . . kneeling at his feet, and imploring his forgiveness."[7] Milton in due course forgave her, and took her back as his wife. He did not, however, forgive her family, whose property he eventually seized in lieu of their debt to him. After the reconciliation Mary had four children, but did not long survive the birth of the fourth (their third daughter). Her death in 1652 was followed shortly by that of their only son. Milton's second wife Katherine Woodcock, whom he married in 1656, gave birth late in 1657 to a daughter; both mother and infant died early in the following year.

Since Milton had completely lost his sight early in 1652, he had by the time of his first wife's death in May of that year become totally dependent upon his household and family, especially for reading and writing. Contemporary accounts of Milton's domestic life indicate that the three surviving daughters increasingly resented being pressed into service as amanuenses to their blind father. His relationship with his daughters deteriorated further after his remarriage in 1663 to Elizabeth Minshull. A strong mutual disliking between the daughters and their second stepmother (who was only six or seven years older than her eldest stepdaughter) appears greatly to have been exacerbated by her severe treatment of them. Not only did Milton respond with anger to his daughters' hostility, but to the end of his life he was unforgiving of his old grudges against their mother's family. His brother affirmed under oath that John Milton intended his chief legacy to his daughters to be Mary Powell's marriage portion, the sum of a thousand pounds which, though promised at the time of the marriage, had never in fact been paid out to him by the debt-ridden Powells.[8]

In *Milton* Blake gives an account of visionary experiences he claims to have had before and during the period he spent at Felpham.[9] The epic hero speaks as "the Inspired Man," Blake's "Bard" who is the artist of true genius in any age.[10] Blake's Milton recognizes

. . . that the Three Heavens of Beulah were beheld
By him on earth in his bright pilgrimage of sixty
   years . . .
In those three females whom his wives, & those
   three whom his Daughters
Had represented and contain'd, that they might be
   resum'd
By giving up of Selfhood. . . .[11]

The "resumption" of the "Three Heavens of Beulah" is to be twofold. In one sense of the word "resum'd" these "States of Humanity in its Repose" are to be "restored" to Milton, while in another they are to be "summed up"—that is, clearly perceived for what potentially they can be: states progressively more threatening to Man's Humanity, capable of degrading him into chaos.

Blake's concept of "Selfhood" is probably influenced, especially in *Milton,* by Boehme's notion of the distinction between the man of the "spirit" and of the "letter" (in St. Paul's sense), and also by Swedenborg's definition of the *proprium* ("that which is one's own") of the individual man.[12] Boehme's distinction is made in *The Signature of All Things:*

Now that he is born from within out of the speaking voice of God in God's will-spirit, he goes in the byss and the abyss everywhere free, and is bound to no form; for he goes not in self-hood, but the eternal will guides him as its instrument, according as it pleases God: but he that is born only in the letter, he is born in the form of the expressed word, and goes on in the self-hood, and is a self-ful voice; for he seeks what he pleases, and contends about the form, and leaves the spirit which has made the form.[13]

To Boehme, the abandonment of this kind of "Selfhood," and the submission of the individual's will to the will of God, is a necessity for the seeker of spiritual enlightenment. Quoting this passage, Robert N. Essick observes, in his linguistic and semiotic study of Blake's work, that "this mystical tradition provides the context for Blake's unqualified assertion, in his annotations of c. 1789 to Swedenborg's *Wisdom of Angels Concerning Divine Love and Divine Wisdom,* that 'Will is always Evil.'"[14] One might logically link this assertion of Blake's to the *involuntary* suspension by Milton's Satan of his evil intent, which renders him, for a moment, "stupidly good."[15] Blake believed, Essick argues, that "a temporary suspension of the will is necessary for poetic composition."[16] The "proprium" of Swedenborg, itself intrinsically willful, still possesses the Milton who first appears in Blake's epic:

What a man loves above all things, that he has for an end: he has regard to it in each and all things: it is in his will like the hidden current of a stream, drawing and bearing him along. . . . A man is entirely of such a quality as is the ruling motive of his life; by this he is distinguished from others: in accordance with this, his heaven is made if it is good, or his hell if it is evil; it is his will itself, his *proprium,* and his nature, for it is the very *esse* of his life. This cannot be changed after death, because it is the man himself.[17]

In this Swedenborgian sense Milton's spirit is shown

. . . wand'ring thro' Death's Vale
In conflict with those Female forms, which in
   blood & jealousy
Surrounded him . . .[18]

Milton himself, in Blake's poem, courageously undertakes to resolve this conflict by relinquishing his "Selfhood." Heroically he prepares to "go to Eternal Death," "Annihilat[ing] the Self-hood of Deceit & False Forgiveness."[19]

An expanded symbolic version of the historical Milton's "forgiveness" of his wife Mary is twice enacted in *Milton.* In book 1 the multitudinous "hosts of Ololon"—Milton's female "Emanation"—express their "repentance" to the "Divine Family" in Eden.[20]

In book 2 Ololon approaches Milton's "Couch of Death" in Eternity:

> They thunderous utter'd all a universal groan,
>   falling down
> Prostrate before the Starry Eight, asking with tears
>   forgiveness,
> Confessing their crime with humiliation and
>   sorrow.[21]

The repentance of the "hosts of Ololon" is received with rejoicing. Ololon's atonement is the necessary precursor to the "at-one-ment" of its multitude into "One Female" and of the "Starry Eight" into "One Man, Jesus the Saviour . . . round his limbs / The Clouds of Ololon folded as a Garment. . . ."[22] In a final "at-one-ment" Jesus, clothed in "The Clouds of Ololon," enters into Albion's bosom to unite with him. The contrition, confession, and forgiveness in Eternity heralds Ololon's descent to earth and Milton's final achievement, after a momentous struggle, of the purged, regenerated and *reintegrated* condition in which his "Selfhood" is annihilated.[23] "Collecting all his fibres into impregnable strength," Milton materializes, as the poem approaches its climax, in Blake's cottage garden at Felpham.[24] He appears to the astonished Blake "clothed in black, severe & silent," in the Puritan garb and sober mien Blake imagines him to have worn during his lifetime.[25] There, in Blake's presence, Milton confronts his own Selfhood in the form of the Miltonic Satan, rebel against the will of God, whom he acknowledges as "my Spectre." He declares

> "I come to discover before Heav'n & Hell the Self
>   righteousness
> In all its Hypocritic turpitude . . .
>   . . . & put off
> In Self Annihilation all that is not of God alone,
> To put off Self & all I have, ever & ever, Amen."[26]

"Discover[ing]" (i.e., revealing by uncovering) hypocritical self-righteousness and "put[ting] off Self," Milton turns at last to his "Emanation" Ololon, who in the form of "a Virgin of twelve years" has preceded him into the garden at Felpham on that morning of wonders. She has already been recognized by Blake, out for an early morning stroll, as "the Virgin Ololon . . . a Daughter of Beulah."[27] Milton sternly declares to Ololon

> "There is a Negation, & there is a Contrary:
> "The Negation must be destroy'd to redeem the
>   Contraries.
> "The Negation is the Spectre, the Reasoning Power
>   in Man:

> "This is a false Body, an Incrustation over my
>   Immortal
> "Spirit, a Selfhood which must be put off &
>   annihilated alway. . . ."[28]

Trembling as Oothoon trembled in her "virgin fears," Ololon in turn responds to Milton's enlightened perception, switching in her reply from the plural of the multitudinous "hosts" to the singular in her self-reference:

> "Is this our Femin[in]e Portion, the Six-fold
>   Miltonic Female?
> "Terribly this Portion trembles before thee, O
>   awful Man.
> "Altho' our Human Power can sustain the severe
>   contentions
> "Of Friendship, our Sexual cannot, but flies into
>   the Ulro.
> "Hence arose all our terrors in Eternity;
>   & now remembrance
> "Returns upon us; are we Contraries, O Milton,
>   Thou & I . . .
> "Thou goest to Eternal Death & all must go with
>   thee."[29]

Ololon distinguishes, as did Mary Wollstonecraft, between the "Sexual" and the "Human," significantly placing the "Human Power" of the "Feminine Portion" on an equal footing with that of the "awful man" before her: it *can* "sustain the severe contentions / Of Friendship," though the "Sexual" cannot.[30] The "Ulro," to which the "Sexual [Power]" of the "Miltonic Female" flies, is the "Seat of Satan" whose inhabitants are plagued by "the terrors of Chastity that they call / By the name of Morality. . . ."[31] Blake coined the name "Ulro," according to Sheila A. Spector, from Hebrew sources meaning "loss of vision":

> Easily identifiable as an aggregate of AL, "negation" and *Ro'EH*, from the root "Vision," Ulro could literally signify darkness, "deepest night" (*Jerusalem*, 42.17), symbolically the loss of vision, "dreams . . . dark delusive" (*FZ*, N7.331), or both (*Milton*, 9.30–35).[32]

The "loss of vision" implied by the name of this "state" in all its manifestations in Blake's work is clearly the worst possible form of punishment for the human soul, and specifically for the soul of the artist/ prophet. It is a condition far more terrible than the loss of eyesight suffered by the historical Milton: it is the terminal "State of Humanity in its Repose," a plunge into spiritual darkness, a living death.

As Ololon declares her intention to make with Milton the same heroic sacrifice as he has

. . . the Virgin divided Six-fold, & with a shriek
Dolourous that ran through all Creation, a Double Six-
fold Wonder
Away from Ololon she divided & fled into the depths
Of Milton's Shadow. . . .[33]

The "Double Six-fold Wonder" that divides and flees away from Ololon departs with the same "shriek" as did that other virgin, Thel, when she fled precipitately back to the sanctuary of the Vales of Har.[34] Like Thel, the sixfold female is a form of the "Female Will." Its "doubleness" in this manifestation is that of Blake's "cruel two-fold Monster," a sinister hermaphrodite: "A Female hidden in a Male, Religion hidden in War, / Nam'd Moral Virtue . . . A Dragon red & Hidden Harlot. . . ."[35] It combines the duplicity and hypocrisy of Spenser's Duessa with the indeterminate sexuality of the traditional evil witch-figure.[36] This "Wonder" embodies the perverted virginal aspect imposed upon Ololon by the malevolent "Female Will."[37] The creature's refuge in "the depths / of Milton's Shadow" lies within the bosom of Satan, the rebel who pitted his own will against the Divine Will, and whom Milton has recognized as his "Spectre."[38]

Blake's "Female Will," the feminine equivalent of the Satanic "Selfhood" of his personage Milton, had its origin (as we have seen) in the rebellious will of the Eve of *Paradise Lost,* and of Genesis. Because of it Eve had persisted in the "error" (according to the Scripturally-based patriarchy espoused no less by Blake than by Milton) of foolish self-assertion. Instead of combining her creative energies with those of Adam in wifely support, she had insisted on "dividing" her labors from his in the Garden of Eden, by this means exposing herself to the seduction of the Satanic tempter.[39] Blake treats this act of willfulness as a usurpation:

> "There is a Throne in every Man, it is the Throne
>   of God
> "This, Woman has claim'd as her own, & Man is
>   no more! . . .
> "O Albion, why wilt thou Create a Female
>   Will? . . ."[40]

In *Milton* the "Female Will" is embodied in the five daughters of the biblical Zelopehad, Tirzah and her four sisters, who had demanded that their father's inheritance be given to them.[41] To these five Blake adds a "mother," Rahab, to make up the "Six-fold Miltonic Female."[42] In "Eternity" the six surround Milton in the form of "rocky masses terrible," "as the rocks of Horeb round the land / Of Canaan."[43]

Fraught with anger and forcibly suppressed resentment, as Blake visualizes the wives and daughters of the historical Milton to have been, "they wrote in thunder, smoke and fire / His dictate," while Milton, responding defensively to the fiercely smoldering hostility of their presence, became "the Rock Sinai" (from which Moses handed down the Law to the Children of Israel—often referred to by Blake as Mount Horeb), disseminating in his dictated works the cruel religion of "Self-righteousness."[44] The six females dominate the "dreadful" depths of the "Ulro," where—under conditions in which Man's visionary faculties are completely suppressed—they create the time-bound material body of man, for Tirzah is the "mother of [man's] mortal part."[45]

Ololon is released from the power of the "Female Will" by her recognition that she is *not* Milton's hostile "Negation," but his complementary "Contrary," and by her consequent act of self-sacrifice in electing to follow Milton to "Eternal Death." Freed from the strictures of the perverse and destructive misconception of the "Femi[ni]ne Portion" implied in the "Female Will," Ololon is enabled to unite with Milton. As befits a man whose genius placed him, in Blake's eyes, among the greatest of artist-creators, at the climax of the epic Milton, united with his "Emanation," becomes one with the supreme Artist and Creator, the Divine Humanity of Jesus.[46]

"So saying, the Virgin divided Six-fold . . . Away from Ololon": the "virginal" aspect of Ololon's femininity is unmasked in all its hypocrisy and flees "into the depths / Of Milton's Shadow, as a Dove upon the stormy Sea." No doubt Blake had in mind the biblical dove that brought hope to Noah of the subsidence of the turbulent Flood; but there seems to have been another element as well. In alchemy, the descending "Dove" is the catalyst in the "hieros gamos" (sacred marriage) of Sol and Luna, which results in the literal fusion of the two sexes into one body.[47] Blake's monstrous hermaphroditic "Wonder" is thus a kind of scourge, an instrument of regeneration bringing about its own destruction. (Blake presents a "contrary" view of the event in the full-page illustration of plate 38 [Copy B] of *Milton.* An eagle hovering in a night sky screeches to arouse and thus to *separate* a pair of lovers, Milton/Los and his "emanation," who lie entwined on a rocky outcrop amidst a calm sea—on the "watery shore" of the material world in the darkness of the night of Time. The eagle opposes the alchemical dove in its symbolism, and is simultaneously Blake's familiar emblem for Genius.)

Ololon now descends into "Felpham's Vale" "as a

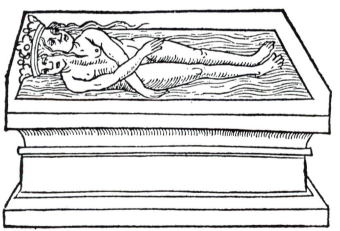

Three stages in the "hieros gamos" (sacred marriage) of Sol and Luna: the descent of the catalytic dove, the union of the Sun-King and Moon-Queen, and the lifeless "Hermaphroditus" lying in its tomb. (From the Rosarium Philosophorum [Frankfurt-on-Mainz, 1551]. Reproduced in C. G. Jung, An Account of the Transference Phenomena Based on the illustrations to the "Rosarium Philosophorum," in Collected Works, vol. 16; fig. 4, 5, and 6, pp. 241, 247, and 265.)

Moony Ark"—one of Blake's persistent symbols of the love that ensures the survival of the human spirit despite the oppression of the material world that threatens to extinguish it.[48] In the poem's apocalyptic conclusion Milton's "Emanation" is transformed into "Clouds . . . folded as a Garment dipped in blood, / Written within & without in woven letters."[49] In this hieratic form Ololon enfolds the body of "One Man, Jesus the Saviour," with whom the "Starry Eight" (the composite of Milton's spirit and the "Seven Angels of the Presence") have combined.[50] An apocalyptic fulfillment of the vision of Blake's great lyric in the "Preface" fills the heavens: as "in ancient time / [he] walk[ed] upon England's mountains green . . . ," so at this moment "Jesus . . . walked forth / From Felpham's Vale clothed in Clouds of Blood to enter into / Albion's Bosom. . . ."[51] Overcome by a momentary swoon of terror, Blake falls "outstretch'd upon the path" of his cottage garden.[52] Recovering, he finds his own "sweet Shadow of Delight" beside him, trembling as did Ololon before the majestic presence of Milton.[53] William and Catherine Blake, reunited, assume the forms of Los and Enitharmon—the inspired artist joined at last by his true feminine counterpart and helpmeet. Together they rise "over the Hills of Surrey" into the visionary heaven inhabited by artists engaged in the labors of creative productivity.[54] "Their clouds roll over London" as Blake's imagery wishfully enacts what he confided to Thomas Butts in a heartfelt letter from Felpham, "That I can alone carry on my visionary studies in London unannoy'd. . . ."[55]

Near the head of plate 12 of *Milton* appears a group of "rocky masses."[56] David Erdman identifies them as human skulls and stones on "the altar of blood sacrifice" associated with the murder of Abel by Cain. But they may also suggest those "Seven rocky masses terrible in the Desarts of Midian": Milton himself as the "Rock Sinai" with the six females "rang'd round him as the rocks of Horeb round the land of Canaan."[57] The "rocky masses" are flanked by two figures, one lying dead with head toward the reader, the other fleeing as Cain did from the murdered Abel.[58] Cain's forward stride in his flight suggests a "Negation" of the mutually supportive fraternal relationship visually depicted in *Milton*, on plates headed "William" and "Robert," between William Blake on earth, his body flung back in a state of visionary receptivity, and his brother Robert in the mirror reflection of this attitude in Eternity.[59] Both brothers receive the starlike "spirit" of Milton, sharing the visionary experience and its inspiration between them as dynamic "Contraries" respectively of

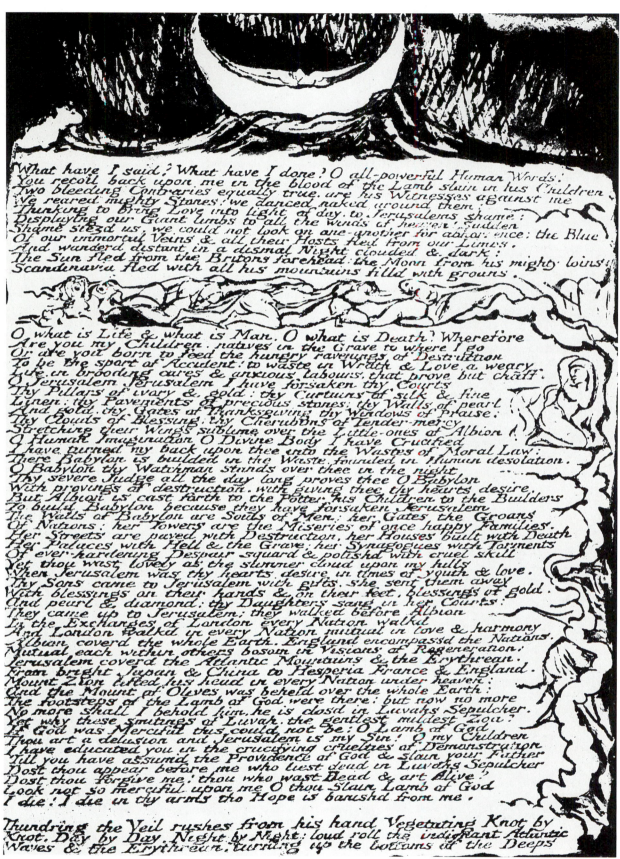

What have I said? What have I done? O all-powerful Human Words!
You recoil back upon me in the blood of the Lamb slain in his Children
Two bleeding Contraries equally true. are his Witnesses against me
We reared mighty Stones: we danced naked around them:
Thinking to bring Love into light of day. to Jerusalems shame:
Displaying our Giant limbs to all the winds of heaven: Sudden
Shame seizd us, we could not look on one-another for abhorrence: the Blue
Of our immortal Veins & all their Hosts fled from our Limbs
And wanderd distant in a dismal Night clouded & dark:
The Sun fled from the Britons forehead: the Moon from his mighty loins:
Scandinavia fled with all his mountains filld with groans.

O what is Life & what is Man. O what is Death? Wherefore
Are you my Children. natives in the Grave to where I go
Or are you born to feed the hungry ravenings of Destruction
To be the sport of Accident! to waste in Wrath & Love, a weary
Life. in brooding cares & anxious labours. that prove but chaff.
O Jerusalem Jerusalem I have forsaken thy Courts
Thy Pillars of ivory & gold: thy Curtains of silk & fine
Linen: thy Pavements of precious stones: thy Walls of pearl
And gold. thy Gates of Thanksgiving thy Windows of Praise:
Thy Clouds of Blessing: thy Cherubims of Tender-mercy
Stretching their Wings sublime over the Little-ones of Albion
O Human Imagination O Divine Body I have Crucified
I have turned my back upon thee into the Wastes of Moral Law:
There Babylon is builded in the Waste, founded in Human desolation.
O Babylon thy Watchman stands over thee in the night
Thy severe Judge all the day long proves thee O Babylon
With provings of destruction. with giving thee thy hearts desire.
But Albion is cast forth to the Potter his Children to the Builders
To build Babylon because they have forsaken Jerusalem
The Walls of Babylon are Souls of Men: her Gates, the Groans
Of Nations: her Towers are the Miseries of once happy Families.
Her Streets are paved with Destruction, her Houses built with Death
Her Palaces with Hell & the Grave: her Synagogues with Torments
Of ever-hardening Despair squard & polishd with cruel skill
Yet thou wast lovely as the summer cloud upon my hills
When Jerusalem was thy hearts desire in times of youth & love.
Thy Sons came to Jerusalem with gifts. she sent them away
With blessings on their hands & on their feet. blessings of gold.
And pearl & diamond: thy Daughters sang in her Courts:
They came up to Jerusalem: they walked before Albion
In the Exchanges of London every Nation walkd
And London walkd in every Nation mutual in love & harmony
Albion coverd the whole Earth. England encompassd the Nations.
Mutual each within others bosom in Visions of Regeneration:
Jerusalem coverd the Atlantic Mountains & the Erythrean.
From bright Japan & China to Hesperia France & England.
Mount Zion lifted his head in every Nation under heaven:
And the Mount of Olives was beheld over the whole Earth:
The footsteps of the Lamb of God were there: but now no more
No more shall I behold him, he is closd in Luvahs Sepulcher.
Yet why these smitings of Luvah. the gentlest mildest Zoa?
If God was Merciful this could not be: O Lamb of God
Thou art a delusion and Jerusalem is my Sin! O my Children
I have educated you in the crucifying cruelties of Demonstration
Till you have assumd the Providence of God & slain your Father
Dost thou appear before me who liest dead in Luvahs Sepulcher
Dost thou forgive me! thou who wast Dead & art Alive?
Look not so merciful upon me O thou Slain Lamb of God
I die! I die in thy arms tho Hope is banishd from me.

Thundring the Veil rushes from his hand Vegetating Knot by
Knot. Day by Day. Night by Night: loud roll the indignant Atlantic
Waves & the Erythrean. turning up the bottoms of the Deeps

William Blake, Jerusalem, *1804, plate 24 (Copy "A").*
(By permission of the Trustees of the British Museum.)

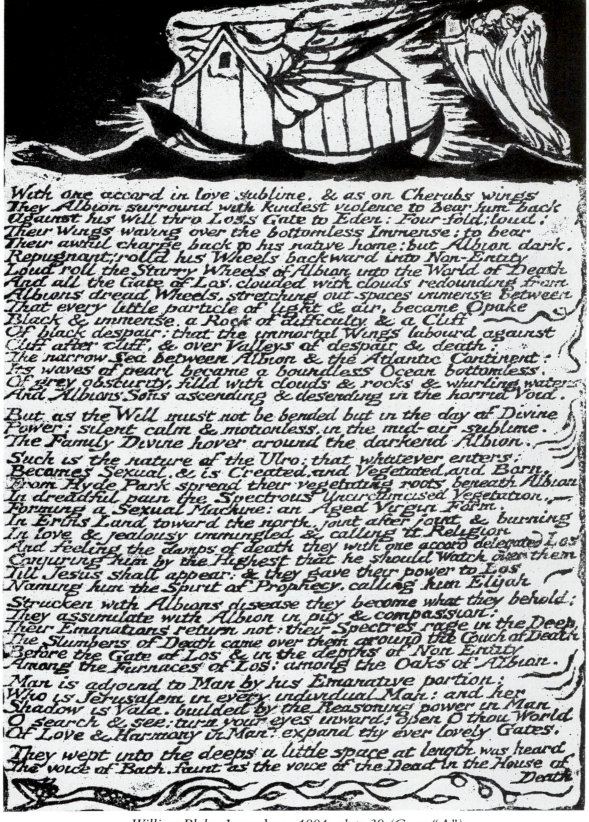

With one accord in love sublime. & as on Cherubs wings
They Albion surround with kindest violence to bear him back
Against his Will thro Los's Gate to Eden: Four-fold; loud!
Their Wings waving over the bottomless Immense: to bear
Their awful charge back to his native home: but Albion dark,
Repugnant; rolld his Wheels backward into Non-Entity
Loud roll the Starry Wheels of Albion into the World of Death
And all the Gate of Los, clouded with clouds redounding from
Albions dread Wheels, stretching out spaces immense between
That every little particle of light & air, became Opake
Black & immense, a Rock of difficulty, & a Cliff
Of black despair: that the immortal Wings labourd against
Cliff after cliff, & over Valleys of despair & death:
The narrow Sea between Albion & the Atlantic Continent:
Its waves of pearl became a boundless Ocean bottomless,
Of grey obscurity, filld with clouds & rocks & whirling waters
And Albions Sons ascending & descending in the horrid Void.

But as the Will must not be bended but in the day of Divine
Power; silent calm & motionless, in the mid-air sublime,
The Family Divine hover around the darkend Albion.

Such is the nature of the Ulro: that whatever enters:
Becomes Sexual, & is Created, and Vegetated, and Born,
From Hyde Park spread their vegetating roots beneath Albion
In dreadful pain the Spectrous Uncircumcised Vegetation.
Forming a Sexual Machine: an Aged Virgin Form.
In Erins Land toward the north, joint after joint & burning
In love & jealousy immingled & calling it Religion
And feeling the damps of death they with one accord delegated Los
Conjuring him by the Highest that he should Watch over them
Till Jesus shall appear: & they gave their power to Los
Naming him the Spirit of Prophecy, calling him Elijah

Strucken with Albions disease they become what they behold:
They assimilate with Albion in pity & compassion:
Their Emanations return not: their Spectres rage in the Deep
The Slumbers of Death came over them around the Couch of Death
Before the Gate of Los & in the depths of Non Entity
Among the Furnaces of Los: among the Oaks of Albion.

Man is adjoind to Man by his Emanative portion:
Who is Jerusalem in every individual Man: and her
Shadow is Vala, builded by the Reasoning power in Man
O search & see: turn your eyes inward: open O thou World
Of Love & Harmony in Man: expand thy ever lovely Gates.

They wept into the deeps a little space at length was heard
The voice of Bath, faint as the voice of the Dead in the House of
Death

William Blake, Jerusalem, 1804, *plate 39 (Copy "A").*
(By permission of the Trustees of the British Museum.)

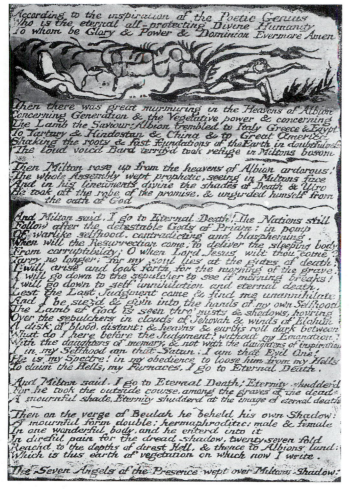

William Blake, *Milton, 1804, plate 12 (Copy "B,"*
RB54041). (By permission of the Huntington Library,
San Marino, California.)

the material and spiritual worlds. Elsewhere in the
poem, Blake shows a "negative" female response to
that same event: at the foot of plate 14 (as numbered
in Copies A and B) the nude "William" figure is
struck by the starlike form of Milton to the left of
Cain's crumbling altar, while to its right a clothed
female form—be it wife, sister, or daughter—cringes
in fear away from the supernatural visitant.

Similarly, on the title page of "Book the Second,"
two robed figures, male and female—Milton and
Ololon—their toes touching, seem to flee in panic in
opposite directions. Their positions are exactly opposed to those in which the "William" and "Robert"
contraries are shown in the plates thus titled, which
Blake in all copies placed so that "William" precedes
and "Robert" follows this title page. In turn, the figures on the title page of "Book the Second" seem to
comment, in their relationship to the two brother-
collaborators, upon the attempt to separate made by
the nude male and female figures, also touching toes,

who are twisting away from one another under the
title "Book the First" on plate 3. They are the male
"Spectre" and the female "Emanation," the "Self-
hood" and the "Female Will." Willfully they strive
to part despite the undeniable visual evidence that
they are not only *organically* united, springing as they
do from one apparently vegetable source, but are also
jointly receiving spiritual enlightenment from the
Miltonic star of inspiration, which sheds its beams
on *both* figures. The two figures on plate 3 are associated with ears of wheat (the male) and grapes (the
female), symbolizing the bread and wine of the re-
deeming sacrament of forgiveness. The straining of
the two away from one another on plate 3 seems to
express Milton's troubled relationship with his female "Emanation," much in the terms in which Blake
articulated such a conflict and its reconciliation in a
Notebook poem of the same period as *Milton* (to which
he refers on plate 32 of the epic):

> Till [thou *del.*] I turn from Female Love
> And [dig *del.*] root up the Infernal Grove
> [Thou shalt *del.*] I shall never worthy be
> To Step into Eternity . . .
> & Throughout all Eternity
> I forgive you you forgive me
> As our dear Redeemer said
> This the Wine & this the Bread[60]

The "Six-fold Miltonic Female" appears pictorially
at the top of plate 16, just above the lines of text
that speak of "those three females whom [Milton's]
wives, & those three whom his Daughters / Had represented and contain'd."[61] Blake there etched two
groups, each of three women, all clothed in flowing
robes. Those on the left are young and are set against
a background colored like a fiery sunset.[62] One steps
forward as though in the movement of a dance, her
arms lifted, hands resting on the top of her head,
which is turned to her right. Her sisters, one kneeling
on either side of her, bend away from her respectively
to the right and left, their arms upraised to frame
their heads. The movements of their bodies seem to
be expressive of sorrow, but the young woman on
the reader's extreme left bears a knife in her raised
right hand, adding a hint of vindictive aggression.
(Erdman identifies the weapon as the knife of Cain.[63])
To the right of this group, against a background of
dark night, three older women with set, angry faces,
each wearing a scarf that severely covers her hair, sit
on a scrolled couch. The first and third have the right
leg extended and the left drawn back, and all in uni-
son turn their heads and upper bodies away from the
younger women as though in rejection. These two

William Blake, "Cain Fleeing from the Wrath of God."
(Courtesy of the Fogg Art Museum, Harvard University.
Bequest of Grenville L. Winthrop.)

groups are notable for their *separateness:* not only is there a division between the young and the old, but within each group no individual woman seems to touch or respond to another. Blake has here depicted, in a selectively simplified symbolism, the historical relationship of Milton's three wives and trio of daughters to one another (and perhaps also, in a remote symbolic echo, the relationship of his own wife with his younger sister). Through their jealous conflicts, both among themselves and against their husband and father (or father figure), these women had "negated" and hindered the progress of his creative work by their self-assertion, weighing him down toward the vegetative world in the night of Time (symbolized by their background of sunset and gathering darkness) instead of dedicating themselves, as a united feminine "contrary," to sustaining and complementing the labors of a divinely inspired artist so

William Blake, Milton, 1804, plate 29 (Copy "B," RB54041). (By permission of the Huntington Library, San Marino, California.)

William Blake, Milton, 1804, plate 33 (Copy "B," RB54041). (By permission of the Huntington Library, San Marino, California.)

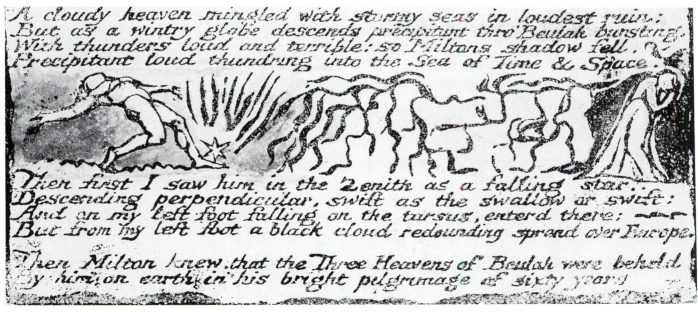

William Blake, Milton, 1804, detail of plate 14 (Copy "B," RB54041). (By permission of the Huntington Library, San Marino, California.)

William Blake, Milton, 1804, plate 30 (Copy "B," RB54041). (By permission of the Huntington Library, San Marino, California.)

William Blake, Milton, 1804, plate 3 (Copy "B," RB54041). (By permission of the Huntington Library, San Marino, California.)

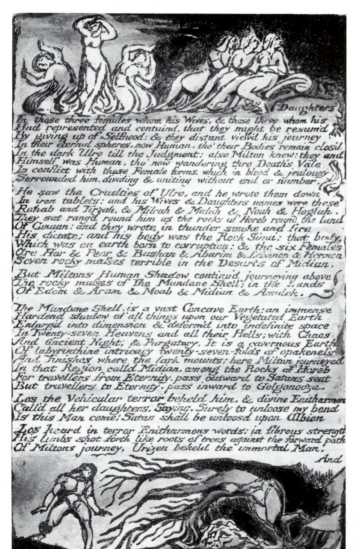

William Blake, Milton, 1804, plate 16 (Copy "B," RB54041). (By permission of the Huntington Library, San Marino, California.)

that, united with them, he is freed "To Step into Eternity."[64]

On the upper part of plate 43, in the midst of Milton's address to Ololon in Blake's garden, Blake depicts the ideally unified state of the "Six-fold Miltonic Female" with whom Ololon associates herself on this plate when tremulously, in her reply to Milton, she acknowledges that she is his feminine "Contrary."[65] Six nude female figures are intertwined in this motif. The first, third, fifth, and sixth from the reader's left face the front, the second and fourth turn their backs to the reader. (Are these latter the two wives who predeceased Milton?) Their arms are raised and linked by holding hands in an intricate pattern, their legs intertwine. Their bodies are set against an oval of glowing yellow light surrounded by a dark irregular border, as though the visionary forms are suspended in the air and are being viewed from within a subterranean cave whose mouth is overgrown with projecting roots and stems of vegetation—the "cavern" in which "man has closed himself up," an alternative form of the enveloping "Mundane Shell" in the "vegetative world."[66] Both the nudity of these figures and their rhythmically patterned physical joining with one another oppose this group to the depiction of the

William Blake, Milton, *1804, plate 13 (Copy "B," RB54041): "Then Milton rose up from the heavens of Albion ardorous. . . . He took off the robe of the promise & ungirded himself from the oath of God." (By permission of the Huntington Library, San Marino, California.)*

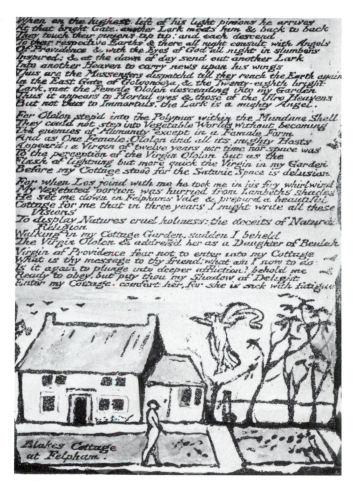

William Blake, Milton, *1804, plate 36 (Copy "B," RB54041). (By permission of the Huntington Library, San Marino, California.)*

William Blake, Milton, *1804, plate 43 (Copy "B," RB54041). (By permission of the Huntington Library, San Marino, California.)*

six women on plate 16, annulling the baleful influence of such feminine conflict as that with which the historical life of John Milton was continually beset.

On the lower third of plate 36, Ololon is shown as a single young female figure with gossamer robes billowing from her shoulders, arms extended as she descends as though flying upright into the garden of "Blakes Cottage at Felpham"—so denoted by lettering on the patch of lawn in front of it.[67] Blake himself (or, perhaps simultaneously, Milton in his Puritan garb), a figure walking contemplatively toward the path on which Ololon will alight, appears in the foreground. In contrast to the previous description of "the multitudes of Ololon . . . their great sway reaching from Ulro to Eternity," Ololon is here an apparently simple unity:

> . . . as One Female Ololon and all its mighty Hosts
> Appear'd, a Virgin of Twelve Years . . .[68]

In this form she is the positive "contrary" to Oothoon as that heroine will appear on the second-last plate of the poem. Like Oothoon, Ololon will overcome her "virgin fears" and advance into maturity, acquiring the courage to pluck the flower of "sweet delight."[69] In so doing she will surrender herself in an unconditional dedication of her own will and her sexual and creative energies to the worthy task of complementing and supporting the creative labors of a divinely gifted and inspired artist, William Blake infused with the spirit of Milton.

When Ololon alights in Blake's garden, she is potentially both a "negation" and a "contrary" in the terms of the poem, for the "Six-fold Miltonic Female" may be either. As Milton declares, turning to her "in terrible majesty" before Blake's cottage, "The Negation must be destroy'd to redeem the Contraries."[70] This enigmatic command of "the Inspired Man" is better understood if one looks into the meaning of Ololon's strange name.

Because when first encountered by the reader Ololon "wept" and "lamented," Northrop Frye hinted that Ololon's name might be derived from the word "ululate."[71] Peter Fisher took up this suggestion, associating the name with a Greek word that signified "the crying of women to the gods."[72] Harold Bloom agreed, on the whole, with Frye and Fisher, though noting that

> [Ololon's] function is the ironic reversal of such a meaning, for though she laments over Milton, she shares in his resolving courage, and emulates him by voluntarily abandoning Eden for the perilous struggles of earth.[73]

Donald Reiman and Christina Kraus elaborated on the etymology proposed by Fisher, finding a possible source in an Aristotelian definition of the word (appearing in a Greek and Latin lexicon that may have been available to Blake) in the sense of "the out-cry . . . which male frogs emit when they call the females to coitus."[74]

The introduction by Reiman and Kraus's etymology of a sexual element (even if of the wrong sex) is not unacceptable, in the light of the connections they make with Blake's restless and obsessive preoccupation with Milton's apparent advocacy of chastity in *Comus.* The senses explored by these scholars may have been known to Blake, and their elements may have entered into his creative processes. Nevertheless, I would suggest that they do not explain the whole of his motivation in coining this unusual name. Moreover, the examples adduced by Reiman and Kraus are all taken from classical, not New Testament, Greek sources. Some weight should surely be given to Blake's view as expressed in the "Preface" to *Milton* that he printed with two of the three copies produced in or shortly after 1808:

> The Stolen and Perverted Writings of Homer & Ovid, of Plato & Cicero, which all Men ought to contemn, are set up by artifice against the Sublime of the Bible. . . .[75]

Blake's letter to his brother James in which he describes the ease with which, under Hayley's tuition, he is acquiring Latin and Greek, also mentions his study of the Hebrew language. For both Greek and Hebrew, the Bible is his lexicon:

> I go on Merrily with my Greek & Latin; am very sorry that I did not begin to learn languages early in life as I find it very Easy; am now learning my Hebrew אבנ . I read Greek as fluently as an Oxford scholar & the Testament is my chief master: astonishing indeed is the English Translation, it is almost word for word, & if the Hebrew Bible is as well translated, which I do not doubt that it is, we need not doubt of its having been translated as well as written by the Holy Ghost. . . .[76]

Milton gives ample evidence—if, indeed, any were needed—of the earnest attention Blake paid to the text of the Old Testament and of his intimate knowledge of it in the Authorized Version. His letter to his brother suggests that he began attempting to read it in the original Hebrew while he was in the midst of composing this epic.[77] Hebrew lettering, significantly disintegrating, appears on the two crumbling tablets of the Old Law shown in the hands of the collapsing Urizen on plate 15 of *Milton.* In fact, the only Hebrew word on this plate that can be made out with any degree of certainty is that on the bottom line of the tablet in Urizen's right hand—at the beginning of the line (reading from right to left): the word לֹא ("LO") the Hebrew word of negation in the Decalogue, used thirteen times in the statement of the Ten Commandments in Exodus 20.1–17.

The phrase "Thou shalt not" is inscribed over the shut doors of the Chapel in Blake's "Garden of Love" of the *Songs of Experience,* where it refers to religious prohibitions of freedom of expression—"binding with briars by joys and desires." The reference becomes more clearly focused upon sexual prohibitions in the poem that follows this one on its first appearance in draft form in Blake's *Notebook,* "I saw a chapel all of gold / That none did dare to enter in. . . ."[78] In Blake's *Europe,* in the course of Enitharmon's "female dream" of dominating mankind through her doctrine that "Woman's Love is Sin," she laughs triumphantly in her sleep when she sees "every man bound" and "Thou shalt not" written over the door of every house.[79] I believe that Blake coined the name Ololon from "LO," the word of negation in the "Thou shalt not's" of the Decalogue in the original

William Blake, Milton, *1804, plate 15 (Copy "B," RB54041): "To Annihilate the Self-hood of Deceit & False Forgiveness." (By permission of the Huntington Library, San Marino, California.)*

William Blake, "Job's Evil Dream." From the Butts series of illustrations to the Book of Job *(1805–6). (By permission of the Pierpont Morgan Library, New York.)*

Hebrew of Exodus 20.[80] He conceived this name in direct relationship to the theme that appears between the lines of the title on plate 30 of *Milton,* written backward so that the reader is obliged to read it from right to left as though it were Hebrew script:

Even as Blake begins to describe Beulah, "where Contrarieties are equally True," in the etched text on plate 30 of *Milton,* he communicates covertly to his reader, in the backward-running mirror-writing included in the design, that "Contraries are Positives / A Negation is not a Contrary."[81] The name "Ololon" reverses a transliteration of the Hebrew word "LO" twice repeated, with a reversal of the English "NO!" added as an ending. The six-lettered name stands for the "Six-fold Miltonic Female," and its three elements reverse a triple negation, "NO–LO–LO." Each *reversed* negative element opposes, and annuls, one of the "Three Heavens of Beulah" beheld by Milton on earth "in those three females whom his wives, & those three whom his Daughters / Had represented and contain'd. . . ."[82] By thrice reversing negation in the name "Ololon," Blake "dissevers" it, employing the traditional method by which the Attendant Spirit of Milton's *Comus* would have annulled the malefic power of the wizard: using

> . . . his rod reversed
> And backward mutters of dissevering power . . .[83]

He thus negates the negation, destroying it "that the Contrary may be redeemed."

The fact that the Hebrew word transliterated as "LO" is the negating element in the biblical "Thou shalt not . . ." enables Blake simultaneously to reject, by spelling it backward in Ololon's name, "Milton's Religion."[84] This means of annulment or "dissevering" is borne out by Blake's account of Milton's attempt to "re-form" Urizen:

> . . . Milton took of the red clay of Succoth, moulding it with care,
> Between his palms and filling up the furrows of many years,
> Beginning at the feet of Urizen, and on the bones Creating new flesh on the Demon cold and building him
> As with new clay, a Human form. . . .[85]

Blake describes this creation in a way that suggests that he had in mind the Kabbalistic notion of the *golem,* "a human being made in an artificial way by virtue of a magic act, through the use of holy names."[86] The word *golem* means "shapeless matter," or "clay"; the *golem* was made by taking earth from virgin soil, "building . . . As with new Clay, a Human form."[87] Gershom Scholem gives this account of its creation and "un"-creation:

> Those who took part in the "act of creation" . . . walked around the *golem* "as in a dance," combining the alphabetical letters and the secret Name of God in accordance with detailed sets of instructions. . . . As a result of this act of combination, the *golem* arose and lived, and when they walked in the opposite direction and said the same combination of letters in reverse order, the vitality of the *golem* was nullified and he sank or fell.[88]

In her first words to Milton, Ololon recalls his attempted "re-formation" of Urizen: "I see thee strive upon the Brooks of Arnon: there a dread / And Awful Man I see, o'ercover'd with the mantle of years."[89] She herself, through her very identity as Ololon, the backward spelling of the word of negation that is at the core of "Milton's Religion," provides Milton with his victory over Urizen, the *golem* of his own creation:

> . . . Silent Milton stood before
> The darken'd Urizen, as the sculptor silent stands before
> His forming image; he walks round it patient labouring.
> Thus Milton stood forming bright Urizen. . . .[90]

From the "*darken'd* Urizen" of the eclipsed fallen Reason, Milton attempts to form anew the "*bright* Urizen, my king" recalled by his bereaved "Emanation," Ahania.[91] He strives vainly to sculpt a figure that will be "*homogeneall,* and proportionall," the description of the "body of Truth" in the "Areopagitica" of John Milton.[92] But the slack and bloated embodiment of the Urizenic Religion, the crumbling tablets of its laws of "Thou shalt not . . ." falling from its feeble hands, collapses in plate 15, even as Milton fails in his effort to "re-form" it—like "Calvin and Luther in fury premature."[93] Though Milton in this plate is represented with polled head, apparently as a "Samson shorn by the Churches" (in all other plates his hair is shoulder-length), his energetic movement and his short-cropped hair make him resemble both Blake and Los in plate 21.[94] The likeness actually inheres in what he is attempting—a creative renewal, to which he is inspired by the rising of the "*beatific* vision" behind Urizen's foundering figure.[95] Blake's own "Vision of beatitude," a new age of human realization through the creative achievement of art, "with harp & heavenly song, / With flute & clarion," dawns in Milton's view as the "stony laws" of Urizen sink to the ground.[96] Only the decapitated head of Urizen is still visible at the foot of plate 16, without a body. Blake implies the comment of John Milton in "Areopagitica,"

> he who thinks we are to pitch our tent here, and have attain'd the utmost prospect of reformation, that the mortal glasse wherein we contemplate, can shew us, till we come to *beatific* vision, that man by this very opinion declares, that he is yet farre short of Truth.[97]

At this moment Blake's Milton is "yet farre short of Truth": he must labor on through "Eternity" to find the means of forming, or "re-forming," that harmoniously symmetrical body, "*homogeneal,* and proportionall."

6
Ololon II

"This place is called Beulah. It is a pleasant lovely Shadow
Where no dispute can come. . . .

—William Blake[1]

*B*LAKE'S BEULAH IS A REGION OF CONTRASTING "Realms / Of terror & of mild moony lustre in soft sexual delusions / Of varied beauty."[2] Beulah surrounds the infinite inner Paradise of eternity in the "Portals of [the] brain," and is to the "Sons of Eden . . . a mild & pleasant Rest" from the creative labors of Eternity, a place where inspiration may be found and renewed, though only in Eden can it be given a definite form.[3] W. H. Stevenson notes that

> Beulah had already passed into the folk-lore of evangelical Nonconformity, not directly from its obscure source in *Isaiah* lxii.4, but from Bunyan's *Pilgrim's Progress,* where Christian and Hopeful . . . towards the end of their journey, [enter] "the country of *Beulah,* whose air was very sweet and pleasant [and] solaced themselves there for a season . . . in this land the Shining Ones commonly walked, because it was upon the borders of heaven."[4]

The Book of Isaiah was a source not at all "obscure" to Blake, to whom "Isaiah the Prophet" had been a mentor since childhood. In verse 4 of chapter 62 the prophet declares to the Chosen People "Thou shalt no more be termed Forsaken; neither shall thy land any more be termed Desolate: but thou shalt be called Hephizibah ('my desire is in her'), and thy land Beulah ('a married woman'): for the Lord delighteth in thee (literally, 'the desire of the Lord is in thee'), and

thy land shall be married." The Hebrew noun *be'ulah* is derived from the root meaning "to marry" or "to possess"—the related form *ti'va'eyl* ("shall be married") is employed in Isaiah 62, 4 and *yiv'al* ("marrieth") in the verse that follows it. The masculine equivalent of *be'ulah, ba'al,* means "husband" or "possessor," and also "master" or "lord."

To Blake's "Sons of Eden" Beulah offers a restful temporary withdrawal—a brief Sabbath—from the mighty exertions of Eternity, to which inevitably they soon return to continue their building of "the Universe stupendous."[5] Because of the discord in his home, and his enforced dependence in later years upon the female members of his household, John Milton had never (according to Blake's perception of his personal history) experienced married life as a positive and revitalizing "mild & pleasant Rest" from his strenuous labors in "Great Eternity."[6] On the other hand, from the point of view of one toiling in Eternity, or Eden, the relationship of the *be'ulah* with the *ba'al* implied in the retirement of the "Emanations" to "Beulah" is one of regression from full adult responsibility: for

. . . Beulah to its Inhabitants appears . . .
As the beloved infant in his mother's bosom round
   incircled
With arms of love & pity & sweet compassion.[7]

Blake's Beulah, as Stevenson comments, is "only a place to rest in, and any being who tries to pretend that it is the real life of Humanity—i.e., of Eternity—is committing a serious error."[8] An "Emanation" who elects to remain for long periods, or even permanently, in Blake's Beulah is as an infant—or is even, at a stretch, a parallel for Milton's wife Mary who "went home to Mother" for three years and would evidently have preferred to stay there permanently. A female in the state of Beulah is protected, but is specifically *not* a supportive helpmeet or copartner, either in creative work or at any other level. The theme of "negation" annulled in Ololon's name is displayed in part in the female who neutralizes or "negates" the creative forces of the male. At best she is a hindrance to his work, at worst she may cripple or even paralyze his capabilities. She may weaken her man by becoming a helpless and withdrawn dependent ("sick with fatigue," perhaps, like Blake's over-taxed "Shadow of Delight?").[9] She may attempt to smother or bind him with the shrill possessiveness of the "Shadowy Female," "Jealous" in her "darkness," whose "Howlings [fill] all the desolate places in accusations of Sin."[10] In the latter role she is close to the malevolent "Lilith" of the *Kabbalah,* queen of female demons, who rejoices in laying waste the land.[11] Or, the female "negation" may foolishly, or maliciously, assert herself as the "Female Will" (Rahab, and Tirzah and her four sisters) in an outright desire to dominate.

Ololon herself, in her face-to-face encounter with Milton in Blake's cottage garden, confesses

"Altho' our Human Power can sustain the severe
   contentions
"Of Friendship, our Sexual cannot, but flies into
   the Ulro.
"Hence arose all our terrors in Eternity. . . ."[12]

In the light of Blake's assertion that "*Opposition* is true Friendship" (made in the course of his statement of the necessity to "*Human* existence" of "Contraries"), it is clear that the "severe contentions / Of Friendship" from which the "Sexual" power of Ololon had fled were the "great Wars of Eternity" continually waged in Eden by its inspired "Sons."[13] The feminine nature of the "Emanations" was thrown into "terrors" by the "fury of Poetic Inspiration," before which they

. . . trembled exceedingly, nor could they
Live, because the life of Man was too exceedingly
   unbounded.
His joy became terrible to them; they trembled &
   wept. . . .[14]

So Milton's Emanation Ololon will tremble before

him when he appears "in terrible majesty," speaking as "the Inspired Man."[15] But unlike the other Emanations, who withdraw into "Beulah" and linger there, shrinking from confrontation with "the Eternal Great Humanity," Ololon has courageously emerged from the shelter of the "moony habitations" of that haven where "Contrarieties are equally True" and "no dispute can come."[16] If "no dispute can come" there, then neither can any creative act be performed there—according to Blake's understanding of inspired creative activity as "Mental Fight."[17] Ololon's epiphany is the recognition that she must *leave* Beulah, so that, by her supportive participation as the "contrary" of Milton, she may enable him to fulfill his appointed task, "Mental forms Creating" in the strenuous life of Eden.[18]

"Milton's Religion" had been a "new Religion" woven "in deceit . . . from new Jealousy of Theotormon."[19] The reference to Theotormon reminds the reader that Blake had already, in his *Visions of the Daughters of Albion,* presented his version of the destructive torments of sexual jealousy, arising from hypocritical social mores that constrain the female to chastity. "Milton's Religion" includes—in Blake's view—the doctrine that "Woman's Love is Sin." It arrogates to itself that "Self-righteousness" that "With cruel Virtue mak[es] War upon the Lamb's Redeemed . . . to perpetuate the Laws of Sin."[20] It is this quality that Blake's personage Milton is ultimately to forswear "in all its Hypocritic turpitude" in his comitment to the "Annihilat[ion of] the Selfhood of Deceit."[21]

When Blake thus uses the word "Sin," it is a title, a name—the name of the allegorical female personification whom Milton placed at the Gates of Hell, to be its "portress."[22] In book I of *Milton* the role of Sin is deliberately assumed by Leutha, the "lureing bird of Eden" and "Sweet smiling pestilence" of *Europe.*[23] Leutha "offer[s] herself a Ransom for Satan, taking on her his Sin."[24] Leutha is "a Daughter of Beulah"—inspiring Blake in the same measure as Ololon—but she speaks of Satan as "My Parent power," and "emanates" alternately from Satan's breast and from his head, symbolically expressing a conflict between emotion and intellect.[25] She is hailed by Satan's Gnomes, the "servants of the Harrow," in the same words as Milton's Sin by the "host of heaven" in *Paradise Lost:*

. . . back the Gnomes recoil'd
And call'd me Sin and for a sign portentous held
   me. . . .[26]

Leutha makes a confession before the "Great Solemn

Assembly" of Eden, that she is "the Author of this Sin!"[27] But it becomes clear that Leutha's public admission of guilt is false, and is made for manipulative purposes—it is a "Negation" of the sincere confessions made by Ololon in books I and II. Elynittria, Diana-like personification of cruel chastity and Palamabron's consort, secretly brings Leutha to Palamabron's bed, "In moments new created for delusion. . . ."[28] There Leutha bears "the shadowy Spectre of Sleep & nam'd him Death."[29] She also gives birth "In Lambeth's vales" to "Rahab, the mother of Tirzah, & her sisters"—the reference to Lambeth and the genealogy indicating that Leutha had formed part of Blake's original conception of the mythological structure of his epic before he went to Felpham.[30] The "rainbow-coloured" Leutha is an archetype of female deception, the mother both of Death and of Blake's female figure Rahab who, with *her* daughters, embodies the malevolent aspect of the "Six-fold Miltonic Female," and ultimately appears "in Satan's bosom glowing" at the climax of the epic.[31] She is also a "negation" of Blake's feminine Jerusalem.

"Sin," this female creature with whom Death incestuously consorts, is equated with "Woman's Love" in the creed of "Thou shalt not. . . ." Thus mankind in the thrall of "Milton's Religion" has lapsed into the deluded and benighted condition of Adam when he declared to Eve "if death / Consort with thee, death is to me as life. . . ."[32] To submit to "Sin," with whom Death consorts, is to embrace a life which is deathlike. Los himself acknowledges that he has "embrac'd the falling Death, he is become One with me"; and indeed he did so when he "kissed [Blake] and wished [him] health," upon which Blake became "One Man with him."[33] Los has already "enter'd into [Blake's] soul."[34] The reader is inescapably reminded of Blake's characterization of *himself* by the nickname "Death" in the *Notebook* poem that catalogs the persecutions to which he has been subjected, and their perpetrators.[35]

A life that is a "lively form of death" is the harrowing lot of England, indeed of Europe, as Blake perceives it, in his own time. "There is no end to destruction," lament the "sons of Los," the creative "Contraries" Rintrah the wrathful, and Palamabron the "mild and piteous," as they meet Los / Blake at the "Gate of Golgonooza."[36] They point to the triumph of Rahab and Tirzah, who have "created Voltaire [and] Rousseau, / Asserting the Self-Righteousness against the Universal Saviour" and supporting the rise of the "Natural Religion" that Blake abominated, while perforce such idealists and

visionaries as Whitefield and "Westley" [Wesley] (not to mention William Blake) "devote / Their life's whole comfort to intire scorn & injury & death. . . ."[37] In the raging Napoleonic conflagration in Europe, that Blake despaired of seeing ended, Rahab and Tirzah perpetuate the "War & Glory" originally visited upon mankind by the spite of Enitharmon when she found herself excluded from the "bright world" of the intellect.[38] Meanwhile the fervent apostles of classical art and values, those "silly Greek and Latin slaves of the sword" whom Blake had scathingly rejected in the "Preface" to *Milton,* "With Laws from Plato & his Greeks . . . renew the Trojan Gods / In Albion & . . . deny the value of the Saviour's blood."[39]

Los comforts his "noble Sons" with the recollection of "an old Prophecy in Eden recorded . . . That Milton of the land of Albion should up ascend forward from Felpham's Vale & break the Chain / Of Jealousy from all its roots. . . ."[40] Wordsworth in 1802 had cried out "Milton! Thou shouldst be living at this hour: / England hath need of thee. . . ."[41] Blake's visionary prophecy supplies England's need, visualizing Milton's spirit as Wordsworth had, in the form of a star. The first account in the poem of Milton as a falling star entering Blake's foot is followed immediately by the first great insight attained by Milton's spirit, then walking about in Eternity "intirely abstracting himself from Female loves."[42] At that moment Milton is in the same "abstracted" state as Urizen had been when he had separated himself in vainglory from the other Zoas in his revolt. Milton's initial epiphany is the recognition of his failure to acknowledge his need for his sixfold Emanation.[43] The second reference in the poem to Blake's visionary experience, as he strides forward shod in the "bright sandal" which is the tangible evidence of the event, is followed by the first occurrence of the name Ololon:

There is in Eden a sweet River of milk & liquid
    pearl
Nam'd Ololon, on whose mild banks dwelt those
    who Milton drove
Down into Ulro. . . .[44]

Ololon's brave and compassionate journey of regeneration begins upon the banks of this "sweet River of milk & liquid pearl."[45] Florence Sandler identifies the "liquid pearl" as "the spermatic stream of the Hermeticists."[46] She compares it to the stream of "viscous, fat, mineral water . . . bright like pearls, and transparent like crystal," which Thomas Vaughan sees in his vision in *Lumen de Lumine,* and which is there identified as "the First Matter, and the very natural, true Sperm of the Great World."[47] Milton in *Paradise Lost* had described "a bright sea" flowing beneath the foot of Jacob's Ladder in the sky, "of jasper, or of liquid pearl."[48] This "sea" (the "waters . . . above the firmament" of Genesis 1.8, the "sea of glass" of Revelations 4.6) was also associated with the Hermetic stream of life and is thus masculine in concept. The "milk" of Blake's "sweet River" appears to be his own addition, a balancing female element to the male "liquid pearl," since in "Eden" there is no separation of the sexes. There is here an echo of an earlier Apocalyptic scene visualized by Blake in the imagery of sexual orgasm at the conclusion of the *Song of Los,* when "milk & blood & glandous wine / In rivers rush & shout & dance. . . ."[49] Milton's "sea . . . of liquid pearl" in *Paradise Lost* was the medium that conveyed the Prophet Elijah to Heaven in his chariot of fire.[50] Similarly, Ololon is to become the means by which the "Inspired Man"—Milton, and ultimately Los as another Elijah, the "Spirit of Prophecy, the ever apparent Elias"—approaches the "shining heaven" of fruitful creativity.[51]

On the "living banks" of this river in Eden "dwelt those who Milton drove / Down into Ulro. . . ."[52] These are the "Eternals" who had "[risen] up from the eternal tables / Drunk with the Spirit . . .," and had in wrath "[rent] the heavens round the Watchers [who surround Milton's Couch of Death in Eternity] in a fiery circle," causing them to "flee with cries down to the Deeps" to join "the Watchers of the Ulro."[53] This action aligns the Eternals who perform it with Satan's legions in *Paradise Lost.* Left to their own devices in Hell while Satan seeks an escape route from it, they behave like a rioting mob, and in their "rage . . . rend up both rocks and hills, and ride the air / In whirlwind. . . ."[54] But, as Mary Lynn Johnson points out, after this initial violent response to Milton's transformation, these "Eternals," who will unite to constitute Ololon, are "able to lament, to live through [their] wrath to a new, creative pity."[55] This is the very quality of mercy expressed by the dwellers on the "mild banks" of the "sweet River," who weep in the "long resounding song" of Blake's drawn-out heptameter lines.[56] They repent "that they had in wrath & fury & fire / Driven Milton into the Ulro" and declare "Let us descend also, and let us give / Ourselves to death in Ulro among the Transgressors."[57] Their compassionate atonement evokes the "at-one-ment" of the "Family Divine" into "One Man, even Jesus, / Uniting in One with Ololon, & the appearance of One Man. . . ."[58]

Wailing for Milton "with a great lamentation," the multitudes of Ololon descend into Beulah, whose "Songs" are now added to their lamenting.[59] The Divine Voice is heard in Beulah, speaking with sorrow of the change that has come over the "married woman"—the *be'ulah*—once "lovely, mild & gentle; now . . . terrible / In jealousy & unlovely in my sight. . . ."[60] The Divine Voice presents Milton, "descended to Redeem the Female Shade / From Death Eternal . . . by Annihilation."[61] It prophesies that the "Six-fold Female" "shall relent in fear of death" when she perceives

> . . . that Milton annihilated
> Himself, that seeing all his loves by her cut off, he leaves
> Her also, intirely abstracting himself from Female loves. . . .[62]

The *be'ulah* to whom her *ba'al*—her lord and husband—gave "all [his] whole Soul" at the time of their marriage, had bound him in return with her possessive jealousy.[63] In relenting, she will release those bonds. "Delighting in his delight" she will bring to him "Jerusalem," that is Liberty, and "[will] give her into the arms of God [her] Lord & Husband."[64] Blake's source, once again, is the context of the verse of Isaiah 62 from which he took the name "Beulah":

> . . . as the bridegroom rejoiceth over the bride, so shall thy God rejoice over thee.
> I have set watchmen upon thy walls, O Jerusalem, which shall never hold their peace day or night . . . till he establish, and till he make Jerusalem a praise in the earth.[65]

As the Divine Voice dies away, the "Songs of Beulah" comfort the lamentation of Ololon with a supportive reminder, that these hosts are capable of compassion, that the "thunders & lightnings" of their first wrathful response to Milton have now turned wondrously to "pity."[66]

Now Ololon collectively gains a wider perspective than those "Emanations" can have who remain within Beulah, for they are shown all four of the "States of Humanity in its Repose."[67] Beulah is the first of these, bordering on and surrounding "Eternity" or "Eden," a "mild & pleasant Rest" from that "exceedingly unbounded" region where inspired creative work is conceived. It *has* bounds, and exists *within* Time and Space, but it is nonetheless an intellectual state, "in the Head."[68] Beyond it, and successively further removed from "Eden," lie "Alla," governed by the passions, "in the Heart," and "Al-Ulro," a state created by sexual experience, "in the Loins."[69]

Blake further expanded his concept of the "Three

Heavens of Beulah" on the latest plate of *Milton:*

> And this is the manner of the Daughters of Albion
> in their beauty.
> Every one is threefold in Head & Heart & Reins, &
> every one
> Has three Gates into the Three Heavens of Beulah,
> which shine
> Translucent in their Foreheads & their Bosoms &
> their Loins
> Surrounded with fires unapproachable: but whom
> they please
> They take up into their Heavens in intoxicating
> delight;
> For the Elect cannot be Redeem'd, but Created
> continually
> By Offering & Atonement in the crue[l]ties of
> Moral Law.
> Hence the three Classes of Men take their fix'd
> destinations.
> They are the Two Contraries & the Reasoning
> Negative.[70]

The "Three Heavens of Beulah" are here Gardens of Paradise. Adam and Eve, expelled from Paradise after their Fall, looked back to see the hilltop garden "Waved over by that flaming brand, the gate / With dreadful faces thronged and fiery arms. . . ."[71] But the "Heavens" of Beulah are equivocal in their meaning. To those restored to the wholeness of the regenerated state of mankind, those who both "please," *and are pleased by,* "the Daughters of Albion in their beauty" (the phrasing of 5.9–10 permits the intentional ambiguity) through recognizing the necessary coexistence of the "Two Contraries," these "Three Heavens" are sources of "intoxicating delight." To the "Reasoning Negative," Milton's unredeemable "Elect" whose continual "offering & Atonement in the crue[l]ties of Moral Law" forever restrains them from "delight," these "Heavens" are places of infernal torment, and their fiery "Gates" open, like those of Milton's Hell, into a terrifying Chaos.

The "Or-Ulro" is the furthest of all these states from the living core of creativity. There the unregenerate, the moralists and materialists who "cannot Believe in Eternal Life . . .," are bound "separate," in self-imposed exile from the life of the imagination.[72] Such "separate"-ness is a development of the "abstract" state of the divided Urizen. To those other than the "Elect"—the "Reprobate who never cease to Believe" and the "Redeem'd / Who live in doubts and fears perpetually tormented by the Elect"—the Or-Ulro appears "dreadful," a primitive condition that consists in merely vegetating, "in the Stomach & Intestines terrible, deadly, unutterable," a bare physical existence in which Man is no higher than the beasts.[73] It is in this last of the four "States . . . of Repose," which Ololon courageously seeks out in "a long journey & dark thro' Chaos in the track of Milton's course," that the most dangerous implications of the progressive withdrawal from the vital arena of creativity, accompanied by the loss of visionary perception, become apparent.[74]

Jakob Boehme cataloged the correspondences of parts of the body with aspects and properties of the universe: thus, "the entrails or guts signify the operation of the stars. . . ."[75] In the edition of the works of Boehme that Blake knew, an illustration by Dionysius Freher which he especially admired offers an elaborate multilayered diagram of the human body showing Man as a microcosm, his body containing the sun, moon, and stars.[76] But when "the Starry Heavens are fled from the mighty limbs of Albion," when Man relinquishes his visionary powers and the entrails are *only* viscera and no more than that, then Chaos is literally come again.[77] The "fiery Gates" of the Or-Ulro then parallel the opened gates of Hell in *Paradise Lost,* "belching outrageous flame / Far into chaos . . ." as Sin and Death prepare to make their way through the abyss to establish their dominion on the fallen Earth.[78] Here, Ololon sees "the Contrarieties of Beulah War beneath Negation's Banner."[79] This line was compounded by Blake from the Miltonic passage in which Satan stands upon the "brink of hell" contemplating the "wild abyss" where "eldest Night / And Chaos, ancestors of Nature, hold / Eternal anarchy, amidst the noise / Of endless wars, and by confusion stand."[80] The condition is "terrible, deadly" and, in addition, "unutterable"—depriving Man of comprehensible means of communication: Milton's Satan approaching the court of Chaos could hear nothing but "a universal hubbub wild."[81] It is in this "dreadful" state that a "Contrary" appears as a "Negation." Los, the "strong Guard" of Albion, protecting him against this appalling threat of reduction to visionless chaos, "his force bends / Along the Valleys of Middlesex . . . / Lest those Three Heavens of Beulah should the Creation destroy."[82]

In the lowest reaches of the Or-Ulro Ololon perceives the "Five Females & the nameless Shadowy Mother" (the Five Daughters of Zelopehad and their "Mother" Rahab, comprising the "Six-fold Miltonic Female"), like a nest of spiders spinning "from their bowels with songs of amorous delight" a "vast Polypus / Of living fibres down into the Sea of Time & Space growing."[83] The "melting cadences" of these females "lure the Sleepers of Beulah down / The River Storge (which is Arnon) into the Dead Sea."[84] Blake's characteristically concentrated symbolism implies that a withdrawal from the fiery heart of creative work, abetted by a soothing affection falsely resembling maternal love (the Greek "storgē" means parental or family affection), can be deadly to the human spirit: his "River Storge" runs down into the Dead Sea.[85] This monstrous excrescence, the "Polypus," is Man's Humanity in its ultimate state of "Repose": it is an inhuman mass of flesh vegetating into soft rottenness. Clearly, Ololon, as Milton's "Emanation" and "female portion," properly his partner in creative enterprise, cannot remain in Beulah, lest that "State of Repose" degenerate into this, and the paradoxically delightful terrors of those Three Heavens of Beulah "should the Creation destroy."[86]

The hosts of Ololon take up their station momentarily in a "dark land of death, of fiery corroding waters," a chaotic universe reflecting that which revealed itself to Satan's legions when they explored their "universe of death" in Hell.[87] From this vantage Ololon perceives with compassion the "six-fold Female," and exclaims "O dreadful Loom of Death! O piteous Female forms compell'd / To weave the Woof of Death!"[88] Ololon sees that the five malevolent daughters and their mother Rahab have extended their dominion not only over Blake's London world, but "over the whole Earth."[89] There in the Or-Ulro, among the "Couches of the Dead" on which even Los and Enitharmon "& all the Sons of Albion / And his Four Zoas" now lie, Ololon seeks out the couch of Milton to beg of him forgiveness.[90]

The asking and receiving of forgiveness opens the way for both Milton and Ololon to descend to the consummation of their union at the climax of the epic. As Susan Fox writes,

> The 'universal groan' Ololon utters at her prostration, echoes the groans we have heard throughout the poem at the inception of apocalypse. It is also a kind of birth cry signalling her incarnation, for by falling down in humility she has entered the polypus.[91]

Ololon's "descent thro' Beulah to Los and Enitharmon," who lie in deathlike condition in the Ulro, has exactly the opposite effect to the journey from Hell to Paradise, in book 10 of *Paradise Lost,* of Sin and Death, sent by Satan with the command that they exercise "dominion . . . on man, sole lord of all declared, / Him first make sure your thrall, and lastly kill."[92] Because Ololon has undertaken this "wondrous journey," a "wide road is now open," extending from the dreaded Chaos of Ulro "to eternity"—an inverted image of the "passage broad," the "wondrous pontifice" thrown across the gulf of Chaos by Sin and Death to link Hell to the Earth and bring its effects into Man's world.[93]

It is a necessary stage in the process of redemption that Ololon must pass through the horrors of the Ulro. Before she (or they) can see Golgonooza, the spiritual city of Art that comprises the corpus of Blake's works, she must view the "vast Polypus / Of living fibres down into the Sea of Time and Space growing," within which sit the "Five Females & the nameless Shadowy Mother, / Spinning it from their bowels . . .":

> For Golgonooza cannot be seen till having pass'd the Polypus
> It is viewed on all sides round by a Four-fold Vision,
> Or till you become Mortal & Vegetable in Sexuality,
> Then you behold its mighty Spires & Domes of ivory & gold.[94]

To become "Mortal & Vegetable in Sexuality" in the persons of Catherine and William Blake, so as to view *and to enter* Golgonooza, Ololon and Milton must descend to earth and enter into Time and Space.

Two "Contraries" meet in dynamic interaction to bring about the meeting of Ololon and Milton in Blake's garden: a "mighty Demon," the Wild Thyme, and a "mighty Angel," the Lark. Both are "Los's Messenger[s]."[95] Time and Space, embodied respectively in the "bright purple mantle" and obvious pun of the Wild Thyme and in the beautiful conceit of the ascending Lark, join in a pulsating union of contraries "at the Gate of Los, at the Eastern / Gate of wide Golgonooza."[96] It is, as David Fuller says, "a moment in and yet out of time such as Eliot describes in *Four Quartets*."[97] When within the poem the poet became "One Man" with Los, he declared that "both Time & Space obey my will," adding in a kind of expansion "Los is by mortals nam'd Time, Enitharmon is nam'd Space."[98] For Blake,

> Time and Space are Real Beings, a Male & a Female. Time is a Man, Space is a Woman, & her Masculine Portion is Death.[99]

The personage whose "Masculine Portion is Death" is, once again, Milton's personification of Sin in *Paradise Lost.* We come round full circle: Sin is the sexual partner of her "author," Satan, as Enitharmon is of her progenitor and consort Los; but Sin also consorts with her offspring Death, with whom Los identifies himself when he declares that he too has "embrac'd" him: "[Death] is become One with me."[100] When Enitharmon consorts with Los she thus joins herself also to Death. Passing into the "vegetative" realm of Time and Space, Milton and Ololon become "Real

Beings, a Male & a Female." In assuming earthly human sexuality, they take on mortality as well: mutually they embrace Death.

Ololon waits, sitting beside the "empty tomb" where "Luvah" the Zoa of the Passions lay in death. Although Blake may have had in mind as well the idea of the tomb from which the united Sol and Luna are resurrected in their mystical union, Ololon at this moment is like the three women who came to seek the body of the risen Christ in the sepulcher in the garden of Joseph of Arimathea as she awaits the message of "awakening" from the "mighty Demon," the Wild Thyme, and the "mighty Angel" the Lark.[101] Both of these symbols have the sexual dimensions that Blake associates with Time and Space. The Wild Thyme, according to Elaine Kauvar, is called by Paracelsus "Mother of Thyme" and is classed by him as a uterine herb (from "mother" in the sense of "womb").[102] Known also as St. John's Wort, it is associated with spiritual purgation and the dispelling of evil spirits. Another of its folk names, "Christ's Ladder," emphasizes its habit of growing along the ground and climbing toward heaven on mountains— mounting, as Blake describes, "from Wimbleton's green & impurpled Hills."[103] Its emblematic values "[underscore] Blake's insistence that human sexuality must triumph over the hypocrisy of holy chastity for man to reside in paradise."[104] Blake's inspiration for the Lark, and for some of the symbolism of this passage, came partly from an old favorite of his, the song from act 2 of Shakespeare's *Cymbeline:*

> Hark, hark, the Lark at heaven's gate sings
>   And Phoebus 'gins arise,
> His steeds to water at those springs
> On chalic'd flowers that lies;
> And winking Mary-buds begin
>   To ope their golden eyes.
> With every thing that pretty bin,
>   My lady sweet, arise;
>   Arise, arise![105]

The Lark, the Fountain, the Gate of Los, and the eastern Gate of Golgonooza, all spring from this lovely lyric. Even the association of the "empty Tomb" where "Luvah slept . . . in death" could have been reinforced for Blake by Shakespeare's adjective "chalic'd" (from the Grail or "chalice" that caught the blood from Christ's side). The "Mary-buds" might have brought to Blake's mind the three women named Mary who came on the first Easter Sunday to find the sepulcher in the garden empty. As Kathleen Raine points out, the same Shakespearean source had probably already contributed to the "Bright Marygold of Leutha's vale," Blake's symbol of sexual

William Blake, "Night Startled by the Lark." From the series of illustrations to Milton's L'Allegro, *ca. 1816–20. (By permission of the Pierpont Morgan Library, New York. Purchased with the Assistance of the Fellows with the special support of Mrs. Landon K. Thorne and Mrs. Paul Mellon. 1949.4:2.)*

awakening in *Visions of the Daughter of Albion.*[106] Joseph of Arimathea, in whose tomb the body of Jesus was laid, had special significance for Blake as the legendary founder of a pure original Christianity in Britain.[107]

Shakespeare's *Cymbeline* itself, set in the period of the Roman occupation of Britain, bears the name of an ancient British king and takes place in "Albion's land, / Which is this earth of vegetation on which Now I write."[108] The play as a whole must have had some part in the genesis in Blake's mind of *Milton,* whose grand theme is the awakening of the sleeping Albion. Ololon's virginal condition as an aspect of "Negation," though obviously owing much to Milton's prudishly virtuous "Lady" in *Comus,* may also have been suggested by Shakespeare's characterization of the beautiful Imogen, "as chase as unsunn'd snow," whose husband Posthumus recalls that in her "pudency" she often "restrain'd" him of his "lawful pleasure."[109] "Hark, hark, the lark" is sung in *Cymbeline* to "awaken" Imogen—as much in the sexual sense as in the sense of arousal from sleep. The musicians who perform the song in the play are commanded to do so by the boorish Cloten, who—aspiring to seduce Imogen—has been "advised to give her music a' mornings; they say it will penetrate."[110] His instructions to them to play and sing are laced with sexual double-entendre: "If you can penetrate her with your fingering, so. We'll try with tongue too. . . ."[111] In the play, Imogen has to undertake a long and perilous journey through savage Wales. Hers is a journey of "discovery" (in the sense of "unmasking" or "revealing," for she finds her two long-lost brothers living under other identities in the mountains of Wales) and of redemption, since its goal is expressed in a fully consummated union with her lover/husband Posthumus. There are obvious parallels with the redemptive journey of Ololon.

As the Lark sings, the stage seems set for the resurrection of Albion as well as that of Luvah, Zoa of the Passions, and of Ololon and Milton. A Lark-messenger meets "the Female Ololon" descending into Blake's garden, where Blake, hailing her "Virgin of Providence," invites her to enter into his cottage.[112] Though he fears that the message she may carry for him is "again to plunge into deeper affliction," and though he is "ready to obey," he begs Ololon to pity and give comfort to "my Shadow of Delight . . . for she is sick with fatigue."[113] The image of Catherine Blake as *Shadow* of Delight is an inversion of Isaiah's imagery, once more from the context of Blake's source for the name "Beulah":

> . . . for Jerusalem's sake I will not rest, until the righteousness thereof go forth as brightness, and the salvation thereof as a lamp that burneth. . . . thou shalt be called Hephzibah . . . for the Lord delighteth in thee. . .[114]

In her withdrawn and occluded state, "sick with fatigue," Blake's wife is a "Shadow" where she has been "brightness," a "lamp that burneth" in his inspiration. The association may have been a literal one. After her husband's death Mrs. Blake described the trials of her supportive role to Frederick Tatham, who knew both the Blakes well in their later years, and in whose home Mrs. Blake spent the last years of her life. Tatham told Alexander Gilchrist that Mrs. Blake recalled that she would "get up in the night, when her husband was under his very fierce inspirations, which were as if they would tear him asunder . . . she had to sit motionless and silent; only to stay him mentally without moving hand or foot: this for hours, and night after night. . . ."[115] The notion of the female catalyst of inspiration and enlightenment

as a "lamp that burneth" may well have been associated in Blake's mind with the image of his wife sitting up near him at night by a burning lamp, patiently "stay[ing] him mentally" with her devotion when he was racked by his "fierce inspirations."[116]

But Ololon seeks only Milton, "Driven from Eternity" by the collective "Act . . . which thou knowest."[117] Upon hearing Ololon's voice, "more distinct than any earthly," Milton follows her descending path into the garden at Felpham.[118] Alighting "from the eastern sky" before Blake's cottage, Milton is immediately confronted by his "Spectre," Satan.[119] While Ololon stands "trembling in the Porch," Milton defies and overcomes Satan, who is his own rebellious will, his "Selfhood."[120] Now Ololon addresses Milton, praising his unflinching "Self-annihilation [in] giving thy life to thy enemies."[121] She, in turn, can do no less. She must acknowledge and confront her own malevolent "Female Will," just as Milton had.

Tremulously, Ololon begins to search out the role of the female "Negation" in creating "this Newtonian Phantasm, / This Voltaire & Rousseau . . . / This Natural Religion, this impossible absurdity."[122] As she cries out her *mea culpa*—"Is Ololon the cause of this? O where shall I hide my face?"—her own "Spectre" appears, just as Satan had come to challenge Milton. The spectral counterpart of Ololon is "Rahab Babylon . . . Glorious as the Midday Sun in Satan's bosom glowing. . . ."[123] She is the "false Body," the "Not Human" that must be discarded and washed away. Rahab, the daughter of Leutha, is Blake's personal version of the Great Harlot of the Apocalypse. It was Rahab, the "Abomination of Desolation," who had suppressed the Divine Humanity of creative Man, "Hiding the Human Lineaments as with an Ark and Curtains."[124] By means of a gradual deceptive concealment of the "Human Lineaments," by the progressive imposition of conditions that degrade from full creative Humanity, Rahab and her daughters had virtually brought the artist to confusion, to the Chaos of the terrible Or-Ulro, where "the Contraries of Beulah War beneath Negations Banner." It is a trackless intellectual wilderness where no features are discernible in the landscape of the mind, since "Mountain, River & Plain, / City & sandy Desart [are] intermingled beyond mortal ken."[125] Through a deception (to which they had themselves progressively, and unknowingly, acquiesced), Milton and his "Emanation" were "led to War the Wars of Death," each treating the other as a hostile "Negation."[126] Now at last, each recognizing in the other a complementary "Contrary," they join as

"One Man, Jesus the Saviour, wonderful! round his limbs / The Clouds of Ololon folded as a Garment dipped in blood. . . ."[127] The blood-stained garment, symbol both of mortality and of the penetration of the virginal hymen, is also (as Robert Essick points out) the "antithesis" of the garment "woven of sighs and heart broken lamentations" by the Shadowy Female.[128] The stained vestment is a token that the *Virgin* Ololon is no more, that she has gone, as she declared she would, to "Eternal Death"—the "death" of sexual climax—to rise again renewed as the sexually awakened Oothoon.[129] Thus Ololon has "become Mortal & Vegetable in Sexuality."[130] The "Clouds of Ololon," the Savior's sexual garment of mortality, are

> Written within & without in woven letters, & the
>   Writing
> Is the Divine Revelation in the Litteral expression
> A Garment of War.[131]

As Robert Essick reads this passage, it constitutes the "redemption of writing" by Christ.[132] The understanding of Milton's life and writings achieved by a fellow poet transforms

> the corpus of Milton's writings ("The Clouds of Ololon") into Christ's flesh in Jesus, the living garment of His body, without loss of its textual nature. . . . Jesus' raiment, a text that is one with his body, achieves that union of being and meaning defining the incarnational sign: Jesus *is* the "Divine Revelation" as well as its "Litteral expression."[133]

The incarnational clothing of Jesus is "A Garment of War."[134] As a united spiritual force, Milton and his "Emanation" Ololon may now turn, in the mortal and sexual embodiment to be given them by William and Catherine Blake, to the conduct of this "War," which is the "Mental Fight" of creative labor for which the poet had summoned his "Bow of burning gold" and his "Arrows of Desire" before the commencement of the epic.[135]

Supporting and presiding over the resurrection of "Milton the Awakener," Ololon has attained a state of enlightened awareness which is both spiritual and sexual.[136] But the actualization of artistic inspiration into a tangible work of art can only be successfully brought about when Los and Enitharmon, *taking the mortal vehicular forms of William and Catherine Blake*, complement and assist one another in their united labors in the practical procedures of designing, etching or engraving, and printing.[137] So Milton, who put on the mantle of mortality—that is, of Death personified—when he entered into the being of William Blake, must unite with *his* "Emanation," Ololon, for the creation of a new Miltonic work, the epic *Milton*. Ololon too must assume mortality and accept Death as her "Masculine Portion." Catherine Blake, embodying the female personages of the poem as comprehensively as her husband "resumes" the male personages, must join her labors to those of her husband for the work to be brought into being. Together they will etch, print, and color each plate and bind the finished pages into a book, this Miltonic illuminated "Prophecy."

In a passage of *The Four Zoas* Los tells Enitharmon:

> . . . Stern desire
> I feel to fabricate embodied semblances in which
>   the dead
> May live before us in our palaces & in our gardens
>   of [pleasure *del.*] labour. . . .

In reply, Enitharmon

> . . . spread her beamy locks upon the wind & said,
> "O [lovely *del.*] Lovely terrible Los, wonder of
>   Eternity, O Los, my defence & guide,
> Thy works are all my joy & in thy fires my soul
>   delights . . .
> Then I can sigh forth on the winds of Golgonooza
>   piteous forms
> That vanish again into my bosom. . . ."[138]

This scene is movingly recalled in the interplay of visual and verbal symbols with which the epic ends. The final textual manifestation of the female is in the form of "soft Oothoon," who in this poem had previously been associated with the duplicitous Leutha.[139] Freed now from Leutha's coy deceptions, Oothoon is sensual, sexually aroused and receptive to her lover. "Pant[ing] in the Vales of Lambeth" as when their union (living together, working together, and making love) first inspired Blake to commence the work, Oothoon "weep[s] o'er her Human Harvest" at the foot of plate 44, the second-last plate of *Milton*.[140] She hovers naked in the sky over a valley full of grain ready for harvesting, her left arm extended and her hair hanging, bringing down fructifying rain as her compassionate tears dissolve the perverse willfulness and obstructive jealousy of the Miltonic female. The weeping of Oothoon is a parallel for the falling of the dew that brings about the renewal of life in the moribund Sol and Luna in the "hieros gamos."[141] Catherine/Enitharmon/Ololon as Oothoon, lover, fertile matrix, indispensable collaborator, and true partner of the "Inspired Man," presides over the materialization of the fruits of his inspiration.

Writing from Felpham, Blake enclosed some lines

Los shudderd at beholding Albion, for his disease
Arose upon him pale and ghastly: and he call'd around
The Friends of Albion; trembling at the sight of Eternal Death
The four appeard with their Emanations in fiery
Chariots: black their fires roll beholding Albions House of Eternity
Damp couch the flames beneath and silent, sick, stand shuddering
Before the Porch of sixteen pillars: weeping every one
Descended and fell down upon their knees round Albions knees,
Swearing the Oath of God! with awful voice of thunders round
Upon the hills & valleys. and the cloudy Oath rolld far and wide

Albion is sick! said every Valley, every mournful Hill
And every River: our brother Albion is sick to death
He hath leagued himself with robbers! he hath studied the arts
Of unbelief! Envy hovers over him! his Friends are his abhorrence!
Those who give their lives for him are despised!
Those who devour his soul, are taken into his bosom!
To destroy his Emanation is their intention:
Arise! awake O Friends of the Giant Albion
They have perswaded him of horrible falshoods!
They have sown errors over all his fruitful fields!

The Twenty-four heard! they came trembling on watry chariots.
Borne by the Living Creatures of the third procession
Of Human Majesty, the Living Creatures wept aloud as they
Went along Albions roads, till they arrivd at Albions House.

O! how the torments of Eternal Death, waited on Man:
And the loud-rending bars of the Creation ready to burst:
That the wide world might fly from its hinges, & the immortal mansion
Of Man, for ever be possess'd by monsters of the deeps:
And Man himself become a Fiend, wrap'd in an endless curse,
Consuming and consum'd for-ever in flames of Moral Justice.

For had the Body of Albion fall'n down, and from its dreadful ruins
Let loose the enormous Spectre on the darkness of the deep,
At enmity with the Merciful & fill'd with devouring fire,
A nether-world must have reciev'd the foul enormous spirit.
Under pretence of Moral Virtue, fill'd with Revenge and Law.
There to eternity chaind down, and issuing in red flames
And curses, with his mighty arms brandish'd against the heavens
Breathing cruelty blood & vengeance, gnashing his teeth with pain
Torn with black storms, & ceaseless torrents of his own consuming fire:
Within his breast his mighty Sons chaind down & fill'd with cursings:
And his dark Eon, that once fair crystal form divinely clear:
Within his ribs producing serpents whose souls are flames of fire.
But glory to the Merciful-One, for he is of tender mercies!
And the Divine Family wept over him as One Man.

And these the Twenty-four in whom the Divine Family
Appeard; and they were One in Him. A Human Vision!
Human Divine. Jesus the Saviour, blessed for ever and ever.

Selsey, true friend! who afterwards submitted to be devourd
By the waves of Despair, whose Emanation rose above
The flood, and was namd Chichester, lovely mild & gentle! Lo!
Her lambs bleat to the sea-fowls cry, lamenting still for Albion.

Submitting to be calld the son of Los the terrible vision:
Winchester stood devoting himself for Albion: his tents
Outspread with abundant riches, and his Emanations
Submitting to be calld Enitharmons daughters, and be born
In vegetable mould, created by the Hammer and Loom
In Bowlahoola & Allamanda where the Dead wail night & day.

(I call them by their English names: English, the rough basement.
Los built the stubborn structure of the Language, acting against
Albions melancholy, who must else have been a Dumb despair.)

Gloucester and Exeter and Salisbury and Bristol: and benevolent
Bath

William Blake, Jerusalem, 1804, plate 36 (Copy "A").
William and Catherine Blake, depicted as Los and Eni-
tharmon in the righthand margin, collaborate in producing
the illuminated text. (By permission of the Trustees of the
British Museum.)

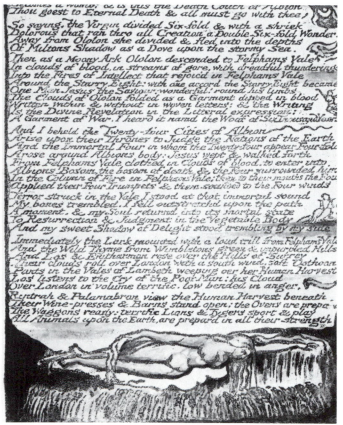

William Blake, Milton, *1804, plate 44 (Copy "B," RB54041). (By permission of the Huntington Library, San Marino, California.)*

a way of consciousness that occurs on another human front while Milton the man is toiling . . . with his alter ego, the Satanic double. These pictures show, through deeds of the chief female characters, how *growth* (rather than masculine contest), abetted by encouragement, fostering and inspiration, leads to human realization.[146]

The generation of the flesh, as an end in itself, lies in the realm of materialism, of the "Not-Human." That is the province of the horrifying "Polypus." Its substance is spun from the bowels of the malevolently spider-like "Shadowy Mother" and her five daugh-

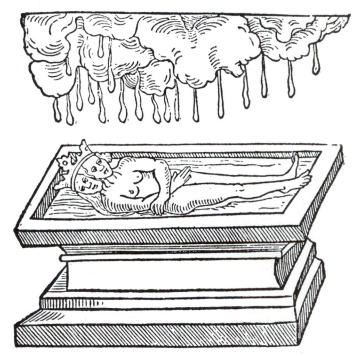

The lifeless corpse is laved and purified by the revitalizing dew of heaven. (See chapter 5, n. 47.) (From the Rosarium Philosophorum *[Frankfurt-on-Mainz, 1551]. Reproduced in* C. G. Jung, An Account of the Transference Phenomena based on the Illustrations to the "Rosarium Philosophorum," *in* Collected Works, *vol. 16, fig. 8, p. 273.)*

to the wife of his patron Thomas Butts, in a letter to her husband:

> Go on in Virtuous Seed sowing on Mold
> Of Human Vegetation, & Behold
> Your Harvest Springing to Eternal life
> Parent of Youthful Minds, & happy Wife![142]

He addresses Mrs. Butts as a wife and mother.[143] There is an obvious parallel between these lines, the "Human Harvest" of Oothoon, and the illustration of the last two plates of *Milton.* This is Blake's poetic depiction of a truly fruitful marital relationship, a suggestion strengthened by his use within the work of parallels with the "hieros gamos" of Sol and Luna.[144] The "Human Harvest" itself appears graphically on the last plate of the poem, in which both male and female have become "Vegetable in sexuality." Two apparently masculine ears of wheat gaze with awe upon a rapt, visionary female figure, emerging from a vegetable stem, who with trancelike unseeing eyes and arms uplifted directs the reader "To go forth to the Great Harvest & Vintage of the Nations."[145] The final plates of *Milton* present what John Grant has called "a feminine awakening,"

William Blake, Milton, *1804, plate 45 (Copy "B,"
RB54041): "To go forth to the Great Harvest & Vintage
of the Nations." (By permission of the Huntington Library,
San Marino, California.)*

PHILOSOPHORVM.

hie ist geboren die eddele Keyserin reich/
Die meister nennen sie jhrer dochter gleich.
Die vermeret sich/gebiert kinder ohn zal/
Sein vnd ötlich rein/vnnd ohn alles mahl.

Die

The resurrected "Hermaphroditus" is elevated on the cres-
cent moon, above the "human harvest." (See Chapter 5,
n. 47.) (From the Rosarium Philosophorum *[Frank-*
furt-on-Mainz, 1551]. Reproduced in C. G. Jung, An
Account of the Transference Phenomena based on the
Illustrations to the "Rosarium Philosophorum," *in*
Collected Works, *vol. 16, fig. 10, p. 305.)*

ters, whose effect on the life of truly creative human-ity is the same as that suggested by the spiders of *Europe*.[147] In her courageous emergence from retreat in "moony shades" into "brightness," Ololon ceases to be a "*Shadow* of Delight," among the "weak & weary," and becomes not merely "Delight" itself, but the fulfillment of desire: "Hephziba," the Hebrew name translated in the Authorized Version as "My delight is in her" in fact means "My *desire* is in her." Ololon sheds and discards the "negative" modes, both of "Rahab Babylon" the hypocritical "Virgin" harlot who embodies the "Female Will," and of the jealous, devouring and corrupting "Shadowy Fe-male" who lays waste the land ("negating" the fruit-ful influence of the loving and sexually yielding Oothoon). Ololon thus becomes the full partner of her "Inspired Man," his true "Contrary." In so doing she enables both of them to attain in their union "*hu-man* realization."

7

The Woman Jerusalem

> ". . . Jerusalem
> "Which now descendeth out of heaven, a City, yet a Woman,
> "Mother of myriads redeem'd & born in her spiritual palaces,
> "By a New Spiritual birth Regenerated from Death."
>
> —William Blake[1]

BLAKE'S JERUSALEM, BOTH MILTONIC AND BIBlical in inspiration, is a complex and comprehensive female presence in his later poetry and art. The eponymous heroine of Blake's last and longest prophecy emerges as an inclusive figure, subsuming in the canon of his work an ideal of which her feminine nature is an essential part, but only a part. As the "lovely Emanation of Albion" Jerusalem is summoned at the conclusion of the epic that bears her name, to "overspread all Nations as in Ancient Time."[2] She thus extends the fulfillment of the poet's undertaking in the lyric that prefaces *Milton,* since the whole of that epic is in an important sense a "Preludium" to *Jerusalem:*

> I will not cease from Mental Flight,
> Nor shall my Sword sleep in my hand
> Till we have built Jerusalem
> In England's green & pleasant Land.[3]

The poem *Jerusalem,* as Hazard Adams points out, is that building—"the establishment of linguistic or metaphorical identity in visionary time and space between holy Jerusalem and resurrected London."[4]

As a City, Blake's Jerusalem arises from the recurring dream vision he knew well from both Old and New Testaments. With the familiar biblical "topos" Blake's imagination continuously incorporated elements gleaned from other historical and literary sources.[5] Two other city concepts, created in the course of Blake's own "visionary studies," are mingled in his prophecy with the holy and heavenly city compounded from the prophetic books of the Bible.[6] One is London, to Blake no less than to Spenser or Milton the "most kyndly Nurse" of his art, the one place where (as Blake confided to Thomas Butts) he could freely "converse with [his] friends in Eternity, See Visions, Dream Dreams & prophecy & speak Parables. . . ."[7] Blake elevates his (and Spenser's, and Milton's) "first native sourse" to the status of a crowning ornament of the idealized Britain represented by the awakened Albion.[8] The other is Golgonooza, the city of "Art & Manufacture" that Los the artist, Blake's alter ego, continually builds.[9]

Golgonooza comprises the whole corpus of Blake's creative work. It is, as Morton Paley says, "the ultimate city," its name "combining the place of Christ's sacrifice of self with the primeval ooze of existence."[10] In its association with "the place of a skull, which is called in the Hebrew Golgotha," the "mind-forg'd" city of Golgonooza links the London

Why wilt thou give to her a Body whose life is but a Shade?
Her joy and love, a shade: a shade of sweet repose:
But animated and vegetated, she is a devouring worm:
What shall we do for thee O lovely mild Jerusalem?

And Los said, I behold the finger of God in terrors!
Albion is dead! his Emanation is divided from him!
But I am living! yet I feel my Emanation also dividing
Such things was never known! O pity me, thou all-piteous-one!
What shall I do! or how exist, divided from Enitharmon?
Yet why despair! I saw the finger of God go forth
Upon my Furnaces, from within the Wheels of Albions Sons:
Fixing their Systems, permanent: by mathematic power
Giving a body to Falshood that it may be cast off for ever,
With Demonstrative Science piercing Apollyon with his own bow:
God is within, & without! he is even in the depths of Hell!

Such were the lamentations of the Labourers in the Furnaces!

And they appeard within & without incircling on both sides
The Starry Wheels of Albions Sons, with Spaces for Jerusalem:
And for Vala the shadow of Jerusalem: the ever mourning shade:
On both sides, within & without beaming gloriously!

Terrified at the sublime Wonder, Los stood before his Furnaces.
And they stood around, terrified with admiration at Erins Spaces
For the Spaces reached from the starry heighth, to the starry depth.
And they builded Golgonooza: terrible eternal labour!

What are those golden builders doing: where was the burying-place
Of soft Ethinthus? near Tyburns fatal Tree? is that
Mild Zions hill's most ancient promontory, near mournful
Ever weeping Paddington? is that Calvary and Golgotha?
Becoming a building of pity and compassion! Lo!
The stones are pity, and the bricks, well wrought affections:
Enameld with love & kindness, & the tiles engraven gold
Labour of merciful hands: the beams & rafters are forgiveness:
The mortar & cement of the work, tears of honesty: the nails,
And the screws & iron braces, are well wrought blandishments,
And well contrived words, firm fixing, never forgotten,
Always comforting the remembrance: the floors, humility,
The cielings, devotion: the hearths, thanksgiving:
Prepare the furniture O Lambeth in thy pitying looms!
The curtains, woven tears & sighs, wrought into lovely forms
For comfort, there the secret furniture of Jerusalems chamber
Is wrought: Lambeth! the Bride the Lambs Wife loveth thee:
Thou art one with her & knowest not of self in thy supreme joy
Go on, builders in hope, tho Jerusalem wanders far away,
Without the gate of Los: among the dark Satanic wheels.

Fourfold the Sons of Los in their divisions: and fourfold,
The great City of Golgonooza: fourfold toward the north
And toward the south fourfold, & fourfold toward the east & west
Each within other toward the four points: that toward
Eden, and that toward the World of Generation,
And that toward Beulah, and that toward Ulro:
Ulro is the space of the terrible starry wheels of Albions sons:
But that toward Eden is walled up, till time of renovation:
Yet it is perfect in its building, ornaments & perfection.

And the Four Points are thus beheld in Great Eternity
West, the Circumference: South, the Zenith: North,
The Nadir: East, the Center, unapproachable for ever.
These are the four Faces towards the Four Worlds of Humanity
In every Man. Ezekiel saw them by Chebars flood.
And the Eyes are the South, and the Nostrils are the East.
And the Tongue is the West, and the Ear is the North.

And the North Gate of Golgonooza toward Generation:
Has four sculptured Bulls terrible before the Gate of iron,
And iron, the Bulls: and that which looks toward Ulro,
Clay bakd & enameld, eternal glowing as four furnaces:
Turning upon the Wheels of Albions Sons with enormous power.
And that toward Beulah four, gold, silver, brass, & iron:

And

William Blake, Jerusalem, 1804, plate 12 (Copy "A").
(See Chapter 7, n. 12.) (By permission of the Trustees of
the British Museum.)

in which Blake lived with the historical Jerusalem where Christ was crucified.[11] While building it the artist labors tirelessly in the renewal of both the contemporary and the ancient cities:

> And they builded Golgonooza: terrible eternal labour!
> What are those golden builders doing? where was the burying-place
> Of soft Ethinthus? near Tyburn's fatal Tree? is that
> Mild Zion's hill's most ancient promontory, near mournful
> Ever weeping Paddington? is that Calvary and Golgotha
> Becoming a building of pity and compassion? . . .
> Go on, builders in hope, tho' Jerusalem wanders far away. . . .[12]

Here is an instance of something characteristic of Blake's poetry, and of his thinking: in the words of Mollyanne Marks, "this opposition of building up and tearing down, of creating and destroying, is going on all the time, with the creative force gaining as Blake goes on with his work."[13]

The site of the notorious Tyburn gallows, where criminals had been executed in the public view until 1783, was a short walk from the lodgings in South Molton Street where Blake and his wife made their home from the time of their return from Felpham in September 1803, until 1821: that is, throughout the period of *Jerusalem*'s composition. Paddington, at this time—as David Erdman records—"a village of poverty-stricken Irish laborers," was surrounded with "the most wretched huts, filled with squatters of the lowest of the community."[14] In 1811–12 "on the Paddington side of old Watling Street some excavation for new houses was made just north of the ancient gallows, and the workers dug up a cartload of Tyburn bones and parts of apparel. . . ."[15] Ethinthus (not—*pace* W. H. Stevenson—"a name only") was the coldly chaste Diana-like "queen of waters . . . [shining] in the sky" in Blake's *Europe* (1794).[16] Her burying place "near Tyburn's fatal tree" is adjacent in Blake's vision to "Mild Zion's hill's most ancient promontory."[17] The association takes the reader back to the Miltonic echoes of the earlier context in *Europe,* in which the waters of Ethinthus "warble round the feet of Enitharmon."[18] Blake was there invoking Milton's image of "Sion and the flowery brooks beneath / That wash thy hallowed feet, and warbling flow."[19] Enitharmon, proclaiming in *Europe* the doctrine that "Woman's Love is Sin," thus identified herself with the Temple of ancient Jerusalem on its Mount, a forbidding edifice enclosing and guarding her Holy of Holies. In *Jerusalem,* the Enitharmon of *Europe* is called a "Female Will . . . [hiding] the most evident God . . . In the shadows of a Woman & a secluded Holy Place. . . ."[20] Ethinthus had been an acolyte of the "Female Will," abasing herself in worship with "warbled" songs of praise before that living shrine of frustrated sexuality. In the *Jerusalem* passage she is laid to rest in earth from which evidence of the savagery of legally sanctioned execution is being dug up, in preparation for the building of dwellings to enable people to live with the dignity of human beings. Two cults that militate against life, the sterile doctrine of "Religious Chastity" and the murderous doctrine of capital punishment, are thus obliterated together in the burial of Ethinthus and the eradication of the memory of the Tyburn tree, as "that Calvary and Golgotha" where humanity had brutally been sacrificed for centuries becomes "a building of pity and compassion." Clearly, the building of Golgonooza and the rebuilding of Jerusalem proceed partly through real urban renewal in the Regency London of Blake's own life experience.[21] On a personal level, the interment of Ethinthus also marks the fading away from Blake's field of concern of the relatively limited cultural issue she represented, since his mind and art are now occupied with the far-reaching social issues implied in the linking of the Tyburn tree with Golgotha, and the relationship of that image to the rebuilding of London.

In visualizing Jerusalem the City, Blake was transcending a historical situation by means that earlier visionaries had employed. St. John, cloistered (according to tradition) in his monastic cell on remote Patmos, at a time when the empire of pagan Rome was at the height of its cruel, covetous, and godless power, recorded his "Revelation" of a heavenly city of sanctity and love that would overspread the earth. At a later period John Milton eagerly and, as it turned out, overoptimistically, visualized London as a beleaguered intellectual Paradise. Though "besieg'd and block't about, her navigable river infested, inrodes and incursions round," Milton's visionary London was populated by citizens.

> . . . wholly tak'n up with the study of highest and most important matters to be reform'd . . . disputing, reasoning, reading, inventing, discoursing, ev'n to a rarity, and admiration, things not before discourst or writt'n of. . . .[22]

In the event, Milton found himself, in 1660, in the midst of a populace who seemed determined to "forgoe & set to sale religion, liberties, honor, safetie, all concernments Divine or human to keep up trading."[23] These people, in summoning back their king, chose for themselves "a Captain back for *Egypt*," spurning the freedom of election and of conscience in whose upholding Milton had expended a lifetime of effort and had even (as he believed) sacrificed his eyesight.[24] A blind prophet without honor in his own country, Milton continued to commend political liberty to his fellow citizens, even risking his own life by publishing "The Readie & Easie Way to Establish a Free Commonwealth" in 1660. Despite all he could say or do, the monarchy was restored in that year. Though virtually under house arrest after a period of imprisonment, John Milton did *not* thereafter withdraw into darkness and silence—the darkness of his loss of physical sight, and the silence enforced by severe official repression that including the banning and public burning of his published tracts. Instead, he set about composing the great poems that were to be his crowning achievement, through which chiefly he spoke, across a century and a half, to William Blake. Surely this heroic personal example of his poetic mentor influenced Blake in his treatment of "Jerusalem [who] is named Liberty" as a figure hidden in darkness, silenced, discredited, and rejected, but awaiting in faith the hour of apocalyptic regeneration.

Each in "the voice of one crying in the wilderness," visionaries like these two named John express their firm faith that, against all probability in practical terms, their redemptive ideals will ultimately be realized.[25] One of the symbolic meanings of Jerusalem is "liberty" in the sense of the artist's freedom to give expression to his own unique vision: as Blake insists,

> In Great Eternity every particular Form gives forth
>   or Emanates
> Its own peculiar Light, & the Form is the Divine
>   Vision
> And the Light is his Garment. This is Jerusalem in
>   every Man . . .
> And Jerusalem is called Liberty among the
>   Children of Albion.[26]

That Los should sing of Blake's vision "in the deadly darkness" of the fallen world, as he keeps his unceasing watch throughout the "night" of Time while tending the furnaces of creativity, is evidence of his dedicated preservation, in common with those other inspired prophets, of "the Divine Vision in time of trouble."[27] The essential difference between the vision of St. John on the one hand, and those of John Milton and William Blake on the other, is that whereas the biblical prophet brought his city of redemption down from heaven at a moment beyond the lifespan of this world, both Milton and Blake desired to build theirs in England, "in the hills &

valleys of Albion . . . embodied in Time and Space."[28]

Milton's idealized metonymic characterization of London as "the mansion house of liberty" in *Areopagitica* influenced Blake's representation of Jerusalem as both City and Woman.[29] Similarly, Milton's personification of ideal "Liberty" as the "consort" of "the spirit of grace" in *Paradise Lost* played a seminal part in Blake's creation of his feminine "Jerusalem."[30] It is in the feminine role that Jerusalem makes her first appearance in Blake's work, on the opening page of *Vala* (later to become *The Four Zoas*), perhaps as early as 1795. Jerusalem, whom Tharmas claims has been taken by Enion from his "inmost Soul," is hidden by him "secret in the soft recess of darkness & silence."[31] The Jerusalem who has thus been put away may represent the "innocence, that as a veil / Had shadowed them [Adam and Eve] from knowing ill."[32] Wilkie and Johnson explain Jerusalem's concealment as a means of protecting her from the taint of fallen nature:

> Rather than following the precedents of biblical and classical myth and allowing Jerusalem, Albion's true Emanation, to fall or cause the fall, Blake hides her away and gives the role of temptress to Vala; in biblical tradition, this would be like preserving Eve's innocence by exposing Lilith as the guilty female. Jerusalem remains uncorrupted as the spiritual side of Albion's feminine being, separated from him by the fall.[33]

Jerusalem as the innocence which "as a veil / Had shadowed them from knowing ill" is hidden and is replaced by Vala, whose name and associations derive from the "veil" of "Mystery" Blake hated—a *veil* that does not *protect* from evil, but masks and conceals it, partly by anagrammatizing the very word "evil." The innocence represented by Jerusalem is in its own way freedom, or liberty; the fallen condition, which overwhelms and destroys innocence, is unquestionably one of bondage or imprisonment, whether by the biblical measure or that of Milton, or in terms of the Blakean myth in which the fallen mind is "Prison'd on wat'ry shore."[34]

Blake's primary association of Jerusalem with liberty is likely to have come from the book of Isaiah. Several passages come to mind:

> Awake, awake, put on thy strength, O Zion; put on thy beautiful garments, O Jerusalem, the holy city. . . . Shake thyself from the dust; arise, and sit down, O Jerusalem: loose thyself from the bands of thy neck, O captive daughter of Zion. . . . (52.1–2)[35]

> The Spirit of the Lord God is upon me; because the

William Blake, Jerusalem, *1804, plate 92 (Copy "A").*
(By permission of the Trustees of the British Museum.)

Lord hath anointed me to preach good tidings . . . to proclaim liberty to the captives, and the opening of the prison to them that are bound. . . . (61.1)

For Zion's sake will I not hold my peace, and for Jerusalem's sake I will not rest, until the righteousness thereof go forth as brightness, and the salvation thereof as a lamp that burneth. . . . (62.1)

The long-standing association of Jerusalem with "Liberty" in Blake's mind would have been augmented for him by Milton's presentation, lighthearted though it appears to be in its context, of "the mountain nymph, sweet Liberty" who is the chief companion of Mirth in his *L'Allegro*.[36] Blake's illustrations to *L'Allegro* were executed in the period 1816–20, while he was still deeply involved in the composition of *Jerusalem*.[37] The first illustration shows "Liberty" as a young girl at the right hand of Mirth, the central figure.[38] The facial expression of "Liberty" is more serious and spiritual than those of any of the other sportive figures in the composition. With eyes uplifted, she seems almost to be relinquishing the hand of Mirth. She wears Grecian robes and sandals—perhaps recalling Milton's association of mountainous Greece with political liberty—and has bound to her back a sheaf of arrows from which, with her right hand, she is drawing one fledged shaft. As the golden clouds of dawn unfold behind her, Liberty/Jerusalem in this painting seems to respond to the poet's injunction in *Milton*, "Bring me my Arrows of desire . . .!" In a sense apparently related

William Blake, "Mirth and Her Companions." From the series of illustrations to Milton's L'Allegro (ca. 1816–20). (By permission of the Pierpont Morgan Library, New York. Purchased with the Assistance of the Fellows with the special support of Mrs. Landon K Thorne and Mrs. Paul Mellon. 1949.4:1.)

to this summons, Jerusalem in *Milton* is the *fulfillment* of desire, redeemed from the opprobrious status of outcast and harlot into which she had fallen; she becomes, literally, the "Hephzibah" of Isaiah 62.4, whose Hebrew name means "My desire is in her."[39] Thus the repentant "Six-fold Female" is commanded by the Divine Voice:

> "[Thou] shalt bring Jerusalem in thine arms in the night watches and
> No longer turning her a wandering Harlot in the streets,
> Shalt give her into the arms of God your Lord & Husband."[40]

In *Jerusalem*, the line "Jerusalem is named Liberty among the Sons [Children] of Albion" occurs twice.[41] In both contexts Jerusalem as Liberty is associated with the capacity for spiritual vision, the "Divine Vision . . . in every Man. . . ."[42] This is the form finally assumed by "the Woman Jerusalem" as she appears both at the opening and near the closure of the work.

In *The Four Zoas* Blake had called Jerusalem "a City, yet a Woman."[43] But in her first pictorial appearance, on the title page of his last great poem, Jerusalem is not in any way a city, nor is she easily identifiable as a woman. At first glance the winged creature extended across the lower part of the title page (attended by other winged forms) seems to be a large and splendid butterfly. Richly colored in "a universal rainbow spectrum," Jerusalem lies supine, sleeping with head thrown back and arms extended behind her head, her long hair trailing between them.[44] On the uppermost of her three gorgeous pairs of wings the sun and the earth appear, like "eye-spots"; on the middle pair the moon waxes to the right and wanes to the left of her body; on the lowest pair, stars are scattered over ribbed vanes into which her legs have almost metamorphosed.

Blake refers in his address "To the Jews," on plate 26 of *Jerusalem*, to the "tradition, that Man anciently contain'd in his mighty limbs all things in Heaven & Earth."[45] The tradition to which he refers is that of the Kabbalistic "Adam Kadmon" or "primordial man." According to Gershom Scholem, the "Adam Kadmon" is a "vessel" created "by a raising and lowering of the 'cosmic measure' which serves as a permanent connection between *Ein-Sof* ('the infinite') and the primordial space of *zimzum* ('contraction')."[46] In the Lurianic system of the Kabbalah the Adam Kadmon, the "first being to emerge after the *zimzum*," serves as

a kind of intermediary link between *Ein-Sof*, the light

whose substance continues to be active in him, and the hierarchy of worlds still to come. In comparison with the latter, indeed, the *Adam Kadmon* himself could well be, and sometimes was, called *Ein-Sof*.[47]

Professor Sheila A. Spector's meticulous research suggests that Blake could hardly have gleaned his own knowledge of Kabbalism from Jewish sources. It is far more probable that he obtained it in distorted and indirect forms from seventeenth- and eighteenth-century Christian sources in English.[48] Blake, indeed, associates the concept he mentions in his address "To the Jews" with his lifelong interest in British Druidism.[49] He asserts that "Abraham, Heber, Shem and Noah . . . were Druids," and that the Jews received their tradition "from the Druids," whom he regarded as proto-Christians, "so near in descent to the fountains of true religion and worship as to have one of Noah's sons for grandsire or great-grandsire. . . ."[50] Yet Blake's concepts of the "limit of contraction," "the infinite" or "infinity," and the intermediary function of primordial or regenerated Man, through whom the light of infinity shines, must have reached him from Kabbalistic origins through the filters of whatever sources were available to him. Scholem notes:

> From the head of the *Adam Kadmon* tremendous lights shone forth and aligned themselves in rich and complex patterns. Some assumed the form of letters while others took on still other aspects of the Torah or the Holy Tongue. . . . Thus, two essentially different symbolisms—that of light and that of language and writing—are here joined.[51]

Blake's understanding of his own inspiration and its dual expression in visual and verbal imagery would surely have found a happy parallel in this particular aspect of the symbolism of the Adam Kadmon. Indeed, in the words of J. A. Wittreich, "in the very act of restoring the arts to union, [*Jerusalem* offers] an image, magnificent and expansive and whole, of the world restored as Jerusalem."[52]

As the poet evokes the condition of the "primordial man" who "anciently contain'd in his mighty limbs all things in Heaven and Earth," he adds in a melancholy refrain, echoed from *Milton* and thrice repeated in *Jerusalem,* that this is so no longer: "But now the Starry Heavens are fled from the mighty limbs of Albion."[53] In the design of plate 25, just preceding this lament, the sun, moon and stars can still be seen on Albion's "mighty limbs," although, through the influence of Vala, stretching out her arms and robe above him, and by the ministrations of Rahab and Tirzah on either side, these heavenly bodies

are about to be stripped away from him. On the lower half of plate 33[37], the divestiture is shown in its ghastly completion, with Albion, extended on his "Couch of Death," vegetating into a gigantic "Polypus" and overhung by a reptilian "Spectre" whose batlike wings mimic the extended arms of Vala in plate 25. The sun, moon, and stars, fled from Albion's decaying limbs, hang in the darkness at either end of his supine body. This design is the antithesis or "negation" of the representation on the title page, of Jerusalem as the regenerated "Eve" to Albion's "Adam Kadmon." "The Starry Heavens," the sun, moon, and stars, are incorporated into her winged form as she appears there. Her breasts, face, and arms are those of a woman, but from the waist downward she has no obvious human sexuality.

The description of Jerusalem in the text that corresponds to the title-page figure occurs late in the work. In the fourth and final Chapter of the poem, Los

> . . . walks upon his ancient Mountains in deadly darkness,
> Among his Furnaces directing his laborious Myriads, watchful
> Looking to the East, & his voice is heard over the whole Earth. . . .[54]

In the song that Los "sings on his Watch" he invokes Jerusalem:

> "O lovely mild Jerusalem! O Shiloh of
>   Mount Ephraim!   22
> "I see thy Gates of precious stones, thy Walls
>   of gold and silver
> "Thou art the soft reflected Image of the
>   Sleeping Man
> "Who, stretch'd on Albion's rocks,
>   reposes . . .   25
> "I see thy Form, O lovely mild Jerusalem,
>   Wing'd with Six Wings   1
> "In the opacous Bosom of the Sleeper, lovely
>   Three-fold
> "In Head & Heart & Reins, three Universes
>   of love & Beauty.
> "Thy forehead bright, Holiness to the Lord,
>   with Gates of pearl
> "Reflects Eternity; beneath, thy azure wings
>   of feathery down   5
> "Ribb'd delicate & cloth'd with feather'd gold
>   & azure & purple,
> "From thy white shoulders shadowing purity
>   in holiness!
> "Thence, feather'd with soft crimson of the
>   ruby, bright as fire,
> "Spreading into the azure, Wings which like a
>   canopy   9

And there was heard a great lamenting in Beulah: all the Regions
Of Beulah were moved as the tender bowels are moved: & they said:

Why did you take Vengeance O ye Sons of the mighty Albion?
Planting these Oaken Groves: Erecting these Dragon Temples
Injury the Lord heals but Vengeance cannot be healed:
As the Sons of Albion have done to Luvah: so they have in him
Done to the Divine Lord & Saviour, who suffers with those that suffer;
For not one sparrow can suffer, & the whole Universe not suffer also,
In all its Regions, & its Father & Saviour not pity and weep.
But Vengeance is the destroyer of Grace & Repentance in the bosom
Of the Injurer: in which the Divine Lamb is cruelly slain;
Descend O Lamb of God & take away the imputation of Sin
By the Creation of States & the deliverance of Individuals Evermore Amen

Thus wept they in Beulah over the Four Regions of Albion
But many doubted & despaird & imputed Sin & Righteousness
To Individuals & not to States, and these Slept in Ulro.

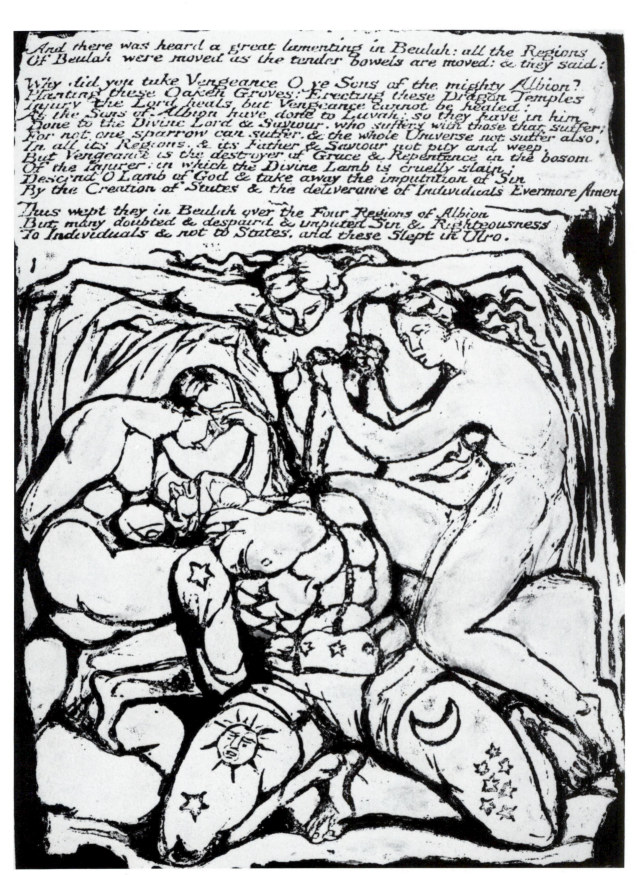

William Blake, Jerusalem, *1804, plate 25 (Copy "A").*
(By permission of the Trustees of the British Museum.)

William Blake, Jerusalem, 1804, *plate 33 (Copy "A").*
(By permission of the Trustees of the British Museum.)

"Bends over thy immortal Head in which
  Eternity dwells . . .
"Thy Bosom white, translucent, cover'd with
  immortal gems,   14
"A sublime ornament not obscuring the
  outlines of beauty,
"Terrible to behold for thy extreme beauty
  and perfection;
"Twelve-fold here all the Tribes of Israel I
  behold
"Upon the Holy Land. I see the River of Life
  & Tree of Life,
"I see the New Jerusalem descending out of
  Heaven,   19
"Between thy Wings of gold & silver,
  feather'd, immortal,
"Clear as the rainbow, as the cloud of the
  Sun's tabernacle.
"Thy Reins, cover'd with Wings and
  translucent, sometimes covering
"And sometimes spread abroad, reveal the
  flames of holiness
"Which like a robe covers & like a Veil of
  Seraphim
"In flaming fire unceasing burns from
  Eternity to Eternity.   25
"Twelvefold I there behold Israel in her Tents;
"A Pillar of a Cloud by day, a Pillar of fire by
  night
"Guides them; there I behold Moab &
  Ammon & Amalek.
"There, Bells of silver round thy knees living
  articulate
"Comforting sounds of love & harmony, &
  on thy feet   30
"Sandals of gold & pearl, & Egypt & Assyria
  before me,
"The Isles of Javan, Philistea, Tyre and
  Lebanon."[55]

Much of this biblically inspired passage is presented through Miltonic perspectives. Jerusalem is "mild"—an adjective repeatedly applied to her—because Blake chose to interpret her name as "vision of peace" or "city [abode] of peace," both traditional etymologies of the Hebrew "Yeru-shalayim."[56] To Blake the vision of the long-desired Jerusalem who wandered far away, lost and unattainable, most eminently expressed his longing for peace during the incessant warfare in Europe of the first decade and a half of the nineteenth century. The alternative phrase of address, "Shiloh of Mount Ephraim" refers to the assembly at Shiloh, near Mount Ephraim, where the holy tabernacle was set up by the twelve tribes of Israel ("Twelve-fold here all the Tribes of Israel I behold / Upon the Holy Land . . ."), after they had entered Canaan and subdued its heathen tribes under the leadership of Joshua.[57] The name "Shiloh" draws on the same root as the second element of "Yerushalayim"—shalom, "peace"—and had for Blake the same symbolic value.[58] Jesus took refuge in "a city called Ephraim" when it became known that Caiaphas was plotting against him.[59] "Shiloh" and "Ephraim" were associated by Blake with the concept of sanctuary, in the dual sense of a consecrated holy place and a resort secure from persecution. Both symbolized as well the eventual triumph of the Chosen People over hostile forces, recalled by the reference to the divine guidance of "Israel in her Tents" through the wilderness by "a Pillar of Cloud by day, a Pillar of Fire by night," and in the catalog of historical enemies and rivals from whom Israel was delivered. Los now faces these hostile forces: "Moab & Ammon & Amalek . . . Egypt & Assyria . . . Javan, Philistea, Tyre and Lebanon."[60] The "Gates of precious stones" and "Walls of gold and silver" attributed to Blake's Jerusalem as City are primarily Miltonic.[61] The gates resemble the one seen by Satan, in the course of his voyage through the sky in book 3 of *Paradise Lost,* at the entrance to that Heaven from which he had been cast out: a "kingly palace gate / With frontispiece of diamond and gold / Embellished, thick with sparkling orient gems."[62] Travelling onward, Satan had viewed the sun, "in splendour likest heaven" (again reminding him of his exclusion from it). Within the sun "part seemed gold, part silver clear," like the walls of Blake's Jerusalem.[63] Los's view of the preciousness and radiance of Jerusalem the City is evidently that of an exile longing to return.

The description of Jerusalem's "Form" on plate 86 was partly inspired by Milton's account, in book 5 of *Paradise Lost,* of the archangel Raphael. This "empyreal minister" is commanded by God the Father to fly to Paradise to warn Adam and Eve of the imminence of Satan's assault upon their happiness.[64] In prompt obedience Raphael springs up "from among / Thousand celestial ardours, where he stood / Veiled with his gorgeous wings."[65] Speeding through the sky on his mission,

> . . . within soar
> Of towering eagles, to all fowls he seems
> A phoenix, gazed by all, as that sole bird
> When to enshrine his relics in the sun's
> Bright temple, to Aegyptian Thebes he flies.[66]

Blake's concept of Jerusalem draws in certain fundamental ways on the legend of the phoenix, from a description of which Milton's account of the angelic form is derived.[67] Milton's passage relating the phoenix to the "towering eagle," traditionally a bird that soars toward the sun and gazes directly at it, influenced Blake in his consistent association throughout his work of the eagle with "Genius."[68] Aspects of the traditional symbolism of the phoenix apear in all three of the "lovely Three-fold . . . universes of love & beauty" Blake attributes to Jerusalem's bodily form, "in Head & Heart & Reins."[69] In Christian symbolism the phoenix, which expired in flames and arose renewed from its own ashes, was emblematic of regeneration, and of the triumph of eternal life over death.[70] The Forehead of Blake's Jerusalem—like the heavenly city of Revelation 21—"with Gates of pearl / Reflects Eternity"; in her "immortal Head . . . Eternity dwells."[71] In her bosom "the River of Life & Tree of Life" appear, drawn from Revelations 22.1–2, but also from Milton's Tree of Life in the Garden of Eden, and his "living streams among the trees of life" in Heaven.[72] Her "Reins" "reveal the flames of holiness / Which . . . in flaming fire unceasing burns from Eternity to Eternity."[73] Consumed in flames and regenerated from its own ashes, the phoenix transcends both mortality and division into sexes. In secular iconography the phoenix symbolized uniqueness, and hence constancy: thus in Jerusalem's bosom Los sees the fulfillment of a series of biblical covenants, including that of God with the Chosen Race—"all the Tribes of Israel I behold / Upon the Holy Land."[74]

Since it was complete in itself, comprising both masculine and feminine, the phoenix became an ideal of true love, hermaphroditic or "neutral" in sex, as in Donne's image of a perfect union:

> The phoenix riddle hath more wit
> By us; we two being one, are it.
> So to one neutral thing both sexes fit
> We die and rise the same, and prove
> Mysterious by this love.[75]

Blake alludes elsewhere in *Jerusalem* to a discussion of angelic sexuality that takes place between Raphael and Adam in *Paradise Lost,* when in response to Adam's curiosity concerning the loves of "heavenly spirits,"

> . . . the angel with a smile that glowed
> Celestial rosy red, love's proper hue,
> Answered. Let it suffice thee that thou know'st
> Us happy, and without love no happiness.
> Whatever pure thou in the body enjoy'st
> (And pure thou wert created) we enjoy
> In eminence, and obstacle find none
> Of membrane, joint, or limb, exclusive bars:
> Easier than air with air, if spirits embrace,

> Total they mix, union of pure with pure
> Desiring . . .[76]

In *Jerusalem,* as in other works, Blake rejects a "Religion of Chastity," calling it "a False Holiness hid within the Center."[77] A loving union ideally takes the form Raphael implies: "Embraces are Comminglings from the Head even to the Feet, / And not a pompous High Priest entering by a Secret Place."[78] Like the phoenix, the Woman Jerusalem is a type of true and constant love: though rejected, she is faithful to Albion throughout his long eclipse. She is also unique in being his only true "Emanation." Yet although she is always spoken of in the feminine gender, has daughters, and is frequently depicted visually as a beautiful nude woman within the poem, Blake's idealization of Jerusalem, in graphic form on the title page, and verbally in the passage under discussion from the fourth chapter of the work, virtually sets her apart from physical sexuality.

Raphael in *Paradise Lost* alights on the eastern cliff of Paradise, where he resumes his "proper shape" and appears as "a seraph winged":

> . . . six wings he wore, to shade
> His lineaments divine; the pair that clad
> Each shoulder broad, came mantling o'er his breast
> With regal ornament; the middle pair
> Girt like a starry zone his waist, and round
> Skirted his loins and thighs with downy gold
> And colours dipped in heaven; the third his feet
> Shadowed from either heel with feathered mail
> Sky-tinctured grain. Like Maia's son he stood,
> And shook his plumes, that heavenly fragrance filled
> The circuit wide.[79]

Each of the angel's three pairs of wings is of a different hue: purple ("regal ornament") at the shoulder, "downy gold" round the "loins and thighs," and "sky-tinctur'd grain" "from either heel." The colors of this "winged hierarch" are symbolic of three spheres in the divinely ordered hierarchy of the heavens.[80] The regal purple of the uppermost wings recalls the "primum mobile," the outermost region of the universe, where God dwells in universal sovereignty. Gold stands for the sphere of the sun, that "great palace . . . of light" from which the stars "in their golden urns draw light"; and indeed the golden middle wings of the archangel are compared to "a starry zone."[81] The blue—"sky-tinctur'd grain"—of the lowest pair of wings represents the sublunar aerial sphere from which the angel, who is pure spirit, becomes embodied so as to become visible to Adam and Eve.[82]

The splendor of Jerusalem's coloration draws not

Leaning against the pillars, & his disease rose from his skirts
Upon the Precipice he stood: ready to fall into Non-Entity.

Los was all astonishment & terror: he trembled sitting on the Stone
Of London: but the interiors of Albions fibres & nerves were hidden
From Los; astonishd he beheld only the petrified surfaces:
And saw his Furnaces in ruins. for Los is the Demon of the Furnaces;
He saw also the Four Points of Albion reversd inwards
He siezd his Hammer & Tongs, his iron Poker & his Bellows,
Upon the valleys of Middlesex. Shouting loud for aid Divine.

In stern defiance came from Albions bosom Hand, Hyle, Koban,
Gwantok, Peachy, Brertun, Slaid, Hutton Skofeld, Kock, Kotope
Bowen: Albions Sons: they bore him a golden couch into the porch
And on the Couch reposd his limbs, trembling from the bloody field,
Rearing their Druid Patriarchal rocky Temples around his limbs.
All things begin & end, in Albions Ancient Druid Rocky Shore.)

*William Blake, Jerusalem, 1804, plate 46 (Copy "A"):
Jerusalem and her daughters (with Vala). (By permission
of the Trustees of the British Museum.)*

only upon Milton's description of the descending archangel, but also upon another, equally significant, moment of perception in *Paradise Lost,* which Milton himself relates to it. This is the glimpse of Eve through the eyes of Satan, delighted to come upon her alone after she has left Adam in the Garden to "divide" her labors from his:

> Beyond his hope, Eve separate he spies,
> Veiled in a cloud of fragrance, where she stood,
> Half spied, so thick the roses bushing round
> About her glowed, oft stooping to support
> Each flower of slender stalk, whose head though gay
> Carnation, purple, azure, or specked with gold,
> Hung drooping unsustained, them she upstays
> Gently with myrtle band, mindless the while,
> Her self, though fairest unsupported flower,
> From her best prop so far, and storm so nigh. . . .[83]

Although her self-assertion, perverse and ill-omened in the patriarchal Miltonic view, is always associated by Blake with the "Female Will," Eve at this moment, exquisitely resembling the delicate flowers "of slender stalk . . . drooping unsustained" about her, appears as a "heavenly form / Angelic. . . ."[84] Like the archangel Raphael, "veiled with his gorgeous wings" which shed "heavenly fragrance," she is "Veiled in a cloud of fragrance."[85] The flowers surrounding her, colored "carnation, purple, azure, or specked with gold," deliberately disorder the purple, gold, and blue of the "winged hierarch."[86] Milton introduces into Eve's "flowery plat" the glow of "roses bushing round / About . . .," and the color "carnation," meaning "flesh-colored" or "ruddy," hinting prophetically at the erotic attraction and the fleshly "link of nature" that will draw Adam into disaster in the *Paradise Lost* context.[87]

The six wings of Blake's Jerusalem are "azure . . . of feathery down / Ribb'd delicate & clothed with feather'd gold & azure & purple, / From thy white shoulders . . . Thence, feather'd with soft crimson of the ruby, bright as fire, / Spreading into the azure. . . ." Although Blake has borrowed from Milton the "starry zone" he shows covering the pair of wings depicted about the loins and thighs of the title-page image of Jerusalem, he does not suggest, either visually or verbally, that each pair of wings is differently colored.[88] Rather, he gives the impression in both media of rainbow coloration, emphasized especially in lines 86.18–21 in which the Woman Jerusalem becomes indistinguishable from the City:

> . . . I see the River of Life & Tree of Life
> I see the New Jerusalem descending out of Heaven
> Between thy Wings of gold & silver featherd
>   immortal

> Clear as the rainbow, as the cloud of the Suns
>   tabernacle. . . .[89]

The elements of this aspect of the vision include Milton's account of the landscape of Heaven before Satan's insurrection, and St. John's description of the descent of the New Jerusalem from Heaven.[90] Blake's customary sparseness of punctuation causes the adjectival phrase "of gold & silver," possibly derived from Satan's perception of the sun (quoted previously), to fluctuate ambiguously between "thy Wings" in line 20 and "the New Jerusalem" in the preceding line. Line 21 takes up Milton's image of primeval Light in its cloudy womb before the creation of the sun, "sphered in a radiant cloud . . . a cloudy tabernacle. . . ."[91] The addition of the rainbow simile to all this recalls God's covenant with Noah after the Flood. The synoptic vision of these lines joins together a moment *before* the beginning of time (the "River of Life and Tree of Life" in Heaven) and the moment when time begins to unfold (when Light is created on the First Day of the week of Creation).[92] It includes a glimpse of time *after* the seven days of creation in the yet unfallen cosmos (Satan's perception of the sun), and a link between the time-bound fallen world and a divinely promised redemption (the rainbow, token of God's "Covenant never to destroy / The earth again by flood . . . till fire purge all things new, / Both heaven and earth . . .").[93] It focuses centrally upon a point in Eternity, symbolized by the descent of the New Jerusalem, beyond the moment when "Time was Finished."[94] Los, recalling the divine covenants represented variously by the River and Tree of Life, by Light, the Sun, the Rainbow, and the New Jerusalem, affirms his faith on Mankind's behalf in the ultimate return of the lost Jerusalem and her reunion with Albion. The rainbow coloration Blake has chosen for the title page is the visual equivalent both of the covenant of God with fallen Man, and of the visionary dimension of Eternity: it seems to enact in a form perceptible to the eye the *simultaneity* of all Time, after "Time was Finished." Here is a vision that, unlike that of the building of Golgonooza depicted in the passage from Plate 12 discussed earlier, seems to float free of "time present" in the sense of Blake's historical lifetime. Here Blake approaches a cosmic sense of man's relationship with the Divine *within himself,* for Los perceives Jerusalem "in the opacous Bosom" of the "Sleeping Man."[95]

The biblical evaluations of Wisdom (and perhaps of the "virtuous woman") must have been in Blake's mind when he feathered with "soft crimson of the ruby" Jerusalem's upper pair of wings, "which like a canopy / Bends over thy immortal Head."[96] Milton's inclusion of the ruby in the composition of the sun, and its presence among the gems ornamenting the breastplate of Aaron, the high priest, would have been part of Blake's cue for the coloration of these plumes.[97] The crimson or scarlet of the roses and the "carnation"—flesh-color—added by Milton to his paradisal setting for the "heavenly form" of Eve, as well as the "celestial rosy red, love's proper hue" of Raphael's glowing smile when the archangel speaks of love, all contribute to Blake's "crimson of the ruby."[98] The parallels with the phoenix-like angel explored earlier suggest that Blake may also have been playing upon the connotations of the Greek word *phoenix,* since the same word was used for the purpled-red or crimson dye anciently obtained from Phoenicia. Each of these associations—divine wisdom and illumination, holiness and love, humanity, and the emblematic significance of the legendary phoenix, especially in its regenerative power—plays a part in the complex ideal symbolized by the Woman Jerusalem.

Milton's implied parallel of Eve with Raphael hints at the essential *distinction* he makes between angelic and human nature—by surrounding Eve with roses symbolic of erotic love, by placing the "carnation" hue of flesh before those already named in the account of the archangel's plumage, and by suggesting an imperfect or disturbed hierarchy in the ordering of the colors. In Blake's context the two Miltonic descriptive passages are deliberately conflated so as to *mingle* the angelic with the human. By so doing Blake emphasizes and centralizes what in Milton is a minor and momentary effect—Satan's response in *Paradise Lost* to the "angelic" beauty of Eve which "overawed / His malice. . . ."[99] When he recovered from this momentary "awe," Satan saw Eve as

> . . . fair, divinely fair, fit love for gods,
> Not terrible, though terror be in love
> And beauty . . .[100]

But Blake has seized and focused on precisely this concept in his creation of the Woman Jerusalem:

> Thy Bosom white, translucent, cover'd with
>   immortal gems,
> A sublime ornament not obscuring the outlines of
>   beauty,
> Terrible to behold for thy extreme beauty and
>   perfection . . .[101]

Blake's Jerusalem is "terrible" where Milton's Eve is not—at least, not to Milton's Satan. Jerusalem inspires the awe that Eve does not—or does not for long—because Milton's Eve is "merely" human, whereas Blake's Jerusalem is human above all things. She is the essence and the summation of the Divine Humanity within the bosom of Albion. Blake's holy Jerusalem, "soft reflected Image of the Sleeping Man . . . stretch'd on Albion's rocks," is an ideal of redemption based upon a humane aesthetic, not a severe hierarchical moral standard. The divinity and beauty of *humanity* is Jerusalem's "sublime ornament."

Conclusion: Albion's Bow

. . . Enitharmon answer'd in great terror in Lambeth's Vale:
"The Poet's Song draws to its period, & Enitharmon is no more . . .
"My Looms will be no more & I annihilate vanish for ever.
"Then thou wilt Create another Female according to thy Will."
Los answer'd swift as the shuttle of gold: "Sexes must vanish & cease
"To be when Albion rises from his dread repose, O lovely Enitharmon . . ."
—William Blake[1]

As the "eternal day" dawns in the fiery apocalypse that concludes Blake's *Jerusalem,* Blake describes all four of the Zoas arising "into Albion's Bosom."[2] Albion, now "Four fold among the Visions of God in Eternity," stands before Jesus and calls upon his "Lovely Emanation," Jerusalem, to "Awake and overspread all Nations as in Ancient Time"; and his voice "in my hearing," the poet says, is that of the "Universal Father."[3] Stretching his hand "into Infinitude," Albion takes his Bow.[4] Simultaneously each of the Four Zoas reaches in "Fourfold . . . Vision" for his own Bow.[5] Urizen, "bright beaming" in renewed luminosity, turns to the south for "a breathing Bow of carved Gold," while Luvah, stretching eastward "bore a Silver Bow, bright shining."[6] No longer contesting for mastery, no longer impaired by the sexual division—incurring jealousy and further mutual enmity—that resulted from their strife, the Zoas of the Reason and the Passions are now part of the wholeness implied in the creative union of golden Sol and silver Luna. Urizen, once the threatening denizen of the wintry north, looks now to the warm south, the aspect of the golden summer sun.[7] The wrathfully destructive Orc, transformed by the dawning of "immortal day," has become Luvah, whom Albion has now directed "to his

Loom" to take over the essential and formerly "female" task that was Enitharmon's in the fallen state of mankind.[8] Luvah appropriates the silver bow of "silent Elynittria," once associated with the stern chastity of Diana.[9] No trace of either the icy hostility of the latter or the blazing anger of Orc remains as Luvah turns, with ardor and hope, to the east, from which, with the sunrise of the "Eternal Day," "the Breath Divine went forth upon the morning hills."[10] Tharmas seizes from the west "a Bow of Brass, pure flaming," implying his contribution, as Zoa of the body's senses, to the physical "making" of the work of art, so "richly wrought."[11] Brass, the material of Tharmas's bow, is classically an image for an enduring work of art.[12] As a lasting man-made alloy, it also represents in Blake's myth a stable and harmoniously organized social structure, for in his regenerated form Tharmas is a figure representing the Brotherhood of Man.[13] Urthona takes from the north "in thick storms a Bow of Iron, terrible, thundering."[14] His realm of the Imagination reflects the atmosphere that surrounded Los, creatively at work at his furnace in the "deadly darkness" of Time:

. . . tempests muster
Around his head, the thick hail stones stand ready
   to obey

His voice in the black cloud, his Sons labour in
    thunders
At his Furnaces . . .[15]

Urthona's world is no longer, as it was in *The Four
Zoas,* a place of "Solid darkness, shut up in stifling
obstruction, rooted in dumb despair."[16] Now liberated from obstruction, redeemed from despair, unre-
stricted in his freedom of expression, Urthona
performs his powerful but modulated and controlled
part, "in just proportion" and "moderated fury," in
the creative activity of the regenerated Fourfold
Man.[17]

The fourfold Bow, Blake says,

    . . . is a Male & Female, & the Quiver of the
        Arrows of Love
    Are the Children of this Bow, a Bow of Mercy &
        Loving-kindness, laying
    Open the Heart in Wars of mutual Benevolence,
        Wars of Love:
    And the Hand of Man grasps firm between the
        Male & Female Loves.[18]

The Man regenerated to the fullness of Humanity
Divine is—like Donne's perfect union of lovers and
Milton's phoenix-angel—"one neutral thing" to
which "both sexes fit."[19] In the words of Ben F.
Nelms, "the bow within the active agency of the
Hand of Man is a perfect balance of male and female,
not dominated by a Female Will nor undermined by
a spectrous male jealousy."[20]

When Enitharmon expressed her fear of extinction, her words echoed those of the fallen Eve as-
sessing her own situation in relaton to the yet
unfallen Adam:

        . . . I shall be no more,
        And Adam wedded to another Eve,
        Shall live with her enjoying, I extinct;
        A death to think . . .[21]

The solution of Milton's Eve had been the spiteful
and self-serving choice of what Blake was to term
the "Female Will": that Adam must fall with her, so
that both should be condemned together to eternal
death. But Blake sees Eve's choice in a different light.
Diana Hume George, reading Blake's illustrations to
Paradise Lost, comments perceptively: "Once creation
and separation have occurred, Eve's action is the one
necessary to effect redemption, through entering experience. This is Blake's view of the 'fortunate
Fall.'"[22] If Los had assumed a role parallel to that
in which the unfallen Eve had gladly acknowledged
Adam in *Paradise Lost,* he might well, as Enitharmon's "Author and disposer," have "Create[d] an-

other Female according to [his] Will."[23] But Blake
does not allow him to fall into the egocentric trap of
the "self-hood." Instead,

    Los answer'd swift as the shuttle of gold: "Sexes
        must vanish & cease
    "To be when Albion rises from his dread repose, O
        lovely Enitharmon."[24]

On his own behalf and that of his female counterpart,
Los—like Milton in Blake's epic—chooses "To Annihilate the Self-hood" of individual sexuality.[25] He and
Enitharmon go together as one being, not to extinction, but to an abundant fullness of life: to live in the
climate of eternity that enfolds the realm of the artist
engaged in creative work. When "Time [is] Finish'd"
each of the Zoas arises into Albion's bosom united
with his own Emanation.[26] Jerusalem, Albion's Emanation, is an intrinsic part of his regenerated being,
contained just as Los had perceived her in his vision
"in the opacous Bosom of the Sleeper" during the
Night of Time.[27] This inclusive and complete sexuality is the condition of inspired creativity, as Blake
repeatedly makes clear. A "male form'd without a
counterpart," he declares in *The Four Zoas,* is "without a concentering vision"; such a being "ravin[s] /
Without the food of life."[28] Jerusalem is above all the
"concentering vision" of Albion, the *sine qua non,* the
absolutely essential focal concept of Blake's ideal of
humanity; and this is true, *pro rata,* of all the female
Emanations in relation to the faculties of the human
mind to which they are linked. The female counterpart provides the male not only with "the food of
life," but with the indispensable matrix without
which there can be no creative conception, and hence
no meaningfully *human* life at all.

Blake's treatment of femininity and of females in
the course of the unfolding of his myth has, on the
whole, displeased feminist critics. Alicia Ostriker describes Blake's "ideal female function[ing] as a medium of interchange among real, that is to say male,
beings."[29] Anne K. Mellor maintains that "attempts
to read Blake's Eden and the fourfold Man as genuinely androgynous are belied by Blake's consistently
sexist portrayal of women," arguing that even
Blake's portrayal of the convergence of male and female functions in Eden "should not obscure the fact
that, in Blake's metaphoric system, the masculine is
both logically and physically prior to the feminine."[30]
Blake's use of the word "Man" as a capitalized sub-
stantive in his prophetic writings draws on an old
and capacious sense. The *OED* records that in all
Teutonic languages the word had the twofold sense
of "human being" and "adult male human being,"

William Blake, "The Little Boy Found." From Songs of Innocence and of Experience (1794). (By permission of the Trustees of the British Museum.)

that was completely gender-free" in the visual aspect of his work, as critical dispute over the sex of some of the angelic and "regenerated" human figures in his designs attests.[34] As to his use of language, if Blake could have known that "English, the rough basement" upon which Los "built the stubborn structure of the Language" might be invaded by "the pronoun 'per' to refer to all persons, irrespective of sex-gender," one wonders whether he might not conceivably have been reduced to Albion's "Dumb despair."[35] Brenda Webster has failed to observe that the male in Blake's apocalyptic consummations *also* ceases to exist independently. Male *as well as* female sexuality is dispensed with when the dynamically opposed contrary forces, of which male and female are the most obvious pairing, unite in a "Marriage" in "Eternity." The question becomes partly one of perspective. Chaucer's Wife of Bath, a militantly feminist literary critic with whose arguments Blake was very

but that its earliest, and prevailing, sense in Old English, was "A human being (irrespective of sex or age)."[31] Mellor acknowledges that Blake used the word in this sense, but counters that "By continuing to use the sexist language of the patriarchal culture into which he was born, Blake failed to develop an image of human perfection that was completely gender-free."[32] And Brenda S. Webster reads Blake's view of woman in *Milton* and *Jerusalem* as a recommendation that "the female should cease even to exist independently and become reabsorbed into the body of man where she belongs," and that "during the writing of *Jerusalem*, Blake begins to feel that female sexuality can be dispensed with altogether."[33]

There is nevertheless, with the great respect genuinely due to Anne Mellor, evidence that Blake did attempt to develop "an image of human perfection

William Blake, The Marriage of Heaven and Hell, 1790, plate 3. (By permission of the Syndics of the Fitzwilliam Museum, Cambridge.)

William Blake, Jerusalem, *1804, plate 99 (Copy "A").*
(By permission of the Trustees of the British Museum.)

familiar, asserted that the Apostle Paul told her that *she* had exclusive and entire rights over her husband's physical person, but pointedly omitted to note that the same apostle simultaneously gave the equivalent rights to her husband over *her* body.[36] As a parallel for an extreme feminist view of Blake's "Divine Humanity," this is not as flippant as it may sound at first.

It would seem that critics who approach Blake's work with a feminist ideological agenda risk being blinkered by their indignation so as to see only gross deficiencies in his treatment of the female in his mythmaking. The concept and title of the present study of Blake's vision of woman as "Miltonic" imply that in my reading of Blake's work I perceive an agreement, in a very basic sense, with the Scripturally based patriarchy that informs Milton's treatment of woman. The Scriptural account of the creation of woman from the body of man, followed no less by Blake than by Milton, is an attempt, whose authority goes back thousands of years to the beginnings of the Judaeo-Christian culture of Western Man, to violate the biological order of things. It is surely in a negative sense an implicit recognition of the enormous power nature gives to the female through her reproductive function. The reflexive male response to that inherent threat, from the earliest human societies onward, has been to assume control of that function, and even, in this symbolic instance, to arrogate to itself the right to give birth. Seen in this light, Blake's view of woman is not revolutionary at all, but traditional.

Nevertheless, the poet is not given the credit I feel he deserves for a concept of gender that was remarkable for its time in its sensitivity to female sexuality, and its breaking down of sexual stereotypes, notwithstanding that Blake had only in part succeeded in freeing himself from the handicap of the culturally ingrained attitudes of his time. Some of those who recorded their impressions of Blake and his wife, especially in their later life, have conveyed to posterity a sense that in her "obedient, unassuming devotion" Catherine Blake was little more than her husband's faithful servant.[37] Yet this was not Blake's own perception. He saw her not as *his* servant, but as the handmaid of his art: and he himself was no less bound than she in that same service. Thus when he addresses the "Virgin of Providence" Ololon, descending into his cottage garden, he asks

". . . What am I now to do?
"Is it again to plunge into deeper affliction? behold me
"Ready to obey, but pity thou my Shadow of Delight:

"Enter my Cottage, comfort her, for she is sick with fatigue."[38]

It might be argued that Blake had himself *chosen* his thralldom—although he continually presents it as a vocation he has of necessity to accept—and that Catherine, for her part, had effectively had no choice but to fall in with his needs. But the world has known artists of genius whose wives *have* balked at entering into the service of their husbands' creative obsessions: in some sense, at some point, Catherine made her choice. When Blake writes to Hayley to announce ecstatically that after visiting the Truchsessian Gallery he has been "again enlightened with the light [he] enjoyed in [his] youth," he declares joyfully, and totally without self-consciousness, that at last "my feet and my wife's feet are free from fetters."[39] Denouncing the "spectrous Fiend" from whose "annoyance" he has now been delivered as "the enemy of conjugal love," he recalls "the distress I have undergone, and my poor wife with me: incessantly labouring and incessantly spoiling what I had done well."[40] Blake's assumption that "man and wife is one flesh" accords entirely with his conception of "Divine Humanity." At the same time, he shows an awareness of his need as an artist, and as a man, of his wife's devoted support, and expresses an appreciation of the selflessness with which she meets that need: a sensitivity, and a gesture, rare indeed among eighteenth-century husbands.

Enitharmon's threat—

. . .. "This is Woman's World . . .
"A triple Female Tabernacle for Moral Law I weave,
"That he who loves Jesus may loathe, terrified, Female love,
"Till God himself become a Male subservient to the Female"

—is surely neither more nor less tyrannical, as Blake presents it, than Urizen's rhetorical demand "Am I not God? . . . Who is Equal to me?" or the declaration of Tharmas,

"Now all comes into the power of Tharmas. Urizen is fall'n
"And Luvah hidden in the Elemental forms of Life & Death
". . . & Tharmas
"Is God. . . ."[41]

Yet Urizen's self-deification was pronounced at the moment when "his strong right hand came forth / To cast Ahania to the Earth"; and as he did so, and as she fell, there was heard

". . . a universal groan of death, louder
Than all the wracking elements, deafen'd & rended
      worse
Than Urizen & all his hosts in curst despair down
      rushing."[42]

When Tharmas made his claim to deity, it was undercut by his lament for his lost Enion:

"Yet tho' I rage, God over all, A portion of my
      Life
"That in Eternal fields in comfort wander'd with
      my flocks
At noon & laid her head upon my wearied bosom
      at night,
"She is divided. She is vanish'd. . . ."[43]

The division of the sexual Emanation from her male counterpart is not merely the cause of grief, as expressed by Tharmas: it expands the disaster implicit in that split into cosmic proportions, "like a crack across from immense to immense."[44] Enitharmon's declaration amounts to a threat to enforce this sexual division, "Till God himself become a Male subservient to the Female." The true extent of the power of the Female is quite clearly shown here. In the matter of sexual dominance, Blake always was aware that "the hand that rocks the cradle / Is the hand that rules the world," that the female is naturally empowered through her ability to bear and rear a child:

"What may Man be? who can tell! but what may
      Woman be
"To have power over Man from Cradle to
      corruptible Grave?"[45]

As Blake knew, as every man subconsciously has always known, this natural source of the power a woman has because she can bear a child is insidiously reinforced because those services which woman traditionally provides are mankind's most fundamental needs: nourishment and comfort. A universal masculine fear of what could happen if woman were willfully to withdraw these services, and decline to perform her office, lies behind Blake's hostility to what he read as Milton's defense of chastity in *Comus.* This emerges as the earliest embodiment of the "Female Will" in the characterization of Thel, and continues to weave a tortuous strand throughout Blake's poetry in many echoes of *Comus.*

Since woman is also the object of man's desire and the source of his inspiration, her power is indeed immense. Susan Fox, while recognizing that "in his prophetic poems Blake conceives a perfection of humanity defined in part by the complete mutuality of its interdependent genders," comments that throughout the same poems Blake "represents one of

those mutual, contrary, equal genders as inferior and dependent (or, in the case of Jerusalem, superior and dependent), or as unnaturally and disastrously dominant."[46] She concludes that Blake's females "come to represent weakness . . . and power hunger," and that "the metaphoric use Blake makes of femaleness is pejorative."[47] Yet Fox's own perceptive account of the role of Ololon in her fine study of *Milton* implicitly questions this assertion.[48] If it were altogether true, then Blake would be doing no more, in tracing the consequences of the exercise of the "Female Will," than allegorizing the universal threat to the male presented by the innate biological powers of the female, and dealing with that menace by the age-old masculine defense of imposing social restraints and an image of weakness upon the potential female tyrant. Unquestionably, Blake dramatizes that threat in the figure of Enitharmon in *Europe,* in the personages of Rahab, Tirzah, and her sisters in *Milton,* and in the account of Vala in *Jerusalem.* Certainly, he constrains to effective passivity Oothoon, Ahania, and Enion, to name only three such figures. Jerusalem too is rendered as almost entirely passive. In fact, a song from *An Island in the Moon,* written when Blake was in his twenties, contains the principal elements of the conflict evident in *Jerusalem,* composed mainly when he was in his fifties:

"Hail, fingerfooted lovely Creatures!
"The females of our human Natures,
      "Formed to suckle all Mankind.
"'Tis you that come in time of need;
"Without you we should never Breed,
      "Or any comfort find."[49]

The intimation of sexual attraction to the "lovely Creatures" is there, together with the uneasy admission of dependence and the consequent sense of threat: overall, there is already present Blake's awareness that males cannot survive without "the females of our human Natures." One may add to this prescience the fact that the poem from which these lines are quoted, "Hail Matrimony, made of Love . . .," is a burlesque of Milton's paean of praise to "wedded love" in *Paradise Lost.*[50] The permanent features of Blake's treatments of the female and of sexuality are already present in these early lines, and they include the pervading Miltonic influence in his vision of woman.

But in my reading, Blake's treatment of the female personage eventually transcends the images he received from the "Milton tradition." In the figure of Ololon, Blake's Miltonic vision of woman moves beyond the limitations—hallowed by custom, tradition, and the Bible—set upon the female in Milton-the-poet's representations of the personages who are Blake's principal models. Ololon follows Blake's character Milton in sacrificing her "self-hood," by going to "Eternal Death" so as to become the creative "contrary" of her male counterpart, whereas previously she had functioned in a multifarious sense as a "Negation." Ololon's oblation of self is the sacrificial act of self-annihilation necessarily performed by every great artist, regardless of gender. So Los clearly indicates in his reply in *Jerusalem* to Enitharmon's articulation of her fear that as "the Poet's Song draws to its Period," she will cease to be. Los answers, in effect, that in Eternity, *neither* of them will continue to exist in the forms they had possessed in the world of "generation." The Woman Jerusalem, in her own very different manner as Miltonic a female as Ololon, is in her wise passivity a very model for the extinction, not merely of sexuality, but indeed of individual personality, to which the inspired artist must volun-tarily submit so as to be suffused in "Eternity" by the "Breath Divine." The overcoming of differences of sex in the regenerated state of "Man," as David Aers concludes, is "essential in the struggle towards Jerusalem, towards human emancipation which transcends the sexual antagonisms [Blake] studied so profoundly."[51] Milton's Sin, the separated female who carries the "fatal key" to the infernal gates opening into Chaos, is finally obliterated when the "Eternal Day" dawns. Together with the dark tumult of Chaos itself, she is subsumed into Blake's ordered Cosmos of art, the visionary "Heaven" of creativity in which Milton had been his earliest guide. It is inhabited by regenerated, triumphantly human beings, living and moving

> . . . in Eternity as One Man, reflecting each in each
>   & clearly seen
> And seeing, *according to fitness & order.*[52]

Notes

Abbreviations Used in these Notes

The title of John Milton's *Paradise Lost* is abbreviated as *PL*.

The title of Blake's *Vala or The Four Zoas* is abbreviated as *FZ*. The nine "Nights" into which *Vala or The Four Zoas* is divided are referred to as "N" followed by the sequence number of the "Night," with the line number given last. Thus, a reference to line 640 of "Night the Ninth" of *Vala or The Four Zoas* becomes *FZ*, N9.640.

Chapter 1. Blake's Miltonic Vision

1. *An Island in the Moon,* chap. 7 (1784–85), p. 51.
2. *An Island in the Moon,* as this early satirical fragment is called from its opening sentence, remained unpublished during Blake's lifetime. The characters called "Quid the Cynic" and "Suction the Epicurean" are generally agreed to represent William Blake himself and his younger brother Robert, also a gifted artist, who died in 1787. See Martin K. Nurmi, *William Blake* (London: Hutchinson, 1975), pp. 45–49.
3.   "Or sweetest Shakespeare fancy's child,
        Warble his native wood-notes wild . . ."
                    (Milton, *L'Allegro* 133–34, p. 138)
4. Letter to John Flaxman (12 September 1800), line 5, in *Complete Writings,* p. 799.
5. Martin Butlin, *The Paintings and Drawings of William Blake* (New Haven: Yale University Press, 1981), 1:38–40, cat. nos. 101–4 (pls. 108–16 in vol. 2).
6. Frederick Tatham, who commissioned the print, gave this information to John Thomas Smith. It first appears in Smith's *Nollekens and His Times* (London, 1828) and is repeated in Tatham's own manuscript *Life of Blake* (ca. 1832). My source is G. E. Bentley, *Blake Records* (Oxford: Clarendon Press, 1969), pp. 527–28.
7. Butlin, *Paintings,* cat. nos. 201–14, 1:84–113. A photographic and typographic facsimile of Blake's *Notebook* has been edited by David V. Erdman, with the assistance of Donald K. Moore (Oxford: Clarendon Press, 1973).

8. Butlin, *Paintings,* cat. nos. 527–46, 1:373–404; 2: pls. 616–732. Both the *Comus* and *Nativity* series, each commissioned originally by the Reverend Joseph Thomas, were repeated, in reinterpreted versions, for Thomas Butts. Three versions of the *Paradise Lost* series are extant, executed successively for Rev. Thomas, for Butts, and in the 1820s, for John Linnell (the latter set consisting of only three scenes).
   Blake's Milton illustrations have been the subject of numerous studies. Three recent books on this topic are: Pamela Dunbar, *William Blake's Illustrations to the Poetry of Milton* (Oxford: Clarendon Press, 1980); Stephen C. Behrendt, *The Moment of Explosion: Blake and the Illustration of Milton* (Lincoln: University of Nebraska Press, 1983); and Bette Charlotte Werner, *Blake's Vision of the Poetry of Milton* (Lewisburg, Pa.: Bucknell University Press, 1986).
9. Werner, *Blake's Vision,* p. 19, suggests a parallel between Blake's personage Ololon, the "sixfold emanation" of the hero of his epic *Milton,* and the six Miltonic works illustrated by Blake. She relates Blake's creative critique to *Milton* itself: "Through the severe contentions of Blake's spiritual friendship with Milton, and in the fires of Blake's own, sometimes revisionary thought, the clouds of Ololon are purified, and Milton's sixfold emanation emerges redeemed in the designs of Blake."
10. *The Faerie Queene,* bk. 4, canto 2, line 34, p. 440.
11. *Milton,* 15.49, p. 497. David Erdman notes the parallel between the conversion of Saul of Tarsus to Paul (Acts 9) and the entry into Blake's tarsus of "the divine imagination." *The Illuminated Blake,* p. 248. See Chapter 5.
12. Joseph Anthony Wittreich, Jr., "'Sublime Allegory': Blake's Epic Manifesto and the Milton Tradition," *Blake Studies* 4 (1972): 16.
13. *Angel of Apocalypse: Blake's Idea of Milton* (Madison: University of Wisconsin Press: 1975), p. xvii.
14. Robert E. Gleckner's *Blake and Spenser* (Baltimore: Johns Hopkins University Press, 1985) explores in detail the Spenserian contexts of Blake's poetry.
15. Wittreich, "'Sublime Allegory,'" p. 44.
16. *The Faerie Queene,* bk. 2, canto 9, stanza 50, p. 257.
17. Ibid., bk. 2, canto 11, stanza 8, p. 273.
18. Ibid., bk. 2, canto 9, stanza 49, p. 256. Blake's Merlin, who appears, inter alia, in *Jerusalem* 36[32].23, 42, p. 663, is numbered "among the Giants of Albion" at 93.13, p. 740. See Edward J. Rose, "Blake's Metaphorical States," *Blake Studies* 4 (1971): 26–29.
19. S. T. Coleridge, *Biographia Literaria,* ed. George Watson (London: J. M. Dent, 1975), p. 167.

20. See W. Rossky, "Imagination in the English Renaissance: Psychology and Poetic," *Studies in the Renaissance* 5 (1958): 49–53.

21. *The Faerie Queene,* bk. 2, canto 12, stanzas 22–26, p. 285.

22. "A Vision of the Last Judgement," pp. 604, 606.

23. Gleckner, *Blake and Spenser,* p. 360, n. 56.

24. *The Marriage of Heaven and Hell,* pl. 6, p. 150, and pl. 24, p. 158.

25. *PL* bk. 1, lines 742–45, p. 505. (Italics mine.)

26. *Milton,* 15.47–48, p. 497.

27. *Milton,* 22.6, p. 505. The event is illustrated in pl. 21 of Copy B, pl. 47 of A (Erdman, *The Illuminated Blake,* p. 263).

28. Mitchell points out the relationship between the depiction of Milton in Blake's poem as a falling star, and Milton's own description of the fall of Mulciber in *Paradise Lost,* bk. 1, lines 740–51, p. 505, but does not comment on the sun as a symbol in this passage. (W. J. T. Mitchell, "Style and Iconography in the Illustrations of Blake's *Milton,*" *Blake Studies* 6 [1973]: 47–71.) In *Angel of Apocalypse,* pp. 14–16, Wittreich explores in brilliant detail the significance of Blake's usage of the star as a symbol for Milton's spirit, but also excludes the sun from his discussion.

29. This sense of the name and function of Los is made clear in Blake's verses in his letter to Thomas Butts, 22 November 1802:

> Then Los appear'd in all his power:
> In the Sun he appear'd, descending before
> My face in fierce flames; in my double sight
> 'Twas outward a Sun: inward Los in his might.
>
> (lines 55–58, *Complete Writings,* p. 818)

Blake also perceives "Los" as a name punning on "loss," since Los, the fallen human imagination, is *less* than Urthona, the imagination in its "Eternal" condition.

30. Hamlet's condemnation of his own suspicions (if they should be false) about the guilt of Claudius—"my imaginations are as foul / As Vulcan's stithy" (*Hamlet* 3.2, lines 81–82, p. 1049)—was another element in Blake's conception of this aspect of Los. Hamlet's suspicions are in fact correct; and as to the "foulness" of the "stithy," or smithy, of the imagination, the principle "Fair is foul, and foul is fair" (*Macbeth* 1.1, line 10, p. 999) applies to Blake's domain of the imagination in a way related to the approximation of the forces of good and evil described in this chapter. Blake was fascinated by the witches and the witch-goddess Hecate in *Macbeth,* and by the ghosts in both *Macbeth* and *Hamlet;* he sketched and painted the scenes in which they appear. (The works of Shakespeare are cited from W. Shakespeare, *The Complete Works,* ed. Peter Alexander [London: Collins, 1951], to which page numbers refer.)

31. *The Four Zoas* (henceforth abbreviated to *FZ*), Night the Fourth, lines 63–64, p. 299; and *FZ,* Night the Ninth, lines 775–76, p. 377. ("Nights" of *The Four Zoas* are henceforth abbreviated to "N4," etc.)

32. *PL,* bk. 1, lines 710–37, pp. 502–4.

33. The term *faber* is repeatedly used in the sense of "a forming or creating power" in translations available to Blake of works by the Gnostic Jakob Boehme (or Behmen: d. 1624), whose work may have been known to Milton as well. See, for instance, the seventeenth-century translation by John Ellistone of Boehme's *De Signatura Rerum,* included in the "William Law" edition of Boehme's works known to Blake. (The "William Law" edition of Boehme's works was *The Works of Jacob Behmen,* ed. G. Ward and T. Langcake [London: M. Richardson, 1764–81], 4 vols. The Ellistone translation of *De Signatura Rerum* has been reprinted as *The Signature of All Things* [Cambridge: James Clarke, 1969].) For Boehme's possible influence on Milton, see Margaret L. Bailey, *Milton and Jakob Boehme: A Study of Mysticism in Seventeenth Century England* (New York: Oxford University Press, 1914); for that on Blake, see Bryan Aubrey, *Watchmen of Eternity: Blake's Debt to Jacob Boehme* (Lanham, Md.: University Press of America, 1986).

34. The most comprehensive surveys of Blake's paintings and graphic work are those of Butlin (see n. 5) and of David Bindman, *The Complete Graphic Works of William Blake* (London: Thames and Hudson, 1978).

35. For instance, his engravings of the "Portland Vase" for Erasmus Darwin's *The Botanic Garden* in 1791, and his illustrations for the catalogs of the Wedgewood potteries, made in 1816. Blake's earliest extant paintings and drawings are of memorial sculptures in Westminster Abbey. One of the "Portland Vase" engravings is reproduced in Kathleen Raine's *William Blake* (London: Thames and Hudson, 1970), p. 31. The Wedgewood catalog drawings are discussed by Butlin (*Paintings,* 1: cat. no. 677, 487), who also provides reproductions of the Westminster Abbey drawings (*Paintings,* 1: cat. nos. 1–47, 2–14; 2: pls. 1–43).

36. *The Marriage of Heaven and Hell,* pl. 24, p. 158. Blake evidently intended to conclude *The Marriage of Heaven and Hell* by making this announcement of the imminent publication of "The Bible of Hell." "A Song of Liberty," on three plates numbered by Blake 25, 26, and 27 and attached to the end of all extant copies of the work, is regarded as having been composed at a later date. See Keynes's note, p. 888 of *Complete Writings.*

37. The "Lambeth book" now known as *The Book of Ahania* was intended as "The Second Book of Urizen," but Blake changed his mind, deleting the word "First" in the title of some copies of *Urizen.*

38. Like Milton's "Mulciber" (*PL,* bk. 1, lines 730–40, pp. 504–5), Urizen is an architect (*FZ,* N2. 166, p. 284, *Jerusalem* 66.4, p. 702). The "Mulciber" passage from bk. 1 of *Paradise Lost* was seminal in Blake's conception of both Los and Urizen.

39. Butlin, *Paintings,* cat. nos. 529.8, 536.8 and 537.2; 1:380, 387, 389.

40. *Milton,* 30.5 and 31.1–2, pp. 518–19.

41. *The Signature of All Things,* chap. 8, par. 32, p. 85; chap. 9, par. 25, pp. 96–97.

42. See my discussion, in Chapter 5, of Blake's use of the "hieros gamos" or mystical union of Sol and Luna.

43. Blake's dabbling in alchemical symbolism is further touched upon in Chapter 5. See especially n. 47 of Chapter 5.

44. *PL,* bk. 8, lines 471–73, p. 839.

45. *PL,* bk. 8, lines 460–71, pp. 838–39. (Italics mine.)

46. *PL,* bk. 9, lines 457–66, pp. 883–84. (Italics mine.) For Blake's reading of the significance of the "heavenly form" of "angelic" Eve, see Chapter 7.

47. *PL,* bk. 8, line 451, p. 838.

48. *PL,* bk. 3, lines 493–98, p. 590; bk. 9, line 103; bk. 4, lines 505–11, p. 642.

49. The realm of "the Eternals" corresponds largely to the Gnostic "divine pleroma." But Blake cannot be categorized as a Gnostic. It is at his or her own peril that Blake's reader ignores either the declaration of Los, "I must Create a System or be enslav'd by another Man's. / I will not Reason & Compare: my business is to Create," or Blake's description of the work of Los as "Striving with Systems to *deliver* Individuals from those Systems." (*Jerusalem,* 10.20–21, p. 629, and 11.5, p. 630.) (Mitchell, "Style and Iconography," pp. 69–70, discusses Blake/Los's "striving with Systems.") Blake never did permit his own creative "business" to be restrained by any "system," but took from Gnosticism only what he found useful for his own artistic purposes. Stuart Curran reached this conclusion in his scholarly survey of possible Gnostic influences in "Blake and the Gnostic Hyle: A Double Negative," *Blake Studies* 4 (1972): 117–33. In a more recent survey of the problem, William Dennis Horn, approaching Blake's "Gnosticism" through "Gnostic rhetoric," argues that Blake's *Book of Urizen* "revives in theme and trope the Gnostic genre of Genesis parody" and that Blake "uses Gnostic narrative techniques in the service of his critique of the Enlightenment metaphysics of Newton and Locke." (William Dennis Horn, "Blake's Revisionism: Gnostic Interpretation and Critical Methodology," in *Blake and the Argument of Method,* ed. Dan

Miller, Mark Bracher, and Donald Ault [Durham, N.C.: Duke University Press, 1987], 77, 80.)

50. *Urizen*, 3.4, p. 222.

51. *Urizen*, 4.16–18, p. 224.

52. *PL*, bk. 1, lines 68–69, p. 466.

53. *PL*, bk. 7, lines 211–12, and bk. 2, lines 910–11; pp. 787, 550.

54. *PL*, bk. 7, lines 242, p. 789.

55. *Urizen*, 6.8, p. 226.

56. Andrew Marvell, "The Definition of Love," lines 17–24:

> And therfore [Fate's] Decrees of Steel
> us as the distant Poles have plac'd,
> (Though Loves whole World on us doth wheel)
> Not by themselves to be embrac'd,
>
> Unless the giddy Heaven fall,
> And Earth some new Convulsion tear;
> And, us to joyn, the World should all
> Be cramp'd into a *Planisphere*.

In *The Metaphysical Poets*, ed. Helen Gardner (Harmondsworth: Penguin Books, 1972), p. 253.

57. *Urizen*, 7.3, p. 226.

58. *Urizen*, 10.15–18, p. 227.

59. *Urizen*, 7.9, 3.20, and 10.31–11.19, pp. 226, 223, and 228–29.

60. *FZ*, N4.284–87, p. 305. At this point in the manuscript of *The Four Zoas* Blake wrote a note to himself: "Bring in here the Globe of Blood as in the B. of Urizen." See Keynes's note on lines 280–95 of N4, pp. 901–2 of *Complete Writings*.

61. *Urizen*, 13.50–51, p. 230.

62. *Urizen*, 13.51–53, p. 230.

63. *Urizen*, 13.58–59, p. 230.

64. In Copy B of *The Book of Urizen* (printed in the 1790s, reproduced by Erdman in *The Illuminated Blake*, p. 117), blood drains from veins shown in the loins and in the head. In Copy G (printed ca. 1818) blood pours through veins clearly depicted over the whole of Los's back as well as around his loins and head. (Copy G is reproduced by K. Easson and R. Easson, *Blake: The Book of Urizen* [London: Thames and Hudson, 1978]. See p. 27 of their edition.)

65. *The Faerie Queene*, bk. 2, canto 9, stanza 49. Cf. Chaucer, "biforen, in his celle fantastyk" ("The Knight's Tale," *Canterbury Tales* A 1372–76, in Chaucer, *Complete Works*, ed. W. W. Skeat [London: Oxford University Press, 1912], p. 436).

66. In the version in the Fitzwilliam Museum, which was evidently the third "pull" of the design, this feature was not retouched so as to make it clear. Butlin reproduces all three versions of "The House of Death" in *Paintings*, 2: pl. 397–99, cat. nos. 320–22.

67. Lines 479–93, p. 1007. Werner notes the similarity of the posture of this "bent sufferer," whom she identifies as one of the inmates of the "Lazar house," to that of Los in pl. 17 of *Urizen*, and suggests that "the similar figure here may also symbolically specify the place of torment to be the fallen world" (*Blake's Vision*, p. 94).

68. *PL*, bk. 8, lines 460–61, p. 838.

69. *Urizen*, 18.1–15, 19.1, p. 231.

70. *Urizen*, pl. 19; Erdman, *The Illuminated Blake*, p. 201.

71. *The Illuminated Blake*, p. 201.

72. *Urizen*, 18.15, p. 231. Blake's concept of the "emanation," like his reinterpretation of the Fall of Man, seems to have been drawn from his readings in Gnosticism, and adapted to his own purposes. Joseph Priestley writes: "The great boast of the Gnostics was their intricate and profound doctrine concerning the derivation of various intelligences from the supreme mind, which they thought to be done by emanation or *efflux*." See *An History of Early Opinions Concerning Jesus Christ . . .* (1786), in *The Theological and Miscellaneous Works of Joseph Priestley*, ed. John

T. Rutt (London: Smallfield, 1817–32), 6:81; quoted by Curran, "Blake and the Gnostic Hyle," pp. 123–24. Curran notes, however, that "an essential distinction . . . separates Blake's from the Gnostic conception of emanations. Blake's emanations testify to a human, if tragically fragmented, reality. The Gnostics concern themselves with heaven" (p. 127, n. 23.). See especially pp. 123–28 of Curran's essay.

73. *PL*, bk. 8, lines 511–20, pp. 841–42.

74. Blake associates Prometheus with the fires of Los and the "generous fire" of the unfallen Urizen. (*The Book of Ahania*, pl. 5, lines 29–34, p. 255; and cf. "The Tyger" of the *Songs of Experience*, lines 5–9, p. 214.) Prometheus was punished for his felony by being bound down on a mountain rock, which partly suggested to Blake the binding of the fiery Orc. (*FZ*, N5.102–9, p. 308.)

75. *PL*, bk. 4, lines 717–19, p. 656.

76. *Urizen*, 18.7 and 11, p. 231; *Hymn on Morning of Christ's Nativity*, line 39, p. 102. This association is more fully discussed in Chapter 3. Tolley identifies Enitharmon in *Europe* with Milton's personification of Nature, though he does not refer to this line in *Urizen*. See Michael J. Tolley, "*Europe* : 'To those ychain'd in Sleep'" in *Blake's Visionary Forms Dramatic*, ed. David Erdman and John E. Grant (Princeton, N.J.: Princeton University Press, 1970), p. 126. Other associations Blake may have had in mind are Spenser's Florimell and the Imogen of Shakespeare's *Cymbeline*. See Chapter 3, n. 58.

77. *Urizen*, 18.5–9, p. 231.

78. *Urizen*, 19.14–16, p. 232.

79. *PL*, bk. 9, lines 780–84, p. 902; bk. 9, lines 1000–1004, pp. 913–14.

80. *PL*, bk. 2, lines 752–60, pp. 543–44.

81. *Urizen*, 19.10–16, pp. 231–32.

82. *PL*, bk. 2, lines 785–96, p. 545.

83. *PL*, bk. 4, lines 477–81, p. 641, and bk. 4, lines 635, p. 650.

84. *PL*, bk. 2, lines 651–53, pp. 538–39.

85. *PL*, bk. 2, lines 783–85, p. 545.

86. *Urizen*, 19.27–29, p. 232.

87. *Urizen*, 19.45–46, p. 232.

88. Zeus was said to have swallowed his pregnant paramour Metis, out of fear that her offspring would be mightier than he. He was later afflicted with an intolerable headache; to relieve it, Hephaistos the smith-god aimed a blow at the forehead of Zeus with his hammer, whereupon the goddess Athene, daughter of Metis and goddess of Wisdom, sprang out fully armed from the head of Zeus.

89. *PL*, bk. 9, lines 953–57, pp. 911–12.

90. From his reading of the works of Jakob Boehme, if from no other source, Blake was familiar with the notion of the separation of the Gnostic Sophia, "Divine Wisdom," from the Godhead. "She is his image, his celestial spouse, with whom he must unite himself, whom he must realize in himself." Alexandre Koyré, *La Philosophie de Jacob Boehme* (Paris: J. Vrin, 1929), pp. 214–15. (Quoted and translated by Leopold Damrosch, Jr., *Symbol and Truth in Blake's Myth* [Princeton, N.J.: Princeton University Press, 1980], p. 189.) Enitharmon's separation from Los, and his subsequent pursuit of and union with her, provide significant parallels.

91. "Annotations to Swedenborg's *Divine Love and Wisdom*" (ca. 1789), p. 90; and "Annotations to Berkeley's *Siris*" (ca. 1820), p. 773. (Blake no doubt read Swedenborg's *Divine Love and Wisdom* around the time of his first association with the Swedenborgian Society in London, in 1788–89; but the copy he annotated is an 1816 reprint of an edition published in 1788. See Chapter 4, note 19.)

92. *PL*, bk. 2, lines 1024–27, p. 556. See also bk. 8, line 450, p. 838, bk. 9, lines 908–16, pp. 909–10, and bk. 10, line 251, p. 938.

93. Werner, *Blake's Vision*, p. 96. See "The Descent of

Peace," Butlin, *Paintings,* cat. nos. 538.1 and 542.1, 1: 389–90 and 393; 2: pls. 660 and 666.

94. *PL,* bk. 10, lines 209ff., pp. 935–36, and bk. 12, lines 411–19, p. 1047. See Butlin, *Paintings:* "So Judged He Man", pls. 641 and 654 (cat. nos. 529.10 and 536.10; 1:381 and 387); "Michael Foretells the Crucifixion," pls. 642, 655, and 659 (cat. nos. 529.11, 536.11, and 537.3, 1:381, 387, and 339).

95. The Latin "Orcus," the name of an infernal deity, is also used to refer to Hell. Milton gives this name to one of the attendants upon Chaos, whose court Satan visits in the course of his search for the newly created Earth (*PL,* bk. 2, lines 959–64, p. 553). The scene at the court of Chaos was among Blake's earliest Miltonic subjects; he sketched several versions, some in the *Notebook.* (See Butlin, *Paintings,* cat. no. 102, pl. 112; 1:38–39, 104–5). Other possible sources for the name Orc include the Greek *orchis* ("testicle") and the Latin *orca,* "a whale" (supported by *America* 2.14, p. 196). Blake was doubtless aware of all these possibilities; the names of his "elementals" are repeatedly played upon in his works as situations dictate.

96. The birth of Orc (not there named) as a revolutionary force pitting itself against ancient tyranny is first described in "A Song of Liberty" at the end of *The Marriage of Heaven and Hell,* pls. 25–27, pp. 159–60.

97. *The Marriage of Heaven and Hell,* pl. 6, p. 150.

Chapter 2. Thel

1. *A Masque Presented at Ludlow Castle, 1634* (hereafter "*Comus*"), lines 779–82, p. 215.

2. Butlin, *Paintings,* 1:373–74. The "Thomas" series of *Comus* illustrations (1801) is now in the Huntington Library and Art Collections in San Marino, California. Blake executed a second series for Thomas Butts ca. 1815; this is in the Museum of Fine Arts in Boston. *The Book of Thel* is dated 1789 on its title page, and was probably complete by 1791. On the completion date, see Blake, *The Complete Poems,* ed. W. H. Stevenson 2 ed. (London: Longman Group, 1989), pp. 93–94, 100.

3. *The Marriage of Heaven and Hell,* pl. 20, p. 157; *Milton,* 41.32–33, pp. 533–54; *Comus,* lines 785–86, p. 216. Blake obviously knew nothing of the historical circumstances that in 1634 had suggested the choice of the theme so sensitively treated by Milton. The earl of Bridgewater, Milton's patron, was closely connected by marriage to the notorious Lord Audley, later earl of Castlehaven, who had been tried and executed in 1631 for his involvement in the horrifying sexual abuse especially of his wife and a young step-daughter. It was for the Bridgewater children that Milton had created the parts of the Lady and the Elder and Younger Brothers in his masque. See Barbara Breasted, "*Comus* and the Castlehaven Scandal," *Milton Studies* 3 (1971): 201–24. The views of sexuality offered in *Paradise Lost* do not suggest that Milton himself approved of either prudishness or asceticism.

4. S. Foster Damon was the first modern critic to recognize the link between *Comus* and *The Book of Thel,* in "Blake and Milton," in *The Divine Vision: Studies in the Poetry and Art of William Blake,* ed. Vivian de Solo Pinto (London: Victor Gollancz, 1957), p. 92. Rodger L. Tarr perceives Thel as a kind of "negation" of Milton's doctrine concerning the wisdom of virginity, in "'The Eagle' versus 'The Mole': The Wisdom of Virginity in *Comus* and *The Book of Thel,*" *Blake Studies* 3 (1971): 187–94.

5. *Thel,* 6.5, 22, p. 130. "The vales of Har" (from Blake's earlier poem *Tiriel,* 2.4ff., p. 100) offer scenes of pastoral serenity. Though apparently associated with primal innocence, they prove ultimately to be a setting for the condition of senility, or a form of arrested emotional development. But David Wagenknecht takes a different view of Thel's flight: see nn. 9 and 76.

6. *Thel,* 1.3, 3.21, and 5.12, pp. 127, 129, and 130.

7. *The Faerie Queene,* bk. 3, canto 6, stanza 38, lines 8–9,

p. 362. (See subsequent discussion of the significance of the "sunny" flocks tended by Thel's sisters.) Although my own reading of the poem takes a different line to hers, I do agree with Raine's emphasis on this and other parallels between Blake's poem and Spenser's "Garden of Adonis," and with her assertion that "Mutability is *Thel*'s theme, as it was Spenser's." See Kathleen Raine, *Blake and Tradition,* Bollingen Series 35.11 (Princeton, N.J.: Princeton University Press, 1968), 1:106, 100.

Further Spenserian sources for *The Book of Thel,* employed by Blake in a "contrary" spirit, are explored by Robert F. Gleckner in *Blake and Spenser,* pp. 31–45, 287–302. Gleckner demonstrates convincingly that in *Thel* Blake parodies Spenserian and Petrarchan "sublimations of the senses and desire" (p. 32), both in the *Amoretti* and in the figure of Alma in book 2 of *The Faerie Queene.* Gleckner also relates Thel's wish "to die because she is of no 'use'" (p. 293) especially to the encounter between Spenser's Redcrosse Knight and Despaire in Book I, showing that "*Thel* is a severe attack upon the underpinnings of Spenser's Book I and the language in which it is couched" (p. 288).

8. *Thel,* 3.22, p. 129.

9. S. Foster Damon, *A Blake Dictionary* (London: Thames and Hudson, 1965), p. 401, noting that Thel does not reappear in any other of Blake's writings, commented disarmingly that she is "far too nice a girl to fit in amongst Blake's furious elementals." Damon speculated that Blake's account of Thel may have been an allegorized narrative woven about a miscarriage, or the premature birth and death of an infant, perhaps Blake's own child.

David Wagenknecht, *Blake's Night: William Blake and the Idea of Pastoral* (Cambridge, Mass.: Belknap Press of Harvard University Press, 1973), p. 162, comments on Thel's flight back "unhinderd till she came into the vales of Har" that "of course this last line of the poem represents a failure," but adds that Blake may mean by it "that Thel can return, at will, to however uninspired a condition . . . in short, that she is still a virgin ([though there are] indications that she will not remain one forever), but a wiser one than when she began."

10. Concerning Blake's "idea of pastoral," Wagenknecht writes that "in terms of the *Songs* [*of Innocence and of Experience*] the idea of the pastoral had emerged as the vehicle for conveying Blake's ambiguous and agonized approach to the problem of 'Generation'" (*Blake's Night,* p. 5). This view is congenial to my own approach to *The Book of Thel,* about which Wagenknecht adds that its nature is best appreciated "via the pastoral ironies and ambiguities of the *Songs*" (p. 148).

11. *Thel,* 1.2, 4, p. 127; *Comus,* line 4, p. 175; line 978, p. 225.

12. *Comus,* lines 991–1001, p. 227. Wagenknecht terms the story of Venus and Adonis "a primary myth of pastoralists" (*Blake's Night,* p. 2). Raine points out an allusion to Adonis concealed in the title-page emblem of *The Book of Thel:* "The flowers, from whose centers spring little lovers in amorous pursuit and flight, are pasqueflowers, *Anemone pulsatilla.* . . . The anemone is the flower of Adonis, into which he was, according to tradition, metamorphosed" (*Blake and Tradition,* 1:105). She describes these flowers on the title page as an allusion to the theme of Shakespeare's *Venus and Adonis,* adding that "the association of the flower with Easter *(pasque)* is itself significant" (1:105).

13. *The Faerie Queene,* bk. 3, canto 6, stanzas 43–49, pp. 363–64.

14. In *Paradise Lost,* a river called "Adonis" is named with reference to the annual rites of the fertility god Thammuz. In a gesture appropriate to his conception of Thel, Blake has feminized the name to "Adona." (*PL,* bk. 1, lines 446–52, pp. 488–89).

15. *The Faerie Queene,* bk. 3, canto 6, stanza 39, line 8, p. 362.

16. Ibid., stanza 40, line 9, p. 362.

17. Ibid., stanza 47, lines 4–6, p. 364.

18. *Thel,* 1.8, p. 127; *Comus,* line 991, p. 226.

19. *Thel,* 1.9–11, p. 127.

20. *Thel*, 1.16, 22, p. 127; 2.2, p. 128.

21. *Comus*, lines 861–62, p. 220; lines 823–24, p. 218.

22. *Comus*, lines 860,864, p. 220.

23. *Thel*, 2.3, p. 128. Irene Tayler, "Blake's *Comus* Designs," *Blake Studies* 4 (1972): 45–80, notes Blake's emphasis on the theme of "narcissism" in his first series of *Comus* illustrations. See especially pp. 71–78 of her essay. Werner differentiates between Milton's perception of Sabrina as an agent of grace, and Blake's reading of Milton's imagery in *Comus*, lines 837–39. Blake, Werner says, perceives that "Sabrina's restoration, her sea-change, to immortality has been accomplished, not through the paralysis of virginity but through the opening of her senses" (*Blake's Vision*, p. 35).

24. *Thel*, 2.5–18, p. 228.

25. *Thel*, 3.5–6, p. 128.

26. *Comus*, line 212–14, p. 187.

27. *Comus*, lines 218–19, p. 187.

28. *Thel*, 3.7–8, p. 128.

29. This is the first appearance in Blake's writings of the "Zoa" of the passions called "Luvah" (the name is a version of "lover"), and the earliest mention of any of the "Zoas." (See Chapter 3, n. 7.) Blake seems here to attribute to Luvah the properties of a sun-god, although in *The Four Zoas* Luvah's appropriation to himself of the "Steeds of Light" is treated as a usurpation of the rights of Urizen, Zoa of the Reason, who has charge of them in the Eternal condition of Man. (*FZ*, N5.234–37, p. 311.)

Raine, *Blake and Tradition*, 1:169, points out that this passage of *Thel* is derived from the song of act 2 of Shakespeare's *Cymbeline*,

> Hark, hark! the lark at heaven's gate sings
> And Phoebus 'gins arise
> His steeds to water at those springs
> On chalic'd flow'rs that lies . . .

30. See, for instance, *FZ*, N7.244–48, p. 326. In Blake's illumination on plate 4 of *Thel* the Cloud has the form of a young man, almost naked but with floating drapery about his body. (Erdman, *The Illuminated Blake*, p. 38.) Blake's figure of Antamon (*Europe*, 14.15–20, p. 244), who symbolizes the male seed, is a development of the Cloud of *Thel*.

31. *Comus*, lines 64–66, p. 179. The mother of Comus is Circe, "daughter of the Sun" (lines 46–58, pp. 178–79).

32. *Comus*, line 781, p. 215; *PL*, bk. 6, lines 99–101, p. 734.

33. Compare the teaching of the Mother in "The Little Black Boy," lines 9–12 (*Songs of Innocence, Complete Writings*, p. 125):

> "Look on the rising sun: there God does live,
> "And gives his light and gives his heat away;
> "And flowers and trees and beasts and men recieve
> "Comfort in morning, joy in the noonday. . . .

34. *Comus*, lines 660–61, p. 209.

35. Blake inscribed and illustrated these lines on p. 36 of the *Notebook*, and experimented with another version of the same emblem on p. 12. His watercolor illustrations to *Comus* actually show the Lady "root-bound," seated in the knotty root of an oak tree, both at the time when Comus finds her, and after the incursion of her two brothers has set Comus and his train to flight. Butlin reproduces the relevant paintings as plates 616, 622, 624, 626, and 630, cat. nos. 527.1 and 7, and 528.1, 3, and 7. Tayler comments on the Lady's "rooty chair" in "Blake's *Comus* Designs," p. 53.

36. "This world of Imagination is the world of Eternity; it is the divine bosom into which we shall all go after the death of the Vegetated body." *A Vision of the Last Judgement* (ca. 1810), from p. 69 of the *Notebook* (p. 605).

37. *Thel*, 1.1, p. 127. See n. 7.

38. *Thel*, 1.2–3, p. 127; 2.11, p. 128.

39. *Thel*, 2.14–15, p. 128.

40. *Thel*, 3.7–8, p. 128. Raine's interpretation of the theme of *Thel* as "a debate between the Neoplatonic and alchemical philosophies" (*Blake and Tradition*, 1:99), of Plotinus and Porphyry on the one hand and Paracelsus on the other, dwells especially upon its "wat'ry" imagery, which is "appropriate to the 'watery' world of generation of the naiads and their ever-flowing streams, to the 'moist' souls who attract to themselves the hylic envelope" (1:108). (The "hylic envelope" is "the moist envelope of the soul, the generated body, [which is] called a 'grave' because in it the soul is dead from eternity, or a 'bed,' as the place of the soul's sleep" [1:109].)

41. *Comus*, lines 297–300, p. 191. Blake wrote out the first three lines of this passage beneath a sketch of an emblem on p. 30 of the *Notebook*. See Butlin, *Paintings*, 1:90 ("Emblem 12").

42. Milton's primary sense was "folded," which gives the current English word "pleated." He also offers the undercurrent of meaning that relates the rainbow to the "plighting" of God's covenant with Noah.

43. *Thel*, 3.31, p. 129.

44. *Thel*, 3.14, p. 128. The "Antamon" of *Europe* is likewise "prince of the pearly dew" (*Europe*, 14.15, p. 244). Chrysogone (in *The Faerie Queene*, bk. 3, canto 6, stanzas 3ff., pp. 355ff.) was the mother of Belphoebe and Amoret, twin daughters born "of the wombe of Morning dew" (ibid., stanza 3, line 1, p. 355), miraculously begotten "through influence of th'heauens fruitfull ray" (ibid., stanza 6, line 2, p. 356). Chrysogone is said to have conceived them while sleeping in the sun:

> The sunne-beames bright vpon her body playd,
> Being through former bathing mollified,
> And pierst into her wombe, where they embayd
> With so sweet sence and secret power vnspide,
> That in her pregnant flesh they shortly fructifide.
> (bk. 3, canto 6, stanza 7, lines 5–9, p. 356)

45. *Thel*, 3.12–16 p. 128.

46. *Thel*, 2.18, p. 128.

47. Erdman, *The Illuminated Blake*, pp. 38, 268.

48. Job 7.17. This sketch appears on p. 68 of the *Notebook*; see Butlin, *Paintings*, 1:97.

49. Job 7.5, 9.

50. *Thel*, 3.23, 25, p. 128.

51. *Thel*, 3.26, p. 128.

52. *Thel*, 3.26–27, p. 128.

53. *Thel*, 4.3, p. 129.

54. *Thel*, 4.6, p. 129.

55. *Thel*, 4.8–9, p. 129.

56. Compare "The Clod and the Pebble:" "Love seeketh not Itself to please, / Nor for itself hath any care, / But for another gives its ease. . . So sang a little Clod of Clay / Trodden with the cattle's feet . . ." (*Songs of Experience*, "The Clod and the Pebble," lines 1–3, 5–6, *Complete Writings*, p. 211).

57. *Thel*, 4.10, p. 129.

58. *Thel*, 5.7, 5.16–17, p. 130.

59. *Thel*, 6.3, p. 130. The sketches of royal tombs done in Westminster Abbey during the period 1774–77 are among Blake's earliest extant drawings. Butlin, 1:1–14, 2: pls. 1–47.

60. *Thel*, 6.3–5, p. 130.

61. *Comus*, line 351, p. 193. On p. 58 of the *Notebook* Blake made a sketch that may be an illustration to *Comus*, lines 350–54, showing a small figure huddled beneath a tree.

62. *Comus*, lines 469–72, p. 200.

63. *Thel*, 6.6–8, p. 130.

64. *Thel*, 6.10, p. 130.

65. *Thel*, 6.13–18, p. 130.

66. *Thel*, 6.19–20, p. 130.

67. Wagenknecht (*Blake's Night*, p. 155) relates Thel's concern about transiency to her "sexual anxiety," commenting that "she wants to sleep 'the sleep of death' (so long as it comes

gently), and her sexual misgivings are deflected into concern for the fading of other innocents and into the imagery of God walking in his Garden in the evening time."

68. *Thel*, 1.1–4, p. 127.

69. Tarr proposes this view ("'The Eagle' versus 'The Mole,'" p. 193).

70. Emmanuel Swedenborg, *Divine Love and Wisdom*, anonymous translation (Amsterdam, 1763; rpt., London: Swedenborg Society, 1987), p. 7, par. 14.

71. Annotations to Swedenborg's *Divine Love and Wisdom*, p. 15; *Complete Writings*, p. 90.

72. *The Marriage of Heaven and Hell*, pl. 14, p. 154.

73. Wagenknecht (*Blake's Night*, p. 121) discusses this motif as it appears on both the last plate of *Thel* and plate 11 of *America*, relating it to similar motifs in the "Lyca" poems of the *Songs*. He restates the questions it raises (pp. 158–59), but finds no final answers.

74. *PL*, bk. 8, lines 444–51, p. 838. See discussion of this passage in Chapter 1.

75. *The Faerie Queene*, bk. 3, canto 6, stanza 39, line 1, p. 362.

76. *Thel*, 1.13–14, p. 127. Cf. *PL*, bk. 10, lines 92–99, p. 930:

> Now was the sun in western cadence low
> From noon, and gentle airs due at their hour
> To fan the earth now waked, and usher in
> The evening cool when he from wrath more cool
> Came the mild judge and intercessor both
> To sentence man: the voice of God they heard
> Now walking in the garden, by soft winds
> Brought to their ears, while day declined. . . .

Wagenknecht, while citing the evidence from *Tiriel* for "the usual view that Thel unambiguously retreats from life at the end of her poem" (*Blake's Night*, p. 151), argues that "Thel's return to the 'vales of Har' from the grave that the matron Clay has shown her in a moment of vision cannot be construed as a return to an unreal Beulah, but only as a return to ordinary fallen existence, an ambiguous retreat, perhaps, from both the horror of the grave and from the passionate intensity of her response to that horror" (p. 150). Wagenknecht's suggestion, which is consonant with his reading of *Thel*, implies that Thel's longing for "gentle" experience may be a rejection of the commitment to Romantic "intensity" urged, for instance, in Blake's poem "Day," in which the sun of creativity arises with "wrath increast . . . Crownd with warlike fires & raging desires" (lines 3–5, *Complete Writings*, p. 177)—an obvious "negation" of the "mild judge and intercessor" who comes as the sun sets, without wrath, "to sentence man" to a life depleted of visionary experience in a darkening fallen world.

77. *Thel*, 1.19–20, p. 127.

78. *Thel*, 2.11–12, p. 128.

79. *Thel*, 3.0–11, p. 128.

80. *Thel*, 5.10–11, p. 129; *The Marriage of Heaven and Hell*, pl. 27, p. 160; *Visions of the Daughters of Albion*, 8.10, p. 195; *FZ*, N2.366, p. 289.

81. *Thel*, 4.11–12, 5.1–2, p. 129.

82. *Jerusalem*, 34.31, p. 661; *PL*, bk. 8, line 451, p. 838.

Chapter 3. Enitharmon

1. *Vala, or The Four Zoas*, was in fact completed and also illustrated with many sketches by Blake during the period 1795–1805, though the title page of the manuscript bears the date 1797. Since it was never engraved, it has no final form. Numerous alterations, additions and alternatives are incorporated into the text of the unique ms., now in the British Museum. Blake worked many of its passages into *Milton* and *Jerusalem*. Facsimiles have been published by G. E. Bentley, Jr., ed., *William Blake's Vala or The Four Zoas: A Facsimile of the Manuscript, a Transcript*

of the Poem and a Study of Its Growth and Significance (Oxford: Clarendon Press, 1963), and by David Erdman and Cettino Tramontano Magno, eds., *Blake's The Four Zoas: A Photographic Facsimile of the Manuscript with Commentary on the Illustrations* (Lewisburg, Pa.: Bucknell University Press, 1987). Important studies of the poem include those of Northrop Frye in *Fearful Symmetry* (Princeton: Princeton University Press, 1947), chap. 9, "The Nightmare with Her Ninefold," pp. 269–309; Brian Wilkie and Mary Lynn Johnson, *Blake's Four Zoas: The Design of a Dream* (Cambridge, Mass.: Harvard University Press, 1978); and Donald Ault, *Narrative Unbound: Revisioning William Blake's The Four Zoas* (Barrytown, N.Y.: Station Hill, 1987).

2. *FZ*, N9.640–41, p. 374.

3. *FZ*, N9.628–30, p. 374.

4. *FZ*, N9.621–25, p. 373.

5. Michael Ackland, "The Embattled Sexes: Blake's Debt to Wollstonecraft in *The Four Zoas*," *Blake / An Illustrated Quarterly* 16 (1982–83): 179. Blake may actually have known Mary Wollstonecraft through their mutual acquaintance Joseph Johnson, a London bookseller and publisher whose shop both frequented in the early 1790s. (Bentley, *Blake Records*, p. 40.) Whether or not they had met personally, Blake read and was deeply impressed by Wollstonecraft's *A Vindication of the Rights of Women* (1792). Parallels between this work and Blake's *Visions of the Daughters of Albion* are traced by Mark Schorer, *William Blake: The Politics of Vision* (New York: Henry Holt, 1946; rpt., New York: Knopf, 1959), pp. 187, 251; and by David Erdman, *Blake: Prophet against Empire*, 3d ed. (Princeton N.J.: Princeton University Press, 1977), pp. 156, 243–44.

6. Ackland, "Embattled Sexes," p. 179. (Italics mine.)

7. *FZ*, N9.849–54, p. 379. Blake took the name "Zoa" from the Greek plural noun translated as "beasts," referring to the Four Beasts about the Throne of the Lamb of God in Revelations 4, 6–9, and the four "living creatures" of Ezekiel 1, 5ff. He used the word "Zoa" as a singular noun to denote one of the "four fundamental aspects of Man." (Damon, *Dictionary*, p. 458.) The Hebrew word *chayot*, used in the original of the Ezekiel passage, can be rendered as "living creatures," "beasts" or "animals." Blake chose to use the latter version in the final prose paragraph of *Jerusalem*, pl. 27, p. 652.

8. The dating of the composition of *Vala* or *The Four Zoas* is comprehensively discussed by Bentley and by Erdman and Magno in the facsimile editions cited in n.1.

9. *FZ*, N1.484–518, pp. 277–78.

10. *FZ*, N5.205–25, p. 310–11.

11. See Chapter 2. For the associations of the "Divine Humanity," see *Milton*, 2.7–8, p. 481; 14.1–3, p. 495; 32.14, p. 521; and *Jerusalem*, 43 [38].19–21, p. 672; 61.43, p. 695.

12. *FZ*, N5.218–22, pp. 310–11; N4.29, p. 298.

13. *FZ*, N5.234–37, p. 311.

14. *FZ*, N5.225–26, p. 311. The triple fall depicted on pl. 6 of Copy A (pl. 7 of Copy G) of *The Book of Urizen* (Erdman, *The Illuminated Blake*, p. 188) is clearly related to Milton's description of the transformation of Satan and his host into serpents in *PL*, bk. 10, 504–84, pp. 951–56, especially 512–13 and 539–42. Blake had earlier painted a different version of the same event, without the serpents, ca. 1793. (The latter version is in the Fogg Art Museum of Harvard University, and is reproduced by Butlin, *Paintings*, as pl. 306 [cat. no. 256].)

15. *FZ*, N4.129–32, p. 301.

16. *Urizen*, 5.39, p. 226; Wilkie and Johnson, *Blake's Four Zoas*, p. 237.

17. *FZ*, N1.9, p. 264.

18. *FZ*, N1.24, p. 264.

19. The opening pages of *Vala* or *The Four Zoas* are so heavily revised that it is often difficult to perceive Blake's final intention. See Andrew Lincoln, "*The Four Zoas*: The Text of Pages 5, 6, & 7, Night the First," *Blake / An Illustrated Quarterly* 12 (1978): 91–95; and John B. Pierce, "The Shifting Characterization of

Tharmas and Enion in Pages 3–7 of Blake's *Vala or The Four Zoas*," *Blake / An Illustrated Quarterly* 22 (1988–89): 93–102.

Northrop Frye suggests that Tharmas and Enion may be the Thaumas and Eione of Hesiod's *Theogony*, where (as in Ovid's *Metamorphoses*) Thaumas is the father of Iris, the rainbow. (Hesiod, *Theogony*, 237, 255, 780; Ovid, *Metamorphoses*, 4.480; Frye, *Fearful Symmetry*, pp. 284, 445.) Enitharmon—whose name comprises elements of the names "Enion" and "Tharmas," and who is their daughter in "Night the First"—is in fact associated with the rainbow in *The Four Zoas*, for instance in N2.380–82, p. 290. (In *Milton* Leutha, in taking upon herself the role of Satan's Sin, also takes on the identification with the rainbow [*Milton*, 11.32, p. 492]). The rainbow association is ultimately transferred to Jerusalem (see Chapter 7). The connection between the names of Enion, Tharmas, and "ENItharmON" was pointed out by Margoliouth in his edition: H. M. Margoliouth, ed., *Vala, Blake's Numbered Text* (Oxford: Clarendon Press, 1951).

20. *The Book of Ahania*, 1.31–37, pp. 249–50; *FZ*, N3.106–38, pp. 294–95.

21. Frye, *Fearful Symmetry*, p. 274.

22. This is the suggestion of Damon (*Dictionary*, p. 124); but Blake may not have known much Greek before he began studying it intensively, together with the Hebrew language, in Felpham in 1802–3 (see Chapter 5). See also n. 19.

23. Blake's mother, née Catherine Harmitage, had probably been his teacher in his early years, since his only formal schooling had been his training for his profession of engraving.

William Blake and Catherine Sophia Boucher were married in 1782, at which date Catherine may have been illiterate. Blake taught her to draw and paint, and perhaps also to read and write. (Crabb Robinson said that Catherine "had been formed by [her husband]," by which he seems to have meant "educated"; see subsequent discussion.) He trained her as his assistant in every phase of the engraving and printing processes. They had no children; Catherine worked beside her husband for the whole of their forty-five years of marriage. See Bentley, *Life Records*.

Blake's only sister Catherine Elizabeth, who never married, traveled to Felpham with her brother and sister-in-law when they went to take up residence there under Hayley's patronage in September 1800. She apparently returned to London shortly, but rejoined them from time to time during the three years they spent there—a period of intense creativity but also of great stress, for Blake. (See Chapter 5.) Damrosch (*Symbol and Truth*, p. 193) draws attention to the coincidence of the names of Blake's mother and sister with that of his wife.

24. *The Marriage of Heaven and Hell*, 25.1, p. 159; *FZ*, N8.36–38, p. 342.

25. *FZ*, N8.36–39, p. 342; *Milton*, 26.31–36, p. 512; *Jerusalem*, 73.50–52, p. 714. The "sanctum sanctorum" appears on f. 22v. of the manuscript of *The Four Zoas*. It is reproduced and thus described by Klonsky, who links the image with the *Notebook* poem "I saw a chapel all of gold . . .," p. 163. (Milton Klonsky, *William Blake: The Seer and His Visions* [London: Orbis Publishing, 1977], p. 79.) Damrosch discusses the poem and its association with the sketch in *The Four Zoas* in a somewhat broader context, using it as a comment on the ambivalence and complexity of Blake's attitudes towards sex. (Damrosch, *Symbol and Truth*, pp. 204–9).

26. *Visions of the Daughters of Albion*, 6.16, p. 194; *Europe*, 14.22, p. 244. I am indebted to Ms. Joan Bellis for pointing out to me the "triptych" form of the shrine, with its implications.

27. Hayley in letters to Lady Hesketh, 10 June and 15 July 1802. H. N. Fairchild, *Studies in Philology* 25 (1928): 4–6. Quoted by Erdman, *Blake: Prophet against Empire*, p. 382.

28. By 1792 Blake and his wife had been married for ten years. See, e.g., "A flower was offer'd to me . . ." (p. 161), the "mirtle" stanzas of the first draft of "Infant Sorrow" (lines 20–43, p. 167), "To my Mirtle" (p. 176), and "Silent, Silent Night" (p. 168), and see "William Bond" in the Pickering Manuscript (pp. 434–36).

29. British Museum Add. MS 36514 f. 97. Quoted by Erdman, *Blake: Prophet against Empire*, p. 524.

30. On the question of Blake's "madness," Northrop Frye (*Fearful Symmetry*, pp. 12–13) wisely observed that

the point is, not that the word "mad" applied to Blake is false, but that it is untranslatable. . . . The sources of art are enthusiasm and inspiration: if society mocks and derides these, it is society that is mad, not the artist, no matter what excesses the latter may commit . . .

31. Henry Crabb Robinson, *Reminiscences*, 1852; quoted by Bentley, *Blake Records*, pp. 542–43.

32. *Jerusalem*, 14.12–14, p. 635. Blake applies the same distinction to Los, who in certain situations is differentiated from "the Spectre of Urthona." See n.40.

33. *FZ*, N7.447–48, p. 331.

34. *FZ*, N7.465–68, p. 332.

35. *PL*, bk. 9, lines 953–56, pp. 911–12.

36. Blake's *Notebook*, p. 22, lines 16–43, in *Complete Writings*, p. 537.

37. Cf. *Milton*, 5.5–8, p. 484. See Chapter 1.

38. *FZ*, N1.518–19, 522–26, p. 278. Bentley regards this passage as one of the last additions to the poem, made possibly some time after 1805. See his facsimile edition.

39. *FZ*, N4.56–62, p. 299. In a similar separation in *The Book of Urizen*, Urizen is "rent" from the side of Los, who experiences "anguish" and howls "in a dismal stupor" at the "wrenching apart." *Urizen* 6.3–4, 7.1–4, p. 226. Los is shown on plate 7 of *The Book of Urizen*, wrapping his arms about his own neck in the self-involvement of the fallen condition, as he howls and writhes in agony. (Erdman, *The Illuminated Blake*, p. 189.)

40. *FZ*, N4.59–64, p. 299. This fall parallels the fall of Milton's "Mulciber" (Vulcan/Hephaistos). See Chapter 1. Blake distinguishes in this passage of *The Four Zoas*, as also elsewhere, between Los the artist—his own alter ego—and the "Spectre of Urthona."

41. *FZ*, N4.65, 98–99, pp. 299–300.

42. Frye identifies Ahania, "Emanation" of Urizen, Zoa of the Reason, with "the Sophia, or Bride of Wisdom, her name being a 'faint echo' of Athene" (*Fearful Symmetry*, p. 277).

43. *FZ*, N1.132–33, p. 268; compare *PL*, bk. 1, lines 571–73, p. 495; bk. 2, lines 5–6, p. 509; and bk. 9, lines 539–48, p. 889.

44. *FZ*, N1.173, 176–78, p. 269.

45. *FZ*, N1.179–92, p. 269.

46. *FZ*, N1.191–92 and 238, pp. 269–70. The reference is both to Genesis 3: 10 and 16, and to Milton's version in *PL*, bk. 9, lines 1091–98, pp. 919–20, and bk. 10, lines 193–95, p.935.

47. Milton, "On the Detraction which Followed upon my Writing certain Treatises," sonnet 12, lines 6–7, p. 295.

48. See my reference to the Los/Sol and Enitharmon/Luna association in Chapter 1.

49. *FZ*, N1.237–38, p. 270.

50. *Comus*, lines 437–51, pp. 198–99.

51. Brian Wilkie and Mary Lynn Johnson describe both Los and Enitharmon in these first stages of their existence in *The Four Zoas* as "repellent figures," commenting especially on the "nasty elusiveness" of Enitharmon "that will later half madden Los" (*Blake's Four Zoas*, (pp. 29–30).

52. *Comus*, lines 440–41, p. 198. In his painting "When the Morning Stars Sang Together," also known as "The Creation," in the series illustrating *The Book of Job* (1805–6), Blake depicted the four faculties embodied in the Four Zoas surrounding the Creator. Urizen, Zoa of the Reason, is a nude young male driving a team of radiant steeds. Luvah, the Zoa of the Emotions, is represented by a clothed, somewhat feminized figure with a crescent-moon headdress, driving a team of serpents: the moon association evokes the tides of the sea and the waxing and waning of emotional states.

53. *FZ*, N1.237–38, p. 270, and 239–42, p. 271. The "Sun" of creative inspiration arises in the important *Notebook* poem called "Day," written probably in 1792 or 1793: *Complete Writings*, p. 177:

> Day
> The [day *del.*] Sun arises in the East,
> Cloth'd in robes of blood & gold;
> Swords & spears & wrath increast
> All around his [ancles *del.*] bosom roll'd,
> Crown'd with warlike fires & raging desires.

Blake represents this "Sun" as a sceptered Apollo in the third of his series of illustrations to Milton's *L'Allegro*, "The Sun at the Eastern Gate," Butlin, *Paintings*, pl. 674 (cat. no. 543.3).

54. *A Vision of the Last Judgement*, p. 614. Dated by Blake "For the Year 1810." *Complete Writings*, pp. 604 and 917.

55. *Urizen*, 18.10–12, p. 231.

56. *Hymn on the Nativity of Christ*, lines 32–44, pp. 102–3.

57. As with many key terms, when "wanton" is used in *Paradise Lost* it has both an "unfallen" or innocent sense, and a "fallen" or corrupt sense. The "unfallen" sense appears in its adjectival usage in the "wanton growth" of bk. 4, lines 628–29, p. 649, describing the exuberantly flourishing vegetation of Paradise, which resembles the "wanton ringlets" of the hair of Eve in her innocence (bk. 4, line 306, p. 632). The "fallen" sense is evident in the "wanton wreath[s]" in which the Satanic Serpent curls his body when approaching Eve to tempt her in bk. 9, line 517, p. 888: these outwardly imitate the growth of Paradise, but are imbued with Satan's evil. Blake's two versions of "Satan Watching the Endearments of Adam and Eve" (Butlin, *Paintings*, pls. 636 and 657, cat. nos. 529.5 and 537.1) suggest that he read this fluctuation of sense in Milton's usages. The "fallen" sense applies, obviously, in the *Hymn*.

58. Shakespeare, *Cymbeline*, 2.5, lines 12–13, p. 1211. See my discussion in Chapter 6 of Blake's possible use of this play, and see Chapter 2 for the "Sun" symbolism in *The Book of Thel*.

Another of Blake's sources for the association of the separated Enitharmon with snow was Spenser's Florimell, who in bk. 3 of *The Faerie Queene* flees a lustful pursuer on a palfrey "more white then snow, / Yet she her selfe is whiter manifold" (bk. 3, canto 5, stanza 5, p. 347). Florimell is a figure embodying sexual frigidity, a point Spenser emphasizes when he describes the artificial creation of a "False Florimell," a kind of animated doll whose bodily substance is of "purest snow in massie mould congeald" (bk. 3, canto 8, stanza 6, p. 376).

59. *The Book of Ahania*, 2.34–37, p. 250.

60. *Jerusalem*, 10.42–43, p. 630.

61. See lines 9–24 of "A Little Boy Lost," *Songs of Experience*, p. 218; and the account of "Mystery, Babylon" dwelling in "Satan's Bosom" in *Milton*, 38.15–26, p. 529.

Spenser's account of fruitful love in his "Garden of Adonis" in *The Faerie Queene*, bk. 3, canto 6, stanza 41, p. 362, expresses exactly what Blake approved in sexual relationships:

> For here all plentie, and all pleasure flowes,
> and sweet loue gentle fits emongst them throwes,
> Without fell rancor, or fond gealosie;
> Franckly each paramour his leman knowes. . . .

(See Gleckner, *Blake and Spenser*, pp. 62–63).

Wilkie and Johnson relate Vala's name to the veil of the biblical Temple, which is rent at the moment of Christ's death (*Blake's Four Zoas*, p. 189). The name Vala is first used in *FZ*, N1.260–78, p. 271. Enitharmon there recounts her dream of the "mighty Fallen One," who asks her "Why dost thou weep as Vala & wet thy veil with dewy tears . . .?" (*FZ*, N1.271, p.271).

62. Butlin, *Paintings*, cat. nos. 529.11, 536.11, and 537.3, pls. 642, 655, and 659; cat. nos. 538.1 and 542.1, pls. 660 and 666.

63. *Blake's Vision of the Poetry of Milton*, p. 96.

64. *FZ*, N1.303–5, p. 272.

65. *FZ*, N1.308–11, p. 272.

66. See Chapter 4.

67. Blake depicted the actual *emergence* of Eve from Adam's side as described in Genesis 2.21–23, in *Jerusalem*, pl. 31[35] (Erdman, *The Illuminated Blake*, p. 310). This is distinct from the three versions of the "Creation of Eve," inspired by *PL*, bk. 8, lines 462–77, pp. 839–40, in his three *Paradise Lost* series, in each of which Eve is shown already separated from Adam, as a fully formed woman. (The phrase "with difference discreet" is quoted from Spenser's ambiguous description of the Bower of Bliss in *The Faerie Queene*, bk. 2, canto 12, stanza 71, p. 294.)

68. *FZ*, N1.523–24, p. 278.

69. John 20.24–29. The characterization of Tharmas as "doubting Thomas" makes him the "negation" of the Savior, who bends over the fallen Man (Albion) in his deathlike condition, saying "If ye will Believe, your Brother shall rise again." (*FZ*, N4.264–70, p. 304.)

70. *FZ*, N4.44–62, pp. 298–99. Cf. "Auguries of Innocence," lines 107–10, p. 433:

> He who Doubts from what he sees
> Will ne'er Believe, do what you Please.
> If the Sun and Moon should doubt,
> They'd immediately Go out.

The repeated associations of Los with Sol and Enitharmon with Luna, in the alchemical sense, or respectively as Apollo and Diana, or simply as the Sun and the Moon, all have relevance here.

71. *FZ*, N4.61–4, p. 299.

72. *FZ*, N4.67–73, p. 299. It is tempting to associate the imagery of this passage (and that of several others, especially in *Milton*) with the period of Blake's residence at the seaside village of Felpham, when he was clearly fascinated by the sea in all its moods, and by the creatures of the littoral. A poem composed at Felpham, copied out in a letter to Thomas Butts, includes the line "here is Enitharmon's bower." (Letter to Butts, 22 November 1802, l. 34, in *Complete Writings*, p. 817.)

73. *FZ*, N4.37–41, p. 298.

74. Blake summed the situation up succinctly in a poem in the *Notebook* written during the period 1808–11:

> "O dear Mother outline, [be not in a Rage *del.*] of
>   knowledge most sage,
> "What's the First Part of Painting?" she said: "Patronage."
> "And what is the second? to Please and Engage?"
> She frown'd like a Fury & said: "Patronage."
> "And what is the Third?" she put off Old Age,
> And smil'd like a Syren & said: "Patronage."

Notebook pp. 60–61, "I ask'd my dear Friend, Orator Prigg . . .," lines 16–21, in *Complete Works*, p. 554. (The text in the *Notebook* has no punctuation. I have modified Keynes's editorial punctuation in line 18 ["And what is . . ."] by moving the second pair of a set of inverted commas to the end of the line and adding a second question mark.)

75. Blake's indignation about the exploitation of the gifted artist of his own time by the "Cunning-sures & The aim-at-yours" (p. 548) sputtered all over the pages of his *Notebook* in his later years, expressed in epigrams ribald, vitriolic, or scatological, and in some lengthy prose denunciations of current taste. See (e.g.) pp. 536–59 and 591–603 of the Keynes edition, and see especially his "Annotations to Sir Joshua Reynolds's *Discourses*," pp. 445–79.

David Erdman's *Blake: Prophet against Empire*, subtitled *A Poet's Interpretation of the History of His Own Times*, gives a comprehensive account of the historical factors that influenced and affected Blake. See especially chaps. 14 to 18.

76. *Jerusalem*, 10.17–19, p. 629. "Golgonooza" was the name Blake gave to Los's city of "Art & Manufacture" (*Milton*, 24.50,

p. 509). Blake also means by it his own body of artistic work. See Chapter 7.

77. This is another instance of the distinction Blake made between, on the one hand, Los as his own "alter ego" with Enitharmon as the "alter ego" of his wife Catherine, and on the other the "Spectre of Urthona" as the Imagination in its fallen state, sharing or desiring Enitharmon as its "Emanation."

78. *FZ*, N4.93–107, p. 300.

79. See Chapter 1.

80. *FZ*, N4.280–83, p. 304, *Urizen* 13.20–27, p. 229.

81. *PL*, bk. 2, line 921, p. 551; *FZ*, N4.284–87, p. 305.

82. *FZ*, N4, between lines 287 and 288, p. 305.

83. *FZ*, N5.12, p. 305.

84. Milton, "Hymn on the Nativity . . .," line 115, p. 106; *FZ*, N5.41–42, p. 306.

85. *FZ*, N5.240, p. 311.

86. *FZ*, N7.148–51, p. 324, N7b.246–49, p. 339.

87. *The Book of Los* (1795), 3.27–30, p. 256.

88. Milton, *Comus*, 671–77, pp. 209–10.

89. *FZ*, N5.225–26, p. 311.

90. Butlin, *Paintings*, pl. 306 (cat. no. 256); Erdman, *The Illuminated Blake*, p. 188.

91. *PL*, bk. 10, lines 504–84, pp. 951–56.

92. *PL*, bk. 10, lines 512–13, p. 951. Milton's Satan's "arms clung to his ribs" (line 512) as well, but Blake leaves Urizen the free use of his arms and hands, with which he reaches out to Luvah and Urthona falling on either side of him. Even though Urizen uses his free hands to compel the other two to fall with him, Blake's falling Zoas are not totally deprived, as Milton's Satan is, of creative potential.

Blake's "Elohim Creating Adam" and "Satan Exulting over Eve" (Butlin, *Paintings*, cat. nos. 289 and 292, pls. 388 and 389) are closely related to the images of pl. 6 of *Urizen*. The fourth painting of the *Paradise Lost* series of 1807, "Satan Spying on Adam & Eve . . .," is probably derived from this complex of images and ideas.

93. *FZ*, N5.225–37, p. 311.

94. *Paradise Regained*, bk. 2, lines 350–53, p. 1110.

95. "Ganymede" as a common noun is a term used for an effeminate man or a homosexual lover. (See *OED*, sense 2.) Cf. the choice by Rosalind in Shakespeare's *As You Like It* of that name for herself in her masculine disguise.

96. Spenser, *The Faerie Queene*, bk. 1, canto 4, stanzas 16–36, pp. 67–71. Gleckner associates Lucifera's chariot and the allegorical beasts that draw it with the apocalypse in *Jerusalem*, 98.40–45, p. 746. (Gleckner, *Blake and Spenser*, pp. 219–20.)

97. *The Book of Los*, 3.7–13, p. 256. (My italics.) Cf. as well *The Marriage of Heaven and Hell*, 8.2–4, p. 151:

> The pride of the peacock is the glory of God.
> The lust of the goat is the bounty of God.
> The wrath of the lion is the wisdom of God....

98. Cf. *Jerusalem*, 82.80–84, p. 727.

99. "And his legs carried it like a long fork . . ." (about 1809), *Notebook*, p. 22, in *Complete Writings*, pp. 536–37:

> The Examiner, whose very name is Hunt,
> Call's Death a Madman [deadly the affront *del.*] trembling for the affront . . .
> [And *del.*] Yorkshire Jack Hemp & gentle, blushing Daw,
> Clap'd Death into the corner of their jaw,
> And Felpham Billy rode out every morn
> Horseback with Death over the fields of corn,
> [And *del.*] Who with iron hand cuff'd in the afternoon
> The Ears of Billy's Lawyer & Dragoon . . .
> For how to starve Death we had laid a plot. . . .
>
>   (lines 16–28, p. 537)

An attack on Blake's exhibition of 1809 had appeared in the *Examiner*, a journal edited by Leigh Hunt. "Yorkshire Jack Hemp"

is the artist John Flaxman, long a friend of Blake's, but at this moment perceived as an enemy, along with "gentle blushing Daw," perhaps one of brothers George and Henry Dawe, both artists. "Felpham Billy" is William Hayley, Blake's well-meaning patron at Felpham. Blake paranoiacally accuses Hayley of having set upon him the drunken "Dragoon," Schofield, whom Blake had cuffed when he stumbled into Blake's cottage garden at Felpham in September 1803. Schofield had consequently laid a charge of sedition against Blake, obliging him to stand trial.

100. *PL*, bk. 1, line 61, p. 465.

101. *FZ*, N5.241, p. 311.

102. *Jerusalem* 91.18, p. 738. Cf. Satan's soliloquy at *PL*, bk. 4, line 508–11, p. 642:

> ". . . I to hell am thrust,
> Where neither joy nor love, but fierce desire
> Among our other torments not the least,
> Still unfulfilled with pain of longing pines. . . ."

103. *PL*, bk. 2, lines 752–58, pp. 543–44; *The Book of Urizen*, pl. 19: Erdman, *The Illuminated Blake*, p. 201.

Orc's fiery birth is described in *Urizen*, 19.45–46, p. 232, and depicted on pl. 20 (*The Illuminated Blake*, p. 202). In "Night the Fifth" of *FZ* Orc "[springs] forth . . . In thunder, smoke & sullen flames, & howlings & fury & blood" (*FZ*, N5.38, p. 306).

104. *FZ*, N7.456–63, pp. 331–32.

105. The emblem, inscribed "Forthwith he rears from off the pool / His mighty stature . . .," was sketched on p. 91 of the *Notebook*. It became no. 5, "Fire," in *The Gates of Paradise* series. See Erdman, *The Illuminated Blake*, p. 271. On the facing page of the *Notebook*, p. 90, Blake illustrated Milton's lines shortly preceding this passage, in which Satan lifts his head from the lake of fire—*PL*, bk. 1, lines 192–96, p. 473. See Erdman's facsimile and transcript of the *Notebook*.

The systematic breaking down of "the whole regulatory, associative machinery of experience" in Milton's descriptions of Hell, evident in such phrases as "darkness visible" (bk. 1, line 63, p. 465) and "fiery deluge" (line 68, p. 466), is pointed out by Harry Blamires, *Milton's Creation: a Guide through "Paradise Lost"* (London: Methuen, 1971), p. 8.

106. Compare *Jerusalem*, 40.59–60, p.668.

107. See *The Marriage of Heaven and Hell*, pl. 24, p. 158, and *Milton*, 30.19, p. 519. "Golgonooza," Blake's visionary city of "Art & Manufacture" (*Milton* 24.49–50, p. 509), is discussed in Chapter 7.

108. *FZ*, N7.464–73, p. 332.

109. *FZ*, N7.464–66, p. 332.

110. *FZ*, N4.99–100, p. 300.

111. See the figure of Eve in "Michael Foretells the Crucifixion" in Blake's three series of illustrations to *Paradise Lost*.

112. *PL*, bk. 12, lines 411–20, p. 1003.

113.   . . . let Eve (for I have drenched her eyes)
> Here sleep below while thou to foresight wakest,
> As once thou slept'st, while she to life was formed.

PL, bk. 12, lines 367–69, pp. 998–99. Cf. bk. 8, lines 452–73, pp. 838–39.

114. *FZ*, N7.463, 469, 471, p. 332.

115. Damrosch, *Symbol and Truth*, p. 179. See his thoughtful discussion of this apparently irresolvable split in Blake's thought in chap. 5, "The Problem of Dualism," pp. 165–243.

116. David Erdman defines the "soft bosom translucent" of Enitharmon as "the inner folds of Blake's allegory's matrix" (*Blake: Prophet against Empire*, p. 381).

117. Boehme, *The Signature of All Things*, chap. 9, par. 25–26; p. 97. See my Chapter 1.

118. *FZ*, N5.42, p. 306. Frye explicates the "Orc cycle" at length in chaps. 7 and 8 of *Fearful Symmetry*, pp. 187–268.

119. *FZ*, N7.398–99, p. 330. Perhaps it is worth noting that "Sophia" was also the middle name of Blake's wife, who was

baptized Catherine Sophia Boucher.

120. Cf. *The Marriage of Heaven and Hell*, 14.1–2, p. 154: "The ancient tradition that the world will be consumed in fire at the end of six thousand years is true, as I have heard from Hell." See also *Milton*, 29.64, p. 518.

121. *Milton*, 28.62–63, 29.1–2, p. 516.

122. Crabb Robinson recorded this phrase as uttered in what he calls a "rambling state" of Blake's "in which I could not follow him." Bentley, *Blake Records*, p. 544.

123. *FZ*, N4.34–41, 70–73, pp. 298–99.

124. *Milton*, 30.8–31, pp. 518–19; *Jerusalem*, 5.17, p. 623. See my discussion of "Beulah" in Chapter 6.

125. *FZ*, N7.453, 464–75, pp. 331–32.

126. *PL*, bk. 10, line 251, p. 938. See *Europe*, 13.12–19, 14.1–31, pp. 243–44, and my discussion in Chapter 4.

Chapter 4. The Winds of Enitharmon

1. *Europe*, 5.1–3, p. 240.

2. *Fearful Symmetry*, p. 263.

3. *FZ*, N9.152, p. 361. The phrase "the ambiguity of energy" is applied to Blake's *Europe* by Morton D. Paley in *Energy and the Imagination* (Oxford: Clarendon Press, 1970), p. 78. Northrop Frye defined Blake's view of war as "a perversion of the sexual impulse" in *Fearful Symmetry*, pp. 262–63.

4. *Jerusalem*, 68.62–63, p. 707.

5. Milton, *Comus*, lines 440–45, p. 198.

6. See Chapter 3.

7. *Europe*, 1.1, p. 238; *America*, 1.1–4, p. 195.

8. *America*, 1.11–12, p. 196; *Urizen*, 20.21–25, p. 233; *FZ*, N5.97–103, pp. 307–8. Morton Paley quotes David Hume's account in his *Dialogues Concerning Natural Religion* of "the idea of a blind nature, impregnated by a great and vivifying principle, and pouring forth from her lap, without discernment or parental care, her maimed and abortive children." (Paley, *Energy and the Imagination*, pp. 78–79)

9. *Europe*, 1.1, p. 238.

10. *America*, 2.6, p. 196.

11. *Europe*, 1.8–15, 2.1–11, p. 238. The suggestion that the inverted-tree image of *Europe*, 1.8, may be the placenta, is made by Tolley, "*Europe*: 'To those ychain'd in Sleep;'" p. 121.

12. See Spenser, *The Faerie Queene*, bk. 2, canto 1, stanza 53, p. 180; and Chaucer, "The Knightes Tale," *Canterbury Tales* A 2075–86, p. 445.

13. Milton, *Comus*, lines 446–48, p. 198.

14. *Europe*, 1.12–15, 2.1–9, p. 238.

15. *Europe*, 2.10, p. 238.

16. *Europe*, 2.8, p. 238.

17. *Europe*, 1.2, p. 238; *FZ*, N7.460, p. 331. The Hebrew word *ruach* in the phrase *ruach Elohim* in the second verse of Genesis 1, translated in the Authorised Version as "the Spirit of God," literally means "breath" or "wind."

18. *PL*, bk. 6, lines 474–83, pp. 750–51. (My italics.)

19. Emanuel Swedenborg, *Divine Love and Wisdom*, Clifford Harley and Doris Harley. (London: Swedenborg Society, 1969), p. 204. Keynes dates Blake's annotations "about 1789" (*Complete Writings*, p. 89). However, according to the Harleys, the Swedenborg Society's most recent editors of the work, the copy annotated by Blake (now in the British Museum) is an 1816 reprint of the edition published in 1788. (*Divine Love and Wisdom*, p. v.) Nevertheless, internal evidence indicates that Blake had read this work by 1790, when he began to compose *The Marriage of Heaven and Hell*. The general agreement of annotations made in 1816 or later with Blake's thinking as reflected in the work etched in 1790 suggests that there was a greater degree of continuity and consistency in his views during this creative period of many years than some critics would allow. See, for instance, Behrendt, *The Moment of Explosion*, p. 67; and Robert N. Essick,

"*Preludium:* Meditations on a Fiery Pegasus," in *Blake in His Time*, ed. Robert N. Essick and Donald Pearce (Bloomington: Indiana University Press, 1978), p. 2.

20. Annotations to Swedenborg's *Wisdom of Angels Concerning Divine Love and Divine Wisdom, Complete Writings*, p. 96.

21. *Europe*, 4.15, p. 240; 2.4, p. 238; *FZ*, N7.464–69, p. 332.

22. Erdman discusses the illuminations to *Europe*, pls. 1 and 2, and suggests identities for the figures, in *The Illuminated Blake*, pp. 159–61.

23. *FZ*, N1.308–11, p. 272.

24. *FZ*, N7.458–62, p. 331.

25. *FZ*, N7.453–63, p. 331–32.

26. *Europe*, 2.5, p. 238.

27. *Europe*, 1.11, 2.8, p. 238.

28. *Europe*, 2.13–14, p. 239.

29. *Notebook*, p. 96 (Butlin, *Paintings*, 1:103).

30. *PL*, bk. 7, line 224–31, pp. 787–78. *Europe*, i; Erdman, *The Illuminated Blake*, p. 156. Blake made many separate imprints of this plate, which he regarded as a particularly significant image. He is said to have worked on the last of these on his deathbed.

31. *FZ*, N1.306–11, p. 272. Urizen in his fallen condition appears in this form on the plate of "The Human Abstract" in the "Songs of Experience" and throughout the *Book of Urizen*. (Erdman, *The Illuminated Blake*, pp. 89, 183, 187, 191, 194, 204–5, 210.)

32. *FZ*, N1.305, p. 272. Klonsky (*William Blake*, p. 40) draws attention to the detail of the left-handed grasp. Joseph Wicksteed has distinguished the left as the "bodily" and the right as the "spiritual" side in Blake's illustrations. (Wicksteed, *William Blake's "Jerusalem"* [London: Trianon Press, 1954], p. 122.)

33. This passage includes the verse Blake illustrated as "When the morning Stars sang together . . ." in his "Job" series, ca.1805–6. (Butlin, *Paintings*, pl. 746, cat. 551.14.)

34. Werner, *Blake's Vision*, p. 114.

35. *Europe*, 3.1–4, p. 239. Milton, *Elegia Sexta*, line 81, p. 117. Blake's lines derive from lines 29–31, 53–55, and 229–34 of Milton's *Hymn*. Michael J. Tolley explores in some detail these and other Miltonic parallels in *Europe* (though not those in its "Preludium") in "*Europe*: 'To Those Ychain'd in Sleep,'" pp. 119–22. While I agree with Professor Tolley on the thematic importance of the Miltonic parodies, I differ with him in their interpretation and especially on their prophetic significance.

36. Milton, *Hymn*, line 110, p. 106.

37. *FZ*, N1301, p. 272. The illustration referred to is the second of the series now in the Whitworth Art Gallery, University of Manchester, and is reproduced in Butlin, *Paintings*, as pl. 661, cat. no. 538.2. (In Blake's other series of illustrations to the *Hymn*, now in the Huntington Art Gallery in San Marino, Calif., the weapons of the seraphim are omitted. Butlin, 1:393, regards the Huntington series as the later of the two.)

38. Milton, *Hymn*, line 222, p. 112; *FZ*, N1.298, p. 272; *PL*, bk. 3, lines 203–9, pp. 572–73.

39. Milton, *Hymn*, lines 61–63, p. 103; *Europe*, 3.6–7, p. 239; *Paradise Lost*, bk. 3, lines 482–83, p. 590; bk. 6, lines 859–60, p. 771; and bk. 1, lines 741–42, p. 505.

40. *Europe*, 3.7, p. 239. See discussion in Chapter 1.

41. *Blake: Prophet against Empire*, p. 267; and David Erdman and John E. Grant, eds., *Blake's Visionary Forms Dramatic* (Princeton: Princeton University Press, 1970), p. 127, n.9.

42. *Europe*, 3.11–12, p. 239.

43. Milton, *Hymn*, lines 168–69, p. 108.

44. Milton, *Hymn*, lines 69–76, p. 104.

45. *Europe*, 3.12, p. 239.

46. *PL*, bk. 5, lines 685–90 and 755–56, pp. 718 and 722.

47. *Europe*, 3.12, and 4.1–4, p. 239.

48. Milton, *Hymn*, lines 96–97, p. 105.

49. See especially *America*, lines 11–12, p. 196, and its design: Erdman, *The Illuminated Blake*, p. 139.

50. Emmanuel Swedenborg, *Heaven and Hell* trans. J. C. Ager, rev. Doris Harley (London: Swedenborg Society, 1958), par. 69, p. 32.

51. *Europe,* 4.15–16, p. 240.

52. *Europe,* 4.17, p. 240.

53. *PL,* bk. 6, lines 472–83, p. 750.

54. *Europe,* 5.1–3, p. 240.

55. Thomas Otway, *Venice Preserved,* act 1, lines 337–39, in *Complete Works,* ed. J. C. Ghosh (Oxford: Clarendon Press, 1932). Cowper had satirized the same passage in *The Progress of Error* (which Blake, who admired Cowper's work, would have known), lines 271–74:

> 'Tis not alone the grape's enticing juice
> Unnerves the moral powers, and mars their use:
> Ambition, av'rice, and the lust of fame,
> And woman, lovely woman, does the same.

See William Cowper, *Poetical Works,* ed. H. S. Milford, 4 ed., rev. Norma Russell (London: Oxford University Press, 1967).

56. The coloration described is that of copies B and G of *Europe,* reproduced in *Blake's "America: A Prophecy" and "Europe: A Prophecy"* (New York: Dover Publications, 1983).

57. David Erdman identifies the female figures with the queens of England and France, and the male figure with Pitt, prime minister of England (*The Illuminated Blake* pp. 163–64). My own reading of this illumination, and in fact of the whole "Prophecy," is offered as a level of its allegorical meaning additional to the political allegory explicated by Professor Erdman in *Blake: Prophet against Empire.*

58. Milton, *Hymn,* lines 205–10. David Erdman postulated that Blake was working on the illustrations to Milton's *Hymn on the Nativity of Christ* at about the same time as he was composing *Europe* (*Blake: Prophet against Empire,* p. 266). However, I have accepted the later dating from the more recent research of Martin Butlin (*Paintings,* 1:389–90 and 393). But Blake may well have been sketching his ideas for illustrations to the *Hymn* around 1794, just as he was continually occupied (on the evidence of his *Notebook*) with the illustration of passages or ideas from other works of Milton's. He usually executed finished paintings when he found a patron to commission them.

59. Butlin reproduces the paintings illustrating "The Flight of Moloch" as pls. 664 and 670. Milton's references to Moloch on which Blake drew for his representations in the two *Nativity Hymn* series come not only from the *Hymn* itself (lines 205–10, p. 111), but also from *PL,* bk. 1, lines 392–96, p. 485, and bk. 2, lines 43–108, pp. 510–12. See also Damon, *Dictionary,* pp. 283–84.

60. *FZ,* N7.459–62, pp. 331–32.

61. *FZ,* N7.466, 469, p. 332.

62. *The Book of Los,* 3.27–30, p. 256; *FZ,* N7.458–75, pp. 331–32.

63. *PL,* bk. 9, lines 532, 540, pp. 888–89.

64. Milton, *PL,* bk. 9, line 405, p. 879; *Jerusalem,* 90.1–2, p. 736. Erdman, *The Illuminated Blake,* pp. 157, 168, 172.

65. *Jerusalem,* 34[30]:325–33, p. 661.

66. See Chapter 3.

67.
> . . . entre les .II. biaus pilerez,
> con viguereus et legerez,
> m'agenoilloi san demourer,
> car mout oi grant fain d'aourer
> le biau saintuaire honorable
> de queur devost et piteable . . .
> de l'ymage lors m'apressai
> que de saintuaire pres sai. . . .

(". . . between the two fair pillars I knelt without delay, all vigour and agility, for I longed intensely to worship the beautiful, adorable sanctuary with a devout and pious heart . . . I drew closer to the image to know the sanctuary more intimately. . . .")

Guillaume de Lorris and Jean de Meun, *Le Roman de la rose,* ed. Felix Lecoy (Paris: Honoré Champion, 1975), 3:148–49, (lines 21557–72).

Blake, *Jerusalem,* 36.58, p. 668:

("I call them by their English names: English, the rough basement . . .").

68. "The Angel," pp. 213–14; Erdman, *The Illuminated Blake,* p. 83. "The Angel" satirizes Milton's defense of chastity in *Comus,* drawing especially on lines 452–57 of that work. See my essay "'Sunclad Chastity' and Blake's 'Maiden Queens': *Comus, Thel,* and 'The Angel,'" *Blake / An Illustrated Quarterly* 25 (1991–92): 104–16.

69. Edmund Burke, *Reflections on the French Revolution,* ed. W. Alison Philips (Cambridge: Cambridge University Press, 1929), p. 76. Burke is caricatured in one of the figures on plate 1 of *Europe* (Erdman, *The Illuminated Blake,* p. 159).

70. Erdman points out the connection between the passage I have quoted from Burke's *Reflections* and Blake's poem "Let the Brothels of Paris be opened . . ." (p. 185). Erdman, *Blake:Prophet against Empire,* p. 184.

71. *Europe,* 5.5–9, p. 240.

72. *FZ,* N5.241, p. 311.

73. *FZ,* N4.97–100, p. 300.

74. *FZ,* N5.241, p. 311.

75. *The Marriage of Heaven and Hell,* pl. 5, pp. 149–50.

76. *Europe,* 5.8–9, p. 240.

77. Erdman, *The Illuminated Blake,* p. 159.

78. Ibid., p. 170.

79. Ibid., p. 171.

80. Ibid., pp. 170–72.

81. Emanuel Swedenborg, *The Wisdom of Angels Concerning Divine Providence* (London, 1790), pp. 137–38.

82. *The Marriage of Heaven and Hell,* pl. 18, p. 156.

83. Ibid., pl. 19, p. 156.

84. *Urizen,* 25.7–22, p. 235. (My italics.)

85. A. C. Hamilton comments, "The spider is an emblem of touch; Acrasia is seen as the spider in the web." See his edition of *The Faerie Queene,* bk. 2, canto 12, stanza 77, lines 4–7, p. 296. Blake links the sense of touch with sexual sensation in *Thel* 6.11–20, p. 130; Milton does so in *PL,* bk. 8, lines 528–31, p. 843.

86. Spenser, *Muiopotmos,* lines 343–52, in Spenser, *Poetical Works,* ed. J. C. Smith and E. de Selincourt (London: Oxford University Press, 1970), pp. 519–20.

87. *FZ,* N8.209–17, p. 346. All the Emanations go to work at their looms in the joyous climax of *The Four Zoas: FZ,* N9.778–81, pp. 377–78. The concept of the "river of space" or "river of life" is illustrated in Blake's watercolor of ca. 1805, "The River of Life," now in the Tate Gallery, London. (Butlin, *Paintings,* 2: cat. no. 525, pl. 586.)

88. Spenser, *The Faerie Queene,* b. 2, canto 7, stanza 28, lines 7–8, p. 229; canto 12, stanza 77, line 7, p. 296.

89. *PL,* bk. 9, line 214, p. 868.

90. Rintrah first appears as a figure of Wrath in Blake's *The Marriage of Heaven and Hell,* 2.1, 21, pp. 148–49. He reappears, raging, in both *Milton* and *Jerusalem.*

91. Erdman, *The Illuminated Blake,* p. 169.

92. Milton, *Comus* lines 440–41, p. 198.

93. *Europe,* 8.8–12, p. 240.

94. Erdman, *The Illuminated Blake,* p. 167; *The Book of Los,* 3.30, p. 256.

95. *Europe,* 12.22–24, p. 242; *The Marriage of Heaven and Hell,* pls. 17–20, pp. 155–56.

96. *Europe,* 12.25–9, p. 243.

97. *Europe,* 13.4–5, p. 243.

98. The line "Thrice he assay'd presumptuous to awake the dead to Judgement . . ." (*Europe,* 13.3, p. 243) is a comical parody of Milton's account of Satan preparing to speak to his fallen

followers, "Thrice he essayed, and thrice in spite of scorn, / Tears such as angels weep, burst forth . . ." (*PL*, bk. 1, lines 619–20, p. 498). The fall of the "Angelic hosts" (*Europe*, 13.6–7, p. 243) imitates the fallen hosts of Satan, lying "thick as autumnal leaves" (*PL*, bk. 1, lines 301–3, p. 480). Tolley notices these parallels (p. 142).

99. *Europe*, 13.11–15, p. 243.

100. Damon, *Dictionary*, p. 130.

101. *Europe*, 14.1–5, p. 243; *PL*, bk. 3, 30–32, p. 562; *Jerusalem*, 34.33, p. 661.

102. Milton, *Samson Agonistes*, line 934, p. 376; Damon, *Dictionary*, p. 448.

103. *Europe* 14.7–8, p. 244.

104. *Europe* 14.7, p. 244.

105. *Europe*, 14.6–8, p. 244; *Visions of the Daughters of Albion*, 2.17, p. 190.

106. The date of the title page of *Visions of the Daughters of Albion* is 1793, one year earlier than *Europe*.

107. *Visions of the Daughters of Albion*, 1.11–17, 2.1–10, pp. 189–90.

108. *Visions of the Daughters of Albion*, 2.13, p. 190.

109. *Europe*, 14.21–5, p. 244.

110. Leutha appears in *Milton*, where she is associated both with the Rainbow and with "My Parent power Satan" (*Milton*, 11.32–6, p. 492). Sheila Spector derives Leutha's name from Hebrew roots meaning "for a sign of sin" (Sheila Spector, "Blake as an Eighteenth-Century Hebraist," in *Blake and His Bibles*, ed. David V. Erdman [West Cornwall, Conn.: Locust Hill Press, 1990], pp. 208–9.)

111. "Let the brothels of Paris be opened," lines 1–4, 33–34, p. 185.

112. Ibid., lines 31–34, p. 185.

113. *Notebook* p. 99, in *Complete Writings*, p. 184.

114. *Europe*, 14.15–19, p. 244.

115. *Thel*, 2.13–18, 3.1–13, p. 128; see my Chapter 2. *Europe*, 14.8–20, p. 244.

116. *Europe*, 14.26–27, p. 244.

117. *Europe*, 14.32–34, p. 244.

118. *PL*, bk. 9, lines 782–84, p. 902.

119. Frye, *Fearful Symmetry*, p. 263; *Europe*, 14.36, 15.1–8, pp. 244–45.

120. *FZ*, N4.286–87, p. 305.

121. *PL*, bk, 9, lines 1000–1, bk. 10, lines 668–69, pp. 913, 961.

122. *Europe*, 15.9–11, p. 245.

Chapter 5. Ololon I.

In referring to *designs* on the plates of *Milton*, I follow the numbering of Copy B, in the Huntington Library, San Marino, California. This necessarily differs from that of the Keynes edition of the *text*, because in his version of the numbering Keynes does not count in the seven plates that bear illustrations *without* text. (The sequence in which plates are placed also varies to some extent from one to another of the four known copies.)

1. *Milton*, 41.30, p. 533.

2. See Chapter 2.

3. Northrop Frye commented that "the notion that Blake was primarily concerned to 'correct' Milton's theological and domestic difficulties rests on a story of Crabb Robinson's which is much better ignored." Frye explained in a footnote that "Blake is alleged to have complained that Milton was grievously in error in saying that the pleasures of sex arose from the Fall." ("Notes for a Commentary on *Milton*," in *The Divine Vision: Studies in the Poetry and Art of William Blake*, ed. Vivian de Sola Pinto [London: Victor Gollancz, 1957], p. 101.)

In the present chapter I attempt to explore the symbolic relationship between, on the one hand, the historical circumstances of the poet John Milton, and on the other the motives of the hero of Blake's epic. My incentive to do so arose from a study of the poem itself, not from Crabb Robinson's story. Robinson gives—it seems to me—a distinctly reductive view of Blake's pronouncements concerning his relationship with "the spirit of Milton," the more so since he was relying to some extent on long-term memory. He noted down some of Blake's remarks concerning Milton in 1852, over twenty-six years after Blake is supposed to have made them. See Bentley, *Blake Records*, pp. 535–36, 544.

4. Blake's unmarried sister Catherine Elizabeth Blake, seven years his junior, had accompanied her brother and sister-in-law to Felpham (see Blake's letter to Flaxman of 21 September 1800, in *Complete Writings*, p. 802). In a letter to Butts dated 22 November 1802 (pp. 816–18) Blake encloses (at his wife's request, he says) "some Verses . . . Composed above a twelve-month ago, while walking from Felpham to Lavant to meet my Sister. . . ." These autobiographically inspired "Verses" include the lines

> "Must my Wife live in my Sister's bane,
> "Or my Sister survive on my Love's pain?"
>
> (49–50)

referring presumably to family turbulence during the latter half of 1801. The poem "William Bond" (pp. 434–35), copied into the "Pickering Manuscript" in ca. 1803, presents a "William" whose "Sister Jane" is a member of his household. "William"'s sister supports him in a crisis, involving another woman, that affects his relationship with "Mary Green," whom the poem depicts as his future wife or possibly already married to him.

Whatever the validity of what these imaginative poetic flights of Blake's may suggest to the speculatively inclined, Blake's wife and sister did not, in fact, like one another. After the death of Mrs. Blake, Mrs. Anne Gilchrist, who knew the Blakes well, wrote that Blake's wife and his sister "got on very ill together; and latterly never met at all" (Bentley, *Blake Records*, p. 417).

5. William Hayley, *The Life of Milton*, 2nd ed. (London: Cadell & Davies, 1796); repr., with an introduction by J. A. Wittreich, Jr. (Gainesville, Fla.: Scholars' Facsimiles and Reprints, 1970). Wittreich argues that Hayley's presentation of the life and works of Milton, the first "Romantic" biography of the poet, influenced the "Romantic" movement in general.

6. My source is J. Milton French, ed., *The Life Records of John Milton*, 5 vols, (New Brunswick, N.J.: Rutgers University Press, 1948–58).

7. Hayley, *Life of Milton*, p. 91.

8. A deposition to this effect was made shortly after John Milton's death by his brother Christopher, since Milton died intestate. *Life Records*, 5:212–13.

9. Blake tells us in the poem that both Milton and Los appeared to him in Lambeth (*Milton*, 21.4–14, p. 503; 22.4–11, p. 505), and that

> . . . when Los join'd with me he took me in his fi'ry whirlwind;
> My Vegetated portion was hurried from Lambeth's shades,
> He set me down in Felpham's Vale & prepar'd a beautiful
> Cottage for me, that in three years I might write all these
> Visions. . . .
>
> (*Milton*, 36.21–24, p. 527)

Blake lived in Felpham from September 1800 to September 1803, so that presumably the inspiration for the poem came to him before September of 1800. He must have been engaged in composing it while working under Hayley's patronage in Felpham. The date on the title page of *Milton*, 1804, may represent—as it usually does with Blake's illuminated books—the date on which he began engraving the plates, or it "may acknowledge his completion of composition" (William Blake, *Milton*, ed. and with a commentary by K. P. Easson and R. R. Easson [London:

Thames and Hudson, 1979], p. 59). Four copies of *Milton* are extant. Copies A, B, and C are on paper watermarked 1808. Copy C contains five more plates than A and B (but lacks the "Preface," with its superb lyric). Blakc did some further work on the poem some time between 1808 and 1815, since the fourth extant copy of *Milton*, D, is printed on paper watermarked 1815 and contains all the plates included in C, plus one more. (Keynes numbers the additional plates common to C and D as pls. 3, 4, 10, 18, and 32, while the plate found only in D is numbered 5 in his edition of Blake's *Complete Writings*.)

10. *Milton*, 40.29, p. 532; for the "Bard," see 2.21–24, p. 482; 13.50–51; 14.1–3, p. 495, and the "Introduction" to the *Songs of Experience*, lines 1–5, p. 210.

11. *Milton*, 16.51–52, 17.1–3, pp. 498–99.

12. ". . . our sufficiency is of God; who also hath made us able ministers of the new testament; not of the letter, but of the spirit; for the letter killeth, but the spirit giveth life." 2 Corinthians 3.5–6.

13. Boehme, *The Signature of All Things*, chap. 15, par. 22, p. 201. (Ellistone translation.)

14. "There can be no Good Will. Will is always Evil; it is pernicious to others or selfish." *Annotations to Swedenborg's "Wisdom of Angels Concerning Divine Love and Divine Wisdom," Complete Writings*, p. 89. Robert N. Essick, *William Blake and the Language of Adam* (Oxford: Clarendon Press, 1989), pp. 189–90.

15. *PL*, bk. 9, lines 459–66, p. 884; see Chapter 1. Joan Bellis provided me with the link after reading Chapters 1 and 5 in manuscript.

16. Essick, *William Blake and the Language of Adam*, p.190.

17. Emanuel Swedenborg, *The New Jerusalem and Its Heavenly Doctrine*, trans. E. C. Mongredien, rev. Doris Harley (London: Swedenborg Society, 1972), pars. 56–57, p. 31.

18. *Milton*, 17.5–8, pp. 498–99.

19. *Milton*, 14.14, 33, pp. 495–56; and 16.1, p. 497.

20. *Milton*, 21.45–50, p. 504.

The principal of a heavenly "multitude in unity" is Swedenborgian: ". . . the more there are in one society of heaven, all acting as one, the more perfect is its human form, for variety arranged as one, in a heavenly form is perfection . . . and variety results from plurality." Swedenborg, *Heaven and Its Wonders and Hell*, par. 71, p. 32.

21. *Milton*, 35.31–33, p. 525. Fox comments on these scenes that "there is no change in the *dramatis personae* in book 2, only a clarification of the consequences of Ololon's contrition, which has united her with Milton and realized the Divine Humanity." Susan Fox, *Poetic Form in Blake's "Milton"* (Princeton, N.J.: Princeton University Press, 1976), p. 151.

22. *Milton*, 42.11–12, p. 534.

23. Wittreich has shown that Blake's principal Miltonic source for the self-annihilation and reintegration of his epic hero was *Paradise Regained*. This is evident from Blake's interpretative illustrations to *Paradise Regained*, executed in 1816–20. (Joseph Anthony Wittreich, Jr., "William Blake: Illustrator-Interpreter of *Paradise Regained*," in *Calm of Mind: Tercentenary Essays on "Paradise Regained" and "Samson Agonistes" in Honor of John S. Diekhoff*, ed. Joseph Anthony Wittreich, Jr. [Cleveland: Press of Case Western Reserve University, 1971], pp. 93–132.)

24. *Milton*, 38.5, p. 529.

25. *Milton*, 38.8, p. 529.

26. *Milton*, 38.43–44, 47–49, p. 530.

27. *Milton*, 36.17, 26–27, p. 527.

28. *Milton*, 40.32–36, p. 533.

29. *Visions of the Daughters of Albion*, iii.3, p. 189; *Milton*, 41.30–35, 42.2, pp. 533–44.

30. Ackland, "The Embattled Sexes," p. 179.

31. *Milton*, 27.45, p. 514; *Jerusalem*, 36.46–47, p. 663.

32. Spector, "Blake as an Eighteenth-Century Hebraist," p. 207. Spector explains that different spellings of the word in Hebrew, while having the same transliteration into Latin characters, may give the compound different senses:

> . . . the root for "ul" could also suggest "God," and "ro," "evil," making Ulro the realm of the God of Evil, Satan, or, if the roots are interchanged, the "God of Vision," or the "Negation of Evil" . . . We have no way of knowing which, if any, Blake intended. (p. 208)

If Blake's knowledge of Hebrew did extend to the linguistic principles on which these Hebrew "roots" operate, it would have been characteristic of him to have intended that these ambiguities remain inherent in the name "Ulro." All the contexts in which this "State" is mentioned agree in suggesting that Blake meant the "Ulro" to be a place of punishment, the ultimate Hell, in the terms of his *own* myth—though it would not be thus seen in an orthodox Christian perspective.

33. *Milton*, 42.3–6, p. 534.

34. *Thel*, 6.21–2 (K 130). See discussion in Chapter 2.

35. *Milton*, 40.20–22, p. 532.

36. Spenser's Duessa reveals her falsity by continually disguising herself:

> Her purpose was not such, as she did faine,
> Ne yet her person such, as it was seene,
> But vnder simple shew and semblant plaine
> Lurckt false *Duessa* secretly vnseene.
> (*The Faerie Queene*, bk. 2, canto 1, stanza 21, p. 174)

Blake's biblical source for the image of the "Dragon red & hidden Harlot which John in Patmos saw" of *Milton* 40.22 (Revelations 17) was undoubtedly augmented by Spenser's account in bk. 1 of *The Faerie Queene* of Duessa robed, crowned, and set by the giant Orgoglio upon a "dreadfull Beast with seuenfold head" which he had "kept longtime in darksome den" (bk. 1, canto 7, stanzas 16–18, pp. 99–100).

On the hermaphrodite witch-figure, see Banquo's reaction to the witches in Shakespeare's *Macbeth*:

> . . . You should be women,
> But that your beards forbid me to interpret
> That you are so.
> (1:3, lines 45–47)

37. Blake uses the word "Wonder" in the sense of "prodigy" or "marvel." See *OED*, s.v. "wonder" sb. I.1.

38. *Milton*, 38.29, p. 529.

39. *PL*, bk. 9, lines 205–411, pp. 868–80. Fowler notes the "strong element of sexual seduction in Milton's presentation of the temptation [of Eve]." (Note to *PL*, bk. 9, line 627, p. 893.)

40. *Jerusalem*, 34.27–28, 31, p. 661.

41. *Milton*, 17.11, p. 498, and 35.8–13, p. 525; also 29.58, p. 517; Numbers 36.33, and 27.1–7.

42. The biblical Rahab of Joshua 2 and 6 was a harlot of Jericho, who, betraying her own people, assisted the Israelites in their siege of the city. When Jericho fell Rahab was protected by Joshua, and "she dwelleth in Israel even unto this day" (Joshua 6.25). Blake linked with this treacherous personage the "Rahab" of Psalm 89.9–10. This other "Rahab" (spelled differently in the Hebrew text) is a sea-monster symbolic of chaos, associated with the "dragon" and "leviathan" of Isaiah 27.1 and Psalm 74.13–14. Blake thus chose to identify Rahab with the Great Whore of Babylon (*Milton*, 40.17–22, p. 532) who is "mother of harlots and abominations of the earth" (Revelations 17.5). In Blake's myth she is the embodiment of falsity and symbolizes the "Female Will."

Florence Sandler points out the distinction between the two "Rahabs" in "The Iconoclastic Enterprise: Blake's Critique of 'Milton's Religion,'" *Blake Studies* 5, no. 1 (1972): 37. See also Damon, *Dictionary*, pp. 338–40.

43. *Milton*, 17.12–13, p. 498.

44. *Milton*, 17.13–14, p. 498; 22.39–45, p. 506.

45. *Songs of Experience*, "To Tirzah," 1.9, p. 220. Sheila Spector proposes that the name Tirzah in Blake may be "a transliteration of 'thou shalt kill,' the key word of the Sixth Commandment. . . . As the 'Mother of my Mortal Part' . . . Tirzah symbolizes death, and along with Rahab could constitute the coordinates of the physical world, Time and Space" (Spector, "Blake as an Eighteenth-Century Hebraist," p. 205). Spector quotes *Milton*, 13.40–43, p. 494, in support of the latter associations.

46. At the apocalyptic ending of *Jerusalem*, Blake places among the "Chariots of the Almighty" in Heaven three poets and three philosophers. The poets are Chaucer, Shakespeare, and Milton, the philosophers—formerly archenemies, but in Eternity "contraries"—Bacon, Newton and Locke. (*Jerusalem* 97.7–9, p. 745.)

47. The stages of the "hieros gamos" of Sol the Sun-King and Luna the Moon-Queen, early phases of which include the descent of the catalytic dove, are depicted in engravings from the *Rosarium philosophorum*, published in Frankfurt in 1551, and analyzed by C. G. Jung in *An Account of the Transference Phenomena Based on the Illustrations to the "Rosarium Philosophorum"* (reprinted in his *Collected Works*, ed. by Herbert Read, Michael Fordham, and Gerhard Adler, Bollingen Series 20 [New York: Pantheon, 1954], 16:203–330, to which page and figure numbers in this note refer). The symbolic events, and some of the illuminations, of Blake's *Milton*, especially in its closing plates, so closely parallel some elements of the "hieros gamos" as strongly to suggest that Blake had seen and been influenced by one of the many medieval accounts of this alchemical mystery—as always, taking from it what was useful for his own creative purposes. The following is a brief outline of parallels. The "two Streams" of Blake's "Fountain" (*Milton*, 35.49–50) follow apparently conflicting courses: one appears to be a river of life, flowing through Blake's seats of creativity, "thro' Golgonooza / And thro' Beulah to Eden" (35.49–51), whereas the other passes "thro' the Aerial Void & all the Churches" (35.52) and is associated with the "Terrible, deadly & poisonous . . . presence in Ulro dark" (35.55) of the symbolic Wild Thyme. The "mercurial fountain" (fig. 1, p. 205) with which the account in the *Rosarium* of the mystic union of Sol with Luna begins is captioned

> "The highest tincture of the Art is made through us . . .
> I make both rich and poor men whole or sick.
> For deadly can I be and poisonous."
>
> (p. 203)

The descent of the catalytic "dove" precedes the union of Sol and Luna (figs. 2, 3, 4, pp. 213, 234, 241). The "Tomb" from which Blake's resurrected Luvah has arisen (*Milton*, 35.59) parallels the sarcophagus in which the united Sol and Luna lie "dead," but awaiting resurrection (fig. 6, p. 257); the "Moony Ark" form assumed by Ololon (*Milton*, 42.7) is similar to the crescent-moon vehicle on which the resurrected hermaphrodite figure is elevated in its final phase (fig. 10, p. 305); the life-giving tears of "soft Oothoon" (*Milton*, 42.32–33) parallel the heavenly dew whose falling upon the entombed Sol-Luna brings about the renewal of life (fig. 8, p. 273). Blake's representation on the final plate of *Milton* of the "Human Harvest" (42.33), a female and two males in vegetated forms, may have been suggested in principle by a vegetable form whose blooms have human faces, springing up beside the transcendent hermaphrodite figure (partly identified with the "Sophia") in the final engraving of the *Rosarium* account (fig. 10, p. 305), which is captioned

> Here is born the Empress of all honour /
> The philosophers name her their daughter.
> She multiplies / bears children ever again /
> They are incorruptibly pure and without any stain.
>
> (p. 304)

48. *Milton*, 42.7, p. 534. Damon describes the Ark, which preserved Noah and his family from drowning in the biblical Flood (Blake's constant symbol for the Sea of Time and Space) as Blake's symbol of Love, which he consequently depicted as a crescent moon (Damon, *Dictionary*, p. 300). Damon refers to Blake's pictorial use of the moon-ark symbol in an illustration to Jacob Bryant's *New System . . . of Ancient Mythology* in 1776, and to the illuminations to *Jerusalem*, pls. 24 and 39 (44). (Jacob Bryant, *A New System, or, an Analysis of Ancient Mythology* [London: Payne, Elmsley, White and Walter, 1774–76], 3:601; Erdman, *The Illuminated Blake*, pp. 303 and 318.) But see as well the alchemical symbolism outlined in my n. 47.

49. *Milton*, 42.12–13, p. 534. Grimes says of this transformation: "Ololon is clearly the corpus of Milton's visionary poetry . . . 'the Divine Revelation in Litteral expression' (M42:14). Milton descends to reclaim an alienated part of himself, his Emanation, which in this case is his poetry." See Ronald L. Grimes, *The Divine Imagination: William Blake's Major Prophetic Visions* (Metuchen, N.J.: Scarecrow Press 1972), p. 25.

Robert N. Essick reads these lines as Christ's "redemption of writing in *Milton*." Blake's personage Milton, Essick argues, "serves as the historical and literary experience from which emerges the vision of Jesus. That revelation is accompanied by a transformation of the corpus of Milton's writings ('The Clouds of Ololon') into Christ's flesh in Jesus, the living garment of His body, without loss of its textual nature." See his *William Blake and the Language of Adam*, p. 201.

Blake's possible reference here to the bloody cloth given to Posthumus in Shakespeare's *Cymbeline*, as evidence of the "death" of the chaste Imogen, is discussed later.

50. *Milton*, 42.11, p. 534; 15.3–6, p. 496.

51. *Milton*, 1.2–3, p. 480; 42.19–21, p. 534.

52. *Milton*, 42.25, p. 534.

53. *Milton*, 42.28, p. 534.

54. *Milton*, 42.31, p. 534.

55. Letter to Butts, 25 April 1803, in *Collected Writings*, p. 822.

56. For an explanation of plate-numbers used in referring to the *designs* of Blake's *Milton*, see headnote preceding the notes to this chapter.

57. *Milton*, 17.12–13 and 17, p. 498.

58. Compare with this the figure of Cain in Blake's large print, "The Body of Abel found by Adam and Eve," Butlin, *Paintings,* cat. no. 806.

59. Erdman, in *The Illustrated Blake*, numbers these plates of *Milton* 32 and 37 (from Copy C); Copy B (reproduced in the facsimile edition of K. P. Easson and R. R. Easson) numbers them 29 and 33.

60. See *Milton*, 32.4–5, p. 521; *Notebook* [N12 (2)], c. 1804. I have quoted the text and approximate dating of this poem from Erdman's edition of Blake's *Notebook*, p. 13.

61. *Milton*, 17.1–2, p. 498.

62. The coloring of Copy B, in the Henry E. Huntington Library and Art Collections, San Marino, California, the source of the facsimile edited by K. P. Easson and R. R. Easson, was used as the basis for the present discussion.

63. Erdman calls the dancing group "these Salomes" (*The Illuminated Blake*, p. 235).

64. Milton is shown about to take this "Step into Eternity" both in the title page and on plate 13 of the work.

65. *Milton*, 41, in *Complete Writings*, p. 533.

66. *Milton*, 21.30, p. 504.

> If the doors of perception were cleansed every thing would appear to man as it is, infinite.

> For man has closed himself up, till he sees all things thro' narrow chinks of his cavern.
>
> (*The Marriage of Heaven and Hell*, pl. 14, p. 154)

Cf. also the "dark black Rock & . . . gloomy Cave" Blake metaphorically declares he received in rebuff from his sometime friend Fuseli (Letter to Butts, 22 November 1802; line 40, in *Complete Writings*, p.817).

67. *Milton*, 36, in *Complete Writings*, pp. 526–27.

68. *Milton*, 35.37–38, p. 526; 36.16–17, p. 527.

. . . an entire angelic society, when the Lord manifests Himself as present, appears as one in the human form. . . . (Swedenborg, *Heaven and Its Wonders and Hell*, par.69, p. 32, trans. Ager, rev. D. Harley.)

69. *Visions of the Daughters of Albion*, iii.3, 1.8–13, p. 189.

70. *Milton*, 40.33, p. 533.

71. *Milton*, 21.15–19, p. 503; 22.3, p. 505. Frye, *Fearful Symmetry*, p. 143.

72. Peter Fisher, *The Valley of Vision: Blake as Prophet and Revolutionary* (Toronto: University of Toronto Press, 1961), p. 248.

73. Harold Bloom, *Blake's Apocalypse: A Study in Poetic Argument* (Garden City, N.Y.: Doubleday, 1965), p. 366.

74. Donald H. Reiman and Christina Shuttleworth Kraus, "The Derivation and Meaning of 'Ololon,'" *Blake / An Illustrated Quarterly* 16 (1982): 82. V. A. De Luca, in his article "Proper Names in the Structural Design of Blake's Myth-Making," *Blake Studies* 8 (1978): 5–22, omits consideration of the name "Ololon," though he does discuss other names coined on pl. 34 of *Milton*.

75. *Milton*, 1, p. 480.

76. Letter to James Blake, 30 January 1803, in *Complete Writings*, pp. 821–22.

77. This was by no means Blake's first acquaintance with the Hebrew language, although this may have been his first systematic study of the Old Testament in the original. Sheila A. Spector ("The Reasons for 'Urizen,'" *Blake / An Illustrated Quarterly* 21 [1988]: 147–49) offers evidence that Blake may have consulted John Parkhurst's *An Hebrew and English Lexicon without Points* (1st ed. 1766) "at some point before 1793" (p. 147). She infers that "Blake's earliest source for Hebrew was Parkhurst's *Lexicon*" (p. 148). In her more recently published and more extensive study, Spector offers evidence that Blake was aware of the Hebrew meanings of place-names of the Bible, and that this applied also to his use of biblical personal names. (Spector, "Blake as an Eighteenth-Century Hebraist.")

Blake had attempted to use Hebrew lettering in his artistic work before he began this systematic study. Impressionistic and inaccurately reproduced Hebrew letters appear on a scroll in Blake's engraving to "Night the Third" of Young's *Night Thoughts*, p. 63 (1797; reproduced by Bindman, *Complete Graphic Works*, p. 366). Blake obviously continued his study of Hebrew and improved his mastery of its script. A phrase etched in clear Hebrew script appears in the margin of a plate of *Milton* included in copies C and D (pl. 32 in the Keynes edition). Blake correctly translates the phrase in a marginal note as "as multitudes." (See the note in W. H. Stevenson's 1989 edition, *Complete Poems*, p. 578. Blake's Hebrew script on this plate is misprinted in the transcripts of both Keynes and the Eassons.) Clear and legible Hebrew script is also used in the Book of Enoch lithograph (ca.1806), in the "Laocoön" plate (ca.1820), and in some of the Job engravings (1825). Again, Spector suggests that in certain cases in later works Blake's distortions of Hebrew letters, when he was well aware of their correct forms, may have been deliberate ("Blake as an Eighteenth-Century Hebraist," pp. 198–202). A clear example of this is "Job's Evil Dream."

A page of sketches in which Blake experiments with the transformation of Hebrew letters into human figures, presumably done ca. 1803 while he was learning the Hebrew alphabet, is reproduced by Butlin, *Paintings*, cat. no. 199 (verso).

78. *Complete Writings*, pp. 162–63.

79. *Europe*, 9.5, p. 240; 5.5, p. 240; 12.15–28, p. 243.

80. Professor Sheila A. Spector has pointed out to me, in a personal letter of 12 July 1991, that the name Ololon "was probably coined during the same time [that Blake] completed *Job's Evil Dream*, with its profusion of *lo*'s."

In Blake's painting "Job's Evil Dream" (ca.1805–6, Butlin, *Paintings*, pl. 707, cat. no. 550.11) the tablets of the Mosaic Law are centrally placed above the supine body of the dreaming Job, and the cloven-hoofed and serpent-entwined figure hovering over Job, a Satanic "Elohim," gestures toward them. The Hebrew word "*lo*" is legible in two of the commandments shown.

81. *Milton*, 30.1, p. 518.

82. *Milton*, 14.51–52, 17.1–2, pp. 497–98.

83. *Comus*, 815–16, p. 217. The backward spelling of words or of a name is a traditional means used to annul magical power, as the Attendant Spirit wishes to use it in *Comus*. It was even employed in "black magic" in an attempt to annul or disable divine power. Thus Marlowe's Dr. Faustus uses "Jehovah's name, / Forward and backward anagrammatized . . ." in an attempt to raise the Devil (Christopher Marlowe, *Dr. Faustus* Ed. Roma Gill. London: Ernest Benn, 1965; act 2 sc. 3, line 9). Anagrammatization was a device constantly used in Kabbalism. See subsequent discussion of the Kabbalistic *golem*.

84. *Milton*, 22.39, p. 506.

85. *Milton*, 19.10–14, p. 500.

86. Gershom Scholem, *Kabbalah* (Jerusalem: Keter Publishing House, 1988), p. 351. See also Gershon Winkler, *The Golem of Prague* (New York: Judaica Press, 1980), especially pp. 17–48. (I am indebted to Dr. Steven Kramer for the suggestion that Blake may have been taking up the idea of the *golem*, and for supplying the latter reference.)

87. *Milton*, 19.14, p. 500.

88. Scholem, *Kabbalah*, p. 352. Scholem notes (p. 353) that the legend of the *golem* was linked, in Christian Kabbalism, to ideas concerning the creation of an alchemical man, the "homunculus" of Paracelsus. This may have been one route by which the notion reached Blake.

89. *Milton*, 40.4–5, p. 532.

90. *Milton*, 20.7–10, p. 502.

91. *The Book of Ahania*, 5.7, p. 254. (My italics.)

92. John Milton, *Selected Prose*, ed. C. A. Patrides (Harmondsworth: Penguin Books, 1974), pp. 235–36.

93. *Milton*, 23.47, p. 507. In *Areopagitica* John Milton put forward the view that the English Wycliffe, had he not been suppressed within his own country, might have become the great reformer of Europe:

And had it not bin the obstinat perversnes of our Prelats against the divine and admirable spirit of *Wicklef*, to suppresse him as a schismatic and *innovator*, perhaps neither the *Bohemian Husse* and *Jerom*, no nor the name of *Luther*, or of *Calvin* had bin ever known: the glory of reforming all our neighbours had bin compleatly ours. (*Selected Prose*, pp. 236–37)

Blake's point is that Milton's concept of religious "reformation" did not advance the cause of true "Redemption," serving only to sow "War and stern division between Papists & Protestants" (*Milton* 23.47–52, p. 507).

Northrop Frye had drawn attention to the relevance of this aspect of Milton's *Areopagitica* to Blake's *Milton* in *Fearful Symmetry*, p. 159. Harold Fisch develops Frye's insight in his essay "Blake's Miltonic Moment," in *William Blake: Essays for S. Foster Damon*, ed. Alvin H. Rosenfeld (Providence, R.I.: Brown University Press, 1969), pp. 45–49.

94. *Milton*, 22.50, p. 506; Erdman, *The Illuminated Blake*, p. 263.

95. Milton, *Selected Prose*, p. 234.

96. *Milton*, 25.68–70, p. 511; *The Marriage of Heaven and Hell*, pl. 27, p. 160.

97. Milton, *Selected Prose*, p. 234.

Chapter 6. Ololon II

1. *Milton*, 30.2–3, p. 518.
2. *Milton*, 2.2–5, p. 481.
3. *Milton*, 2.7–8, p. 481.
4. Blake, *Complete Poems*, p. 545.
5. Seymour Kirkup, an artist and friend of the Butts family who through this connection met Blake on many occasions, wrote that Mrs. Blake "told me seriously one day, 'I have very little of Mr. Blake's company; he is always in Paradise.'" (Letter to Lord Houghton, 25 March 1870; quoted by Bentley, *Blake Records*, p. 221.)
6. *Milton*, 30.14, p. 518.
7. *Milton*, 30.10–11, p. 518.
8. *Complete Poems*, p. 545.
9. *Milton*, 36.31–32, p. 527.
10. *Milton*, 18.43, p. 500.
11. Blake would have read chapter 34 of Isaiah in the original Hebrew text, which uses the name of the demon Lilith, the first wife of Adam according to Talmudic legend, in a prophecy that the land will become a wilderness. The Authorized Version translates the Hebrew noun *lilit* as "screech-owl" (the noun does have this sense as well):

> The wild beasts of the desert shall also meet with the wild beasts of the island, and the satyr shall cry to his fellow; the screech owl [*lilit*] shall also rest there, and find for herself a place of rest. (Isaiah 34.14)

Like the "Rahab" of Isaiah 27.1 and Psalms 89.9–10, with whom Blake must have associated her, the dwelling place of Lilith is at the bottom of the sea. See Gershom Scholem, *On The Kabbalah and Its Symbolism*, trans. Ralph Mannheim (New York: Schocken Books, 1965), p. 157, n. 4.

Northrop Frye, whose knowledge of the Bible approached the comprehensiveness of Blake's, mentioned the Lilith association in his "Notes for a Commentary on *Milton*," p. 116. Gershom Scholem discusses the "Lilith" tradition in *Kabbalah*, pp. 356–61, and *On the Kabbalah and Its Symbolism*, pp. 154–57.

12. *Milton*, 41.32–34, pp. 533–34.
13. *The Marriage of Heaven and Hell*, pl. 20, p. 157 (italics mine); *Milton*, 30.19, p. 519.
14. *Milton*, 30.19–23, p. 519. Frederick Tatham told Gilchrist that Mrs. Blake had spoken, after her husband's death, of the terrible force of his "very fierce inspirations, which were as if they would tear him asunder, while he was yielding himself to the Muse, . . . sketching and writing." Quoted by Bentley, *Blake Records*, n.1, p. 526.
15. *Milton*, 41.31, p. 533; 40.28–29, p. 532.
16. *Milton*, 30.15, p. 519; 30.1, 3, p. 518.
17. *Milton*, 1.13, p. 481.
18. *Milton*, 30.20, p. 519. I cannot agree with the generalization of Brenda S. Webster, that "Blake's only positive images of women are totally weak females sequestered in a separate realm called Beulah." See her "Blake, Women and Sexuality," in *Blake and the Argument of Method*, ed. Dan Miller, Mark Bracher, and Donald Ault (Durham, N.C.: Duke University Press, 1987), p. 210. Ololon seems to me to have, in every sense, a "positive image," and the main point of her role in *Milton*, as I read it, is that she does *not* remain "sequestered" in Beulah—which in any case is no "separate realm," but is conceived in intimate relationship with Eden, being "evermore Created around Eternity" (*Milton* 30.8, p. 518).
19. *Milton*, 22.37–38, p. 506.
20. *Milton*, 38.44, p. 530.
21. *Milton*, 22.44–45, p. 506.
22. *PL*, bk. 2, lines 746, 774–77, pp. 543–44.
23. *Europe*, 14.9, 12, p. 244.
24. *Milton*, 11.30, p. 492.
25. *Milton*, 11.36, 12.10, p. 492; 12.38, p. 493.
26. *Milton*, 12.14, 38–39, pp. 492–93; *PL*, bk. 2, lines 759–61, p. 544.
27. *Milton*, 11.35, p. 492.
28. *Milton*, 13.39, p. 494. Blake created Elynittria in *Europe* (8.4, p. 240). See my Chapter 4.
29. *Milton*, 13.40, p. 494.
30. *Milton*, 13.41–42, p. 494.
31. *Milton*, 38.15–27, p. 529; 40.17–22, p. 532. Leutha in her deceptively "varying" coloration and Rahab with her "Mystery" and malevolence are "negations" of Blake's "Jerusalem," who appears within the bosom of Albion in the transfiguring vision of Los in *Jerusalem*. See my Chapter 7.
32. *PL*, bk. 9, lines 953–54, p. 911.
33. *Milton*, 23.33, p. 507; 22.11–12, p. 505.
34. *Milton*, 22.13, p. 505.
35. "And his legs carried it like a long fork . . ."; *Complete Writings*, pp. 536–37.
36. *Milton*, 22.39, p. 506.
37. *Milton*, 22.41–42, 23.1–2, p. 506.
38. *Milton*, 22.45, p. 506; *FZ*, N1.302–11, p. 272.
39. *Milton*, 22.53–54, p. 506.
40. *Milton*, 23.35–38, p. 507.
41. Wordsworth, *National Independence and Liberty*, part 1, 14. "London, 1802," 11.1–2. William Wordsworth, *The Poetical Works*, ed. Ernest de Selincourt, rev. Helen Darbishire. 5 vols. Oxford: Oxford University Press, 1952–59, 3, p. 116.
42. *Milton*, 15.47–49, p. 497; 33.16, p. 522.
43. *Milton*, 15.51–52, 17.1–3, pp. 497–98.
44. *Milton*, 21.14–17, p. 503.
45. *Milton*, 21.15, p. 503.
46. Sandler, "The Iconoclastic Enterprise," p. 21.
47. Ibid. Sandler cites Thomas Vaughan's *Lumen de Lumine, or a New Magical Light*, ed. Arthur Edward Waite (1651; rpt., London [Watkins] 1910), pp. 7–8.
48. *PL*, bk. 3, lines 518–59, p. 592.
49. *Song of Los*, 7.38–39, p. 248.
50. *PL*, bk. 3, lines 519–22, p. 592.
51. *Milton*, 24.71, p. 510, *FZ*, N7.467, p. 332.
52. *Milton*, 21.16–17, p. 503.
53. *Milton*, 20.43–50, pp. 502–3.
54. *PL*, bk. 2, lines 539–41, p. 532.
55. Mary Lynn Johnson analyzes the responses of the Eternals to the Song of the Bard in *Milton* in "'Separating what has been Mixed: A Suggestion for a Perspective on *Milton*," *Blake Studies* 6 (1973): 11–17.
56. *Milton*, 21.17, p. 503.
57. *Milton*, 21.31–32, 45–46, p. 504.
58. *Milton*, 21.58–59, p. 505.
59. *Milton*, 22.3, p. 505.
60. *Milton*, 33.5–6, p. 522. It is surely significant that toward the climax of *Jerusalem*, when "England, who is Britannia" awakens from her death-sleep on the bosom of her husband, Albion, she cries in horror, "I have Slain him in my Sleep with the Knife of the Druid! . . . / O all ye Nations of the Earth, behold ye the Jealous Wife!" (*Jerusalem*, 94.20, 25–26, p. 742.)
61. *Milton*, 33.11–13, p. 522.
62. *Milton*, 33.14–16, p. 522.
63. *Milton*, 33.2, p. 522.
64. *Milton*, 33.18, 23, pp. 522–23. "Jerusalem is called Liberty among the Children of Albion." *Jerusalem*, 54.5, p. 684. See also *Jerusalem*, 26.3, p. 649.
65. Isaiah, 62.5–7.
66. *Milton*, 34.1–7, p. 523.
67. *Milton*, 34.8, p. 523.
68. *Milton*, 34.14, p. 523.
69. *Milton*, 34.14–15, p. 524.
70. *Milton*, 5.5–14, p. 484. (Composed 1815 or later; unique to Copy D.)
71. *PL*, bk. 12, lines 643–44, pp. 1059–60.

72. *Milton*, 35.32–34, p. 511.

73. *Milton*, 25.35–36, p. 511; 34.9–16, pp. 523–24. Sheila Spector glosses as follows the names of these four "states," with reference to John Parkhurst's *Hebrew and English Lexicon* . . . (London: 1762, 1778, 1792), which Blake may have used:

Alla, the next-to-highest state [to Beulah], resembles the traditional Hebrew verb "to ascend or mount upwards," while the Al of Al-Ulro, the state between the "ascending" Alla and the dreadful lower Or-Ulro, suggests Parkhurst's inventive transformation of the Hebrew *el* (meaning God) into "interposer, intervener," or in its verb form, "to interpose, intervene, . . . for protection. . . ." Finally, the prefix for Or-Ulro seems to be a combination of the traditional meaning of *or*, "light" ("the Or-Ulro & its fiery Gates"), and Parkhurst's more innovative coinage, "curse." Hence the "dreadful" fourth state.

See Spector, "Blake as an Eighteenth-Century Hebraist," pp. 226–27, n.49.

The "equivocal" nature of these interpretations supports the reading I have offered of the "Three Heavens of Beulah" as either places of "intoxicating delight" or of degradation and the virtual extinction of humanity, depending entirely on the condition and perspective of the observer.

74. *Milton*, 34.22, p. 524.

75. Jakob Boehme, *The Aurora*, trans. John Sparrow (London: John Watkins, 1960), chap. 2, par. 39, p. 57.

76. Reproduced in Raine, *Blake and Tradition*, 2:252–53.

77. *Milton*, 6.26, p. 486.

78. *PL*, bk. 10, lines 232–33, p. 937.

79. *Milton*, 34.23, p. 524.

80. *PL*, bk. 2, lines 894–96, 917–18, pp. 549–50.

81. *PL*, bk. 2, line 951, p. 552.

82. *Milton*, 39.52, p. 531; 26.18–20, p. 512.

83. *Milton*, 34.24–28, p. 524.

84. *Milton*, 34.29–30, p. 524.

85. The brook Arnon, dividing the Promised Land from the heathen kingdom to the south, runs into the Dead Sea, and is the setting for Milton's contest with Urizen (*Milton*, 19.3–7, p. 500). See Joshua 13.15–16.

86. *Milton*, 26.20, p. 512.

87. *Milton*, 34.44, p. 524; *PL*, bk. 2, lines 614–28, p. 536.

88. *Milton*, 35.7–8, p. 525. Blake recalled this image when he described his own body, emaciated by illness toward the end of his life, "being only bones & sinews, All strings & bobbins like a Weaver's Loom." (Letter to John Linnell, 1 August 1826, in *Complete Writings*, p. 875.)

89. *Milton*, 35.14, p. 525.

90. *Milton*, 35.26–33, p. 525.

91. Fox, *Poetic Form in Blake's "Milton,"* p. 151.

92. *Milton*, 35.36, p. 525; *PL*, bk. 10, lines 393–412, pp. 946–47. Wagenknecht develops this parallel in *Blake's Night*, pp. 252–53, but asserts that Ololon is "enacting the role of Sin and Death," whereas she is actually reversing or annulling their effects.

93. *Milton*, 35.20, 35, p. 525; *PL*, bk. 10, lines 304, 348, pp. 941, 944.

94. *Milton*, 34.24–28, p. 524; 35.22–25, p. 525.

95. *Milton*, 34.54, 67, p. 526.

96. *Milton*, 34.66–67, p. 526. Raine suggests the pun: "it is the wild *time*, the secret moment, that Blake means—the inspired, 'wild' moment 'that Satan cannot find'" (*Blake and Tradition*, 2:161). There may also be a parallel between Blake's "wild thyme" and the "mercurial fountain" of the "hieros gamos." See Chapter 5, n. 47.

97. David Fuller, *Blake's Heroic Argument* (London: Croom Helm, 1988), p. 163. Noting that "For Blake time and space are not absolutes exterior to the perceiving mind but relatives dependent on it," Fuller comments

all the work's shifting locations are . . . aspects of the one human-

divine imagination in which its central experience takes place. *Milton* records . . . a single moment of transcendent awareness, and all the events of the work are shown as taking place simultaneously in that moment of pure being.

98. *Milton*, 22.17, p. 505; 24.68, p. 509.

99. *A Vision of the Last Judgement*, in *Complete Writings*, p. 614.

100. *Milton*, 23.33, p. 507.

101. For the "hieros gamos," see Chapter 5, n. 47.

102. Elaine Kauvar, "Los's Messenger to Eden: Blake's Wild Thyme," *Blake Newsletter* 10 (1976): 82–84.

103. *Milton*, 42.30, p. 534.

104. Kauvar, "Los's Messenger," p. 84.

105. Raine mentions Milton's *L'Allegro* as a source for Blake's lark symbolism, adding "No doubt Blake also thought of Shakespeare's lark, which sings at 'heaven's gate'" (*Blake and Tradition*, 2:162). Blake's illustration of lines 41–44 of Milton's *L'Allegro*, "Night Startled by the Lark," seems also to draw on the Shakespearean lyric (Butlin, *Paintings*, cat. no. 543.2). Morton Paley had suggested the Shakespearean parallel in *Energy and the Imagination*, p. 248.

106. *Visions of the Daughters of Albion*, iii.5 and 1.3–10, p. 189. Raine descries echoes of the *Cymbeline* "Aubade" in both *Visions* and *Thel* (*Blake and Tradition*, 1:169). In her reading of Blake's *Comus* designs, Tayler draws attention to Blake's transformation of the healing herb called "haemony," with its "bright golden flower," offered by Milton's Attendant Spirit for "sovran use / 'Gainst all enchantments" (*Comus*, lines 628–40, pp. 206–8), to a symbol of similar significance to the "Marygold" of *Visions* (Tayler, "Blake's *Comus* Designs," p. 71).

107. "Joseph of Arimathea on the Rocks of Britain," Blake's earliet extant engraving, "done when I was a beginner at Basire's," is dated 1773 (Bindman, *Complete Graphic Works*, pl. 1). Blake sketched "Joseph of Arimathea Preaching to the People of Britain" ca. 1780, and painted at least two later versions of the scene (Butlin, *Paintings*, cat. nos. 76, 262.6, and 286). Dena Bain Taylor ("The Visual Context of 'Joseph of Arimathea among the Rocks of Albion,'" *Blake / An Illustrated Quarterly* 20 [Fall 1986]: 47–48) suggests that Blake's figure of Joseph of Arimathea was influenced by William Stukeley's rendition of a Druid sage in his account of Stonehenge (published 1740), which Blake appears to have known. Stukeley, who was "as greatly alarmed by the rise of Deism in eighteenth-century thought as Blake was later to be," represented the first Druids in Britain, who came "soon after Noah's flood," as proto-Christians, who because of their isolation in Britain "maintained the true traditions of the patriarchal religion intact." Blake's version of the figure made his Joseph "a British Druid." Taylor concludes that "the Christianity which Blake's Joseph brings, embodied in the imagination of the artist, thus represents the forgiveness of sins given again to a land which had known and forgotten it." The implied association of Joseph of Arimathea with "Luvah's tomb" in *Milton* may thus be another appearance of its theme of "forgiveness."

108. *Milton*, 14.40, p. 496.

109. *Cymbeline*, 2.5 lines 11–13, p. 12.11. There is a real, though indefinable, relationship between the plot of *Cymbeline* and Blake's *Notebook* poem associated with *Milton*, "My Spectre around me night & day . . ." (written on a page on which Blake had already sketched a version of the motif inspired by the simile used by Milton's enchanter for the Lady's virginal state of paralysis in lines 660–61 of *Comus*, "As Daphne was Rootbound . . . ,"). See especially the (deleted) stanza

Thou hast parted from my side
Once thou wast a virgin bride
Never shalt thou a [lover *del.*] true love find
My Spectre follows thee Behind
(lines 9–12, in *Complete Writings*, p. 415)

Did Blake perceive Imogen's thwarted bridegroom "Posthumus" as a "Spectre?"

110. *Cymbeline* 2.3, lines 11–13, p. 1207.

111. *Cymbeline* 2.3, lines 14–16, p. 1207.

112. *Milton*, 36.27–28, p. 527. In addressing Ololon as "Virgin of Providence," Blake may be anticipating that her mission will have a negative effect comparable to that of the "Angels of Providence" who guard the sickbed of "William Bond," spreading over him a "Black, Black Cloud" of baleful and paralyzing influence. ("William Bond," lines 13–16, p. 435.) This association may lead the poet to expect Ololon "again to plunge [him] into deeper affliction." (*Milton*, 36.30, p. 527.) On the contrary, the "Clouds of Ololon" prove to be the means of visionary enlightenment.

113. *Milton*, 36.31–32, p. 527.

114. Isaiah 62.1 and 4.

115. Gilchrist, 1863; p. 317; quoted in Bentley, *Blake Records*, p. 526, n. 1.

116. "William Bond" declares in the poem in the *Pickering Ms.* by that name (*Complete Works*, pp. 434–36) that he rejects his betrothed Mary Green—

> ". . . Another I will have for my Wife;
> "Then what have I to do with thee?
>
> "For thou art Melancholy Pale,
> "And on thy Head is the cold Moon's shine,
> "But she is ruddy & bright as day,
> "And the sun beams dazzle from her eyne."

(lines 27–32)

Mary swoons away, then awakens in bed "On the Right hand of her William dear." (line 38) The "Fairies" symbolizing William's inspiration (cf. the "Fairy" who dictates *Europe* [*Europe*, pl. iii, pp. 237–38]), who had been driven away from him by "Angels of Providence" when he went to church, reappear dancing "around [Mary's] Shining Head" upon the pillow. Her luminosity is evidently a sign that William's inspiration has been renewed through her, for he concludes

> I thought Love liv'd in the hot sun shine,
> But O, he lives in the Moony light!

(lines 45–46)

The poem strongly suggests the relationship of "Beulah" to "Eden" in *Milton*, and hints at the identification of Enitharmon with Luna in its "Moon" imagery. The association of the "Fairies" of creative insight with the "Shining Head" of William's true and faithful love gives it a parallel with the recognition and the recovery to "brightness" of Blake's "Shadow of Delight" in *Milton*.

117. *Milton*, 37.2–3, p. 527.

118. *Milton*, 37.5, p. 527.

119. *Milton*, 38.7, p. 529.

120. *Milton*, 39.59, p. 532.

121. *Milton*, 40.8, p. 523.

122. *Milton*, 40.11–13, p. 532.

123. *Milton*, 40.14, 17, and 19, p. 532.

124. *Milton*, 41.25–26, p. 533.

125. *Milton*, 34.23, p. 524; 40.26–27, p. 532.

126. *Milton*, 41.36, p. 534.

127. *Milton*, 42.11–12, p. 534.

128. The garment was partly inspired by the "bloody cloth" brandished by Imogen's husband Posthumus as a sign that she had been put to death (as he believed) at his command, for supposedly yielding to seduction. (*Cymbeline* 3.4, lines 123–25, p. 1217, and 5.1, lines 1–5, p. 1228.) Essick relates the blood-stained garment of Blake's Savior to the account given on plate 24 of *Milton* of the biblical Joseph, "an infant, / Stolen from his nurse's cradle, wrap'd in needle-

work / Of emblematic texture . . ." (24.17–19, p. 508). Essick concludes that "the 'Garment dipped in blood' resonates typologically with the account of Joseph's coat in Genesis 37, 31, but its written character also connects it to the emblematic cloth in Blake's rendering of the Joseph story on Plate 24 of *Milton* and to their shared antithesis, the garment of signs and lamentations woven by the Shadowy Female on Plate 18." Essick, *William Blake and the Language of Adam*, pp. 201–2.

129. *Milton*, 42.2, p. 534.

130. *Milton*, 35.24, p. 525.

131. *Milton*, 42.13–15, p. 534.

132. Essick, *William Blake and the Language of Adam*, p. 201. Hayley, Blake's patron at Felpham, regarded his protégé as a skilled engraver, but did not take his poetry seriously. Blake's assertion in his letter to Thomas Butts of 6 July 1803 is relevant:

> I am determined to be no longer Pester'd with [Hayley's] Genteel Ignorance & Polite Disapprobation. I know myself both Poet & Painter, & it is not his affected Contempt that can move me to anything but a more assiduous pursuit of both Arts. (*Complete Writings*, p. 825)

133. Essick, *William Blake and the Language of Adam*, pp. 201–2.

134. *Milton*, 42.15, p. 534.

135. *Milton*, 1.9–10, 13, p. 481.

136. *Milton*, 21.33, p. 504.

137. See Erdman's commentary to plate 36 of *Jerusalem; The Illuminated Blake*, p. 315.

138. *FZ*, N7.439–52, p. 331.

139. *Milton*, 13.41–44, p. 494; 18.40, p. 500.

140. *Milton*, 42.33, p. 535.

141. See Chapter 5, n.47.

142. Letter to Thomas Butts, 2 October 1800; lines 3–6, in *Complete Writings*, p. 806.

143. Blake sent respectfully formal "Love" to the wife of his faithful patron in most of his extant letters to her husband, frequently joining his wife's name with his own. Sir Geoffrey Keynes conjectured that Mrs. Butts had fallen in love with Blake ca. 1793 (on the evidence of a poem entitled "The Phoenix to Mrs. Butts," first published posthumously by Keynes in the *Times Literary Supplement* in 1984). But there seems no particular reason for this explanation of the relationship between Blake and the "Wife of the friend of those I most revere . . ." (Blake had addressed Butts at the head of the letter as "Friend of Religion & Order," p. 804). See Blake, *The Complete Poems*, ed. Stevenson, pp. 477–78.

144. See Chapter 5, n.47.

145. *Milton*, 43, p. 535; Erdman, *The Illuminated Blake*, p. 266.

146. John E. Grant, "The Female Awakening at the End of Blake's *Milton*: A Picture Story, with Questions," in *Milton Reconsidered: Essays in Honor of Arthur E. Barker*, ed. John Karl Franson, Salzburg Studies in English Literature: Elizabethan and Renaissance Studies 49 (Salzburg: Institüt für Englische Sprache und Literatur, 1976), p. 87.

147. See Chapter 4.

Chapter 7. The Woman Jerusalem

1. *FZ*, N9.221–23, pp. 362–63. The subject of this chapter is distinct from that of David M. Wyatt's essay, "The Woman Jerusalem: *Pictura* versus *Poesis*," *Blake Studies* 7 (1975): 105–24, which focuses on what Wyatt perceives as a dynamic relationship of conflict between text and illustrations in *Jerusalem*. Wyatt distinguishes between the image of Jerusalem as seen respectively by Los and by Albion: to Los she is a "liberating woman," to Albion "an image of entrapment, a femme fatale . . . a siren" (p. 108). He concludes that the final identity of Jerusalem as a "liberating woman" derives from Blake's vision of her "holding

history and apocalypse together in suspension" (p. 123). Jerusalem, Wyatt writes,

> becomes the central locus of this relationship by balancing the Albion and Los perspective against each other, as well as by creating a tension between *Jerusalem*'s poetry and illustrations that finally brings them closer together. (p. 123)

In the course of the closer and more localized focus of my own treatment of "the Woman Jerusalem," I examine in detail the relationship of one important illustration, a figure on the title page, to Los's apocalyptic vision of Jerusalem in his "Watch Song" near the end of the work. My exploration suggests that in this significant and possibly exceptional instance the visual and textual images extend and support one another rather than conflicting as "contraries."

2. *Jerusalem*, 97.1–2, p. 745.

3. *Milton*, 1.13–16, p. 481.

4. Hazard Adams, "Blake, *Jerusalem*, and Symbolic Form," *Blake Studies* 7 (1975): 149–50.

5. Morton Paley usefully summarises Blake's probable models for the "New Jerusalem" in *The Continuing City: William Blake's "Jerusalem"* (Oxford: Clarendon Press, 1983), pp. 136–66.

6. Letter to Thomas Butts, 25 April 1803, in *Complete Writings*, p. 822.

7. Spenser, *Prothalamion*, line 128, in *Poetical Works* p. 602; Letter to Thomas Butts, 25 April 1803, in *Complete Writings*, p. 822.

8. *Prothalamion*, line 129, p. 602.

9. *Milton*, 24.50, p. 509.

10. *The Continuing City*, p. 136.

11. John 19.17; *Songs of Experience*, "London," line 8, p. 216.

12. *Jerusalem*, 12.24–29, 43, pp. 631–32. For a thought-provoking analysis of the design that runs the length of this passage, see Irene H. Chayes, "The Marginal Design on *Jerusalem* 12," *Blake Studies* 7, no. 1 (1974): 51–77. Chayes relates the uppermost figure in the margin of this plate, an elaborately dressed female, to a line in the text beside it in which Los speaks of "Giving a body to Falsehood that it may be cast off for ever" (*Jerusalem*, 12.13). The lower group of a male and a female figure separated by a globe of the world she identifies as an image of the dialectical conflict of Reason (the upper, compass-wielding male figure) with Desire, a clothed female figure "trying to rise out of her grave by her own effort . . . yet in reaching toward joy she is actually aspiring to the delusive heaven of Reason, located in the north where Reason himself is being drawn down" (p. 75). The marginal design is thus partly of local significance to the text on that plate, and partly of wider application to the theme of Los/Blake's lifelong "building of Golgonooza."

13. Mollyanne Marks, "Self-sacrifice: Theme and Image in *Jerusalem*," *Blake Studies* 7 (1974): 33.

14. Erdman (*Blake: Prophet against Empire*, p. 474, n. 4) quotes Charles Knight's description of the squatters around Paddington from M. D. George, *London Life in the 18th Century* (Harmondsworth, Middlesex: Penguin Books, 1966), p. 115.

15. *Blake: Prophet against Empire*, p. 474.

16. Stevenson edition of Blake's *Complete Poems*, 2d ed. (1989); p. 652, note to *Jerusalem*, 12.26; *Europe*, 14.1, p. 243.

17. *Jerusalem*, 12.26–27, p. 632.

18. *Europe*, 14.5, p. 243.

19. *PL*, bk. 3, lines 30–31, p. 562.

20. *Jerusalem*, 34[30].31–33, p. 661. See discussion of Blake's representation of the feminine "sanctum sanctorum" in Chapter 3.

21. Stanley Gardner notes that during the years of *Jerusalem*'s composition "John Nash was opening the way between Westminster and his mansions in Regent's Park by building Regent Street along the mean line of ancient Swallow Street. . . . [This] vast undertaking in dusty demolition and construction went on a

few yards east of Blake's home" (*Blake* [London: Evans Brothers, 1968], p. 141). Quoting Blake's approval of the buildings going up in the wastes of Paddington, Gardner records that "the Grand Junction Canal ended in Paddington Basin, where crowds of casual labourers found work, and John Nash was busy extending the canal through Marylebone, and round his Park. The Regent's Canal was finished in 1820. To the west, Nash's 'golden Builders' were working over the 'mighty Ruin' of Tyburn" (p. 143). Gardner comments that "In writing of Jerusalem, [Blake] demands a rebuilding of the city. . . . When he writes of . . . 'golden builders' he is looking at the whole development that seemed to be transforming suburban villages, royal domains and waste lands into a Jerusalem, while *Jerusalem* was being written" (p. 144).

22. Milton, *Areopagitica* (1644), in *Selected Prose*, p. 239.

23. Milton, *The Readie and Easy Way to Establish a Free Commonwealth* (1660), in *Selected Prose*, p. 357.

24. *The Readie & Easy Way to Establish a Free Commonwealth*, in *Selected Prose*, p. 358. Milton's phrase and image, and his disgust, are recalled in Blake's conclusion to *The First Book of Urizen*, in which the "remaining children of Urizen," dissociating themselves from those of their brethren who have succumbed to the tyranny of their despotic parent, "left the pendulous earth. / They called it Egypt, & left it" (*Urizen*, 28.20–22, p. 237). ("The pendulous earth" is also Milton's "pendent world," about to be invaded by Satan in *PL*, bk. 2, lines 1051–55, pp. 557–58.)

Milton's nephew Edward Phillips, refuting the charges of those of his uncle's adversaries who "[took] occasion of imputing his blindness as a Judgement upon him for his answering of the King's Book" [the *Eikon Basilike* of King Charles I, published posthumously in 1649, to which Milton had replied immediately in his *Eikonoklastes*], asserted that Milton's sight, "what with his continual Study . . . had been decaying for above a dozen years before . . ." (*Selected Prose*, pp. 392–93).

25. John 1.23; Isaiah 40.3.

26. *Jerusalem* 54.1–5, p. 684. Cf. Joanne Witke, *William Blake's Epic: Imagination Unbound* (London: Croom Helm, 1986), p. 142:

> Every work [of art] is a unique expression of the artist's vision, an effect of spiritual perception. This source cut off by Albion's sons "is Jerusalem in every Man" and "is called Liberty among the Children of Albion" because spirit is free. Blake's concept of liberty, therefore, goes beyond practical freedom from bondage of thought and action; it has a metaphysical meaning in Berkeley's sense of a causal principle. Berkeley insisted upon innate human liberty because it concerns moral accountability: unless man be a free agent, he is not answerable for his acts.

For an assessment of parallels between Berkeley's thought and Blake's, see Kathleen Raine's essay, "Berkeley, Blake and the New Age," in *Blake and the New Age* (London: George Allen & Unwin, 1979), pp. 151–79.

27. *Jerusalem*, 85.10–13, p. 730; 95.20, p. 742.

28. *Jerusalem*, 85.26–27, p. 730.

29. *Selected Prose*, p. 237. The title "Mansion House" has a special sense in the City of London as that of the official residence of its Lord Mayor. This application was probably in use in Milton's lifetime. See *OED*, s.v. "Mansion-house," c.

30. *PL*, bk. 12, lines 524–26, p. 1053. Milton writes in this passage of a corrupt church that assumes "secular power, though feigning still to act / By spiritual," taking by force "the spirit of grace itself, and bind[ing] / His consort liberty" (*PL*, bk. 12, lines 515–26). Obviously Milton refers in part to the contemporary political situation of his own lifetime, expressing his disappointment in his own countrymen, in that they acquiesce to a church of which the secular monarch is the head. But Milton was certainly aware that the name John—his own given name and that of both the Baptist and the Evangelist—is a contraction of the Hebrew "Yochanan," meaning "God is gracious." The consorting of "liberty" with "the spirit of grace" can thus be seen,

at one level, as the symbolic espousal of liberty as a redemptive cause by three successive prophetic figures, all bearing a name that declares the grace of God, each crying out in the wilderness. Blake too may have perceived this level of association.

31. *FZ*, N1.30, p. 265.

32. *PL*, bk. 9, lines 1054–55, p. 917.

33. Wilkie and Johnson, *Blake's Four Zoas*, p. 46.

34. *Songs of Experience*, "Earth's Answer," line 6, p. 211.

35. This verse of Isaiah is illustrated on plate 92 of *Jerusalem*. Erdman, *The Illuminated Blake*, p. 371.

36. *L'Allegro*, lines 35–36, p. 134. Milton may have been referring to the mountainous republics of ancient Greece; or to Switzerland, an Alpine country that had long been a democracy; or, perhaps simultaneously, to Geneva, a city lying between two mountain ranges, from which had emanated the religious reforms of Jean Calvin.

37. Blake's twelve illustrations to *L'Allegro* and *Il Pensoroso* are in the Pierpont Morgan Library, New York.

38. Butlin, *Paintings*, pl. 672, cat. no. 543.1.

39. See discussion of this verse of Isaiah in relation to Ololon in Chapter 6.

40. *Milton*, 33.21–23, p. 523.

41. *Jerusalem*, 26.3, p. 649, and 54.5, p. 684.

42. *Jerusalem*, 54.2–3, p. 684.

43. *FZ*, N9.222, p. 362.

44. The coloration of this plate in the only complete colored copy, E, is described by Erdman as "the rainbow's seven sevenfold" (*The Illuminated Blake*, p. 282).

45. *Complete Works*, p. 649.

46. Scholem, *Kabbalah*, p. 130.

47. Scholem, *Kabbalah*, p. 137.

48. Sheila A. Spector, "Kabbalistic Sources—Blake's and His Critics,'" *Blake / An Illustrated Quarterly* 17 (1983–84): 84–101. Harper acknowledges that Blake "is conscious of the occult tradition surrounding Adam Kadmon," but attributes the line "But now the Starry Heavens are fled . . ." (*Jerusalem* 27, p. 649) to Blake's "remembrance of the physiological charts of the Divine Man in William Law's *Boehme*." See George Mills Harper, "The Odyssey of the Soul in Blake's *Jerusalem*," *Blake Studies* 5 (1974): 69, n.9.

49. See Peter Fisher's comprehensive article, "Blake and the Druids," *Journal of English and Germanic Philology* 58 (1959): 589–612.

50. *Jerusalem*, pl. 27, p. 649. Henry Rowlands, *Mona Antiqua Restaurata: An Archaeological Discourse on the Antiquities, Natural and Historical, of the ISLE OF ANGLESEY, the Ancient Seat of the British Druids*, 2d ed. (London, 1766), pp. 45–46. (For Blake's use of this work, see Taylor, "The Visual Context of 'Joseph of Arimathea among the Rocks of Albion.'")

51. Scholem, *Kabbalah*, p. 137.

52. Joseph Anthony Wittreich, Jr., "Painted Prophecies: The Tradition of Blake's Illuminated Books," in *Blake in His Time*, ed. Robert N. Essick and Donald Pearce (Bloomington: Indiana University Press, 1978), p. 111.

53. *Jerusalem*, 27, p. 649. The refrain is first heard in *Milton*, 6.26, p. 486, and is repeated in *Jerusalem*, 70.32, p. 709 and 75.27, p. 716.

54. *Jerusalem*, 85.10–12, p. 730.

55. *Jerusalem*, 85.22–5, 86.1–32, pp. 730–31.

56. The first part of the name is derived in traditional Christian etymologies either from *ro-EH*, meaning "to see," hence "vision," or from *ir*, "a city"; the second element comes from *shalom*, meaning "peace."

57. *Jerusalem*, 86.17–18, p. 731; Joshua 18.1.

58. Blake also identified Shiloh with France, since although England was at war with France, the ideal of both nations was actually peace, as the common source of both names suggests: "Lo, Shiloh dwells over France, as Jerusalem dwells over Albion." *Jerusalem*, 49.48, p. 680. See Damon, *Dictionary*, p. 371.

59. John 11.54.

60. *Jerusalem*, 86.26–32, p. 731.

61. *Jerusalem*, 85.23, p. 730.

62. *PL*, bk. 3, lines 505–7, p. 591.

63. *PL*, bk. 3, lines 572, 595, pp. 596, 598.

64. *PL*, bk. 5, line 460, p. 703.

65. *PL*, bk. 5, lines 248–50, p. 689.

66. *PL*, bk. 5, lines 270–74, pp. 690–91.

67. The details of Raphael's appearance come probably from the description of the phoenix in the *Historia Naturalis* of the Roman naturalist Pliny the Elder. See Fowler's editorial note to *PL* bk. 5, lines 277–85, pp. 691–92.

68. "When thou seest an Eagle, thou seest a portion of Genius; lift up thy head!" (*The Marriage of Heaven and Hell*, 9.15, p. 152). The image of the Eagle of Genius appears as an interlinear symbol throughout all Blake's illuminated books. The attendant form covering her face in mourning at the feet of the title page "Jerusalem" has eagle wings. The Phoenix also appears as an interlinear symbol, for instance on pl. 17 of *The Marriage of Heaven and Hell* (Erdman, *The Illuminated Blake*, p. 114).

69. *Jerusalem*, 86.2–3, p. 730.

70. See Fowler's note to *PL*, bk. 5, lines 270–74 in his edition of *Paradise Lost*, pp. 690–91. Fowler refers to Guy de Tervarent, "Attributs et symboles dans l'art profane 1450–1600," *Travaux d'humanisme et renaissance* 29 (1958): 304–5.

71. *Jerusalem*, 86.4–5, 10, pp. 730–31.

72. *Jerusalem*, 86.18, p. 731; *PL*, bk. 4, lines 218–20, pp. 622–23; bk. 5, line 652, p. 717. See also Milton's *Lycidas*, lines 172–77, p. 253.

73. *Jerusalem*, 86.23–5, p. 731.

74. *Jerusalem*, 86.17–18, p. 731.

75. "The Canonisation," lines 23–27. John Donne, *The Complete English Poems*, ed. A. J. Smith (Harmondsworth: Penguin Books, 1971), p. 47.

76. *PL*, bk. 8, lines 618–28, pp. 848–49.

77. *Jerusalem*, 69.34, 40, p. 708. The Miltonic parallel with Blake's lines was pointed out by Harold Bloom in *Blake's Apocalypse*, pp. 456–57.

78. *Jerusalem*, 69.43–44, p. 708.

79. *PL*, bk. 5, lines 276–87, pp. 691–92.

80. *PL*, bk. 5, line 468, p. 704.

81. *PL*, bk. 7, lines 363–65, pp. 795–96; bk. 5, line 281, p. 692.

82. Raphael explains the process in reverse in *PL*, bk. 5, lines 496–500, pp. 706–7. Donne refers to the principle in "Air and Angels":

> . . . an angel, face and wings
> Of air, not pure as it, yet pure doth wear . . .
> (lines 23–24, *The Complete English Poems*, p. 41)

83. *PL*, bk. 9, lines 424–33, p. 881.

84. *PL*, bk. 9, lines 457–58, pp. 883–84.

85. *PL*, bk. 5, lines 250, 286, pp. 689, 692; bk. 9, line 425, p. 881.

86. *PL*, bk. 9, line 429, p. 881.

87. *PL*, bk. 9, lines 426–27, 429, p. 881; *OED*, s.v. "Carnation" 2 B adj. a. (obs.), and "Carnationed" b.

88. *PL*, bk. 5, line 281, p. 692.

89. *Jerusalem*, 86.18–21; here quoted from Erdman, *The Illuminated Blake*, p. 365. The rainbow coloration of Jerusalem in "eternity" contrasts positively with the evanescent rainbow hues of the deceitful Leutha in *Milton*, 11.32 and 12.14–15, p. 492.

90. *PL*, bk. 5, line 652, p. 717; Revelation 21.10–11.

91. *PL*, bk. 7, lines 247–49, pp. 789–90.

92. Joanne Witke proposed the synoptic vision of the four Gospels as a structural model for *Jerusalem* as a whole in her essay "*Jerusalem*: A Synoptic Poem," *Comparative Literature* 22 (1970): 265–78, expanding the theory in her book *William Blake's Epic: Imagination Unbound*.

93. *PL*, bk. 11, lines 892–93, 900–1, p. 1026. Milton's ac-

count of the Flood and the Covenant between God and Noah symbolized by the Rainbow is lengthy and significant, bringing to a climax the first phase of Michael's narration to Adam of the history of mankind.

94. *Jerusalem*, 94.18, p. 742.

95. *Jerusalem*, 86.2, 85.24, p. 730.

96. *Jerusalem*, 86.8–10, p. 731; Job 28.18; Proverbs 3.15, and 8.11; Proverbs 31.10.

97. *PL*, bk. 3, lines 593–98, p. 598. Milton's "ruby" is a gloss of "sardius," one of the stones of the breastplate of Aaron, (Exodus 28.17) and one of the foundations of the New Jerusalem (Revelation 21.20).

David Fuller, (*Blake's Heroic Argument*, pp. 213–14), noting parallels between the "Watch Song" of *Jerusalem* pls.85–86 and the passages of Exodus (chaps. 28 and 39) describing the priestly vestments of Aaron, comments:

> Blake wants none of the vestments' associations with priestcraftly ritual and legalism. It is the jewels that interest him. In *Exodus* they each signify one of the twelve tribes: in the context of the parallels established between Britain and Israel the jewels are symbols of England's spiritual potential.

98. *PL*, bk. 8, line 619, p. 848. Milton's angel does not blush in embarrassment, but rather shows the "proper hue" of a cherub, traditionally fiery-faced from the exercise of zeal in loving and praising God and performing his will. Cf. the "fiery red" faces of the angelic guard at *PL*, bk. 4, line 978, p. 669.

99. *PL*, bk. 9, lines 460–61, p. 884. See discussion of the passage in Chapter 1.

100. *PL*, bk. 9, lines 489–91, pp. 885–86.

101. *Jerusalem*, 86.14–16, p. 731.

Conclusion: Albion's Bow

In the revision of this chapter, I am especially indebted to Ms. Joan Bellis, who has given me the benefit of her scholarship in feminist criticism and critical theory. However, I alone must be held culpable for the views expressed here.

1. *Jerusalem*, 92.6–14, p. 739.

2. *Jerusalem*, 97.3, 96.41–42, p. 744.

3. *Jerusalem*, 96.42–43, 97.1–2, 5–6, p. 744.

4. *Jerusalem*, 97.6–7, p. 744.

5. *Jerusalem*, 97.7, p. 744.

6. *Jerusalem*, 97.7–9, p. 744.

7. *Europe*, 3.11–12, p. 239.

8. *Songs of Innocence*: "Night," line 40, p. 119; *Jerusalem*, 95.16–17, p. 742.

9. *Europe*, 8.5, p. 240; *Comus*, lines 440–45, p. 198.

10. *Jerusalem*, 97.3, p. 744; 95.2, 5, p. 742.

11. *Jerusalem*, 97.10, p. 744.

12. *"Exegi monumentum aere perennius"* (My work is done, a memorial more enduring than brass): Horace, *Odes*, 3, 30.1.

13. When Man rises, regenerated by Revolution, "his feet become like brass" (*America*, 8.16, p. 199). But in the fallen condition, brass is the metal of tyranny. Cf. the fallen Urizen's "Book / Of eternal brass, written in my solitude," which constrains human society to

> "One command, one joy, one desire,
> "One curse, one weight, one measure,
> "One King, one God, one Law."
>   (*Urizen* 4.31–33, 38–40, p. 224)

See Damon, *Dictionary*, s.v. "Brass," p. 58.

14. *Jerusalem*, 97.11, p. 744.

15. *Jerusalem*, 85.10, 86.35–8, pp. 730–31.

16. *FZ*, N6.268–69, p. 318.

17. *FZ*, N7.449, 453, 456–58, p. 331.

18. *Jerusalem* 97.12–15, p. 744.

19. Donne, "The Canonisation," line 25, in *The Complete English Poems*, p. 47. See Chapter 7.

20. Ben F. Nelms, "'Exemplars of Memory and of Intellect': *Jerusalem*, Plates 96–100," *Blake Studies* 5, no. 2 (1974): 83. Nelms notes that the regenerated hand of Albion corresponds to "Hand" who is the eldest son of the fallen Albion. E. J. Rose describes the fallen "Hand" as "the perverted instrument through which man communicates physically . . . the hand of death, of punishment, of oppression." (E. J. Rose, "Blake's Hand: Symbol and Design in *Jerusalem*," *Texas Studies in Literature and Language* 6 (1964): 51.)

21. *Jerusalem*, 92.8, 11–12, p. 739; *PL*, bk. 9, lines 827–30, p. 904.

22. Diana Hume George, "'Is She Also the Divine Image?': Feminine Form in the Art of William Blake," *Centennial Review* 22 (1979): 138. George adds:

> To "know" good and evil—that is, to separate them—can be sterile and unproductive, but it can also serve as the means of uncovering the veil of mystery. Eve is indeed the Female Will, hungry for dominion and about to ruin herself and man. But she is also Oothoon to Adam's Thel. (pp. 138–39)

23. *PL*, bk. 4, line 635, p. 650; *Jerusalem*, 92.12, p. 739.

24. *Jerusalem*, 92.13–14, p. 739.

25. *Milton*, 16.1, p. 497.

26. *Jerusalem*, 94.18, p. 742.

27. *Jerusalem*, 86.2, p. 730.

28. *FZ*, N7:402, 408–9, p. 330. A male without a female counterpart is one of those "artefacts of division which Blake calls 'negations,' for since negations lack a true opposite, they are inert and incapable of reunion into a higher organization." (M. H. Abrams, *Natural Supernaturalism* [New York: W. W. Norton, 1971], p. 260.)

29. Alicia Ostriker, "Desire Gratified and Ungratified: William Blake and Sexuality," *Blake / An Illustrated Quarterly* 16 (1982–83): 163.

30. Anne K. Mellor, "Blake's Portrayal of Women," *Blake / An Illustrated Quarterly* 16 (1982–83): 148, 153.

31. *OED*, s.v. "Man" I.1. In the headnote to this entry the root of the word "man" is referred to the Indogermanic word meaning "to think," "so that the primary meaning of the sb. would refer to intelligence as the distinctive characteristic of human beings as contrasted with brutes."

32. Mellor, "Blake's Portrayal of Women," p. 154.

33. Webster, "Blake, Women and Sexuality," pp. 210, 222.

34. Examples of androgynous figures are the angel on the plate of "The Little Boy Found," the figure rising regenerated from flames on pl. 3 of *The Marriage of Heaven and Hell*, the figure of the Soul in its union with God on pl. 99 of *Jerusalem*. The archangel Raphael, as depicted in Blake's painting "Raphael Warns Adam and Eve," can be seen as delicately androgyne. See Chapter 7.

35. *Jerusalem*, 36.58–60, p. 668. Anne Mellor, arguing that "A writer who wished to portray a truly androgynous creature or society would have to transform the language we use" ("Blake's Portrayal of Woman," p. 154), quotes this example from Marge Piercy's *A Woman on the Edge of Time* (New York: Alfred Knopf, 1976).

36. Chaucer, "Wife of Bath's Prologue," *Canterbury Tales*, D 158–62, p. 567.

37. Frederick Tatham, *Life of Blake* (1832): quoted by Bentley, *Blake Records*, p. 526, n. 1. Seymour Kirkup commented "His excellent old wife was a sincere believer in all his visions. . . . She prepared his colours and was as good as a servant." (Bentley, *Blake Records*, p. 221.)

38. *Milton*, 36.29–32, p. 527.

39. Letter to William Hayley, 24 October 1804, in *Complete Writings,* p. 852.

40. Ibid., pp. 851–52.

41. *Jerusalem,* 88.16–21, p. 733; *FZ,* N3.106, p. 294; N4.129–32, p. 301.

42. *FZ,* N3.110–11, 150–52, pp. 294, 295–56.

43. *FZ,* N4.137–40, p. 301.

44. *FZ,* N3.149, p. 295.

45. The proverb in this form is attributed to William Ross Wallace (d. 1881), in *John o' London's Treasure Trove.* (*The Oxford Dictionary of Quotations,* 2d ed. [London: Oxford University Press, 1953], p. 557.) *Jerusalem,* 34[30].25–26, p. 661.

46. Susan Fox, "The Female as Metaphor in William Blake's Poetry," *Critical Inquiry* 3 (1976–77): 507.

47. Ibid., pp. 507, 516.

48. Fox, *Poetic Form in Blake's "Milton."*

49. *An Island in the Moon,* "Hail Matrimony, made of Love . . . ," lines 7–12, p. 56.

50. *PL,* bk. 4, lines 750–75, pp. 658–60.

51. David Aers, "William Blake and the Dialectics of Sex," *ELH* 44 (1977): 512.

52. *Jerusalem,* 98.39–40, p. 746.

Bibliography

Abrams, M. H. *The Mirror and the Lamp*. New York: Oxford University Press, 1953.

———. *Natural Supernaturalism*. New York: W. W. Norton, 1971.

Ackland, Michael. "The Embattled Sexes: Blake's Debt to Wollstonecraft in *The Four Zoas*." *Blake / An Illustrated Quarterly* 16 (1982–83): 172–83.

Adams, Hazard. "Blake, *Jerusalem*, and Symbolic Form." *Blake Studies* 7 (1975): 143–66.

Aers, David. "William Blake and the Dialectics of Sex." *ELH* 44 (1977): 500–14.

Aubrey, Bryan. *Watchmen of Eternity: Blake's Debt to Jacob Boehme*. Lanham, Md.: University Press of America, 1986.

Ault, Donald. *Narrative Unbound: Revisioning William Blake's The Four Zoas*. Barrytown, N.Y.: Station Hill Press, 1987.

Bailey, Margaret L. *Milton and Jakob Boehme: A Study of Mysticism in Seventeenth Century England*. New York: Oxford University Press, 1914.

Behrendt, Stephen C. *The Moment of Explosion: Blake and the Illustration of Milton*. Lincoln: University of Nebraska Press, 1983.

Bentley, G. E. *Blake Records*. Oxford: Clarendon Press, 1969.

———. *William Blake's "Vala or The Four Zoas": A Facsimile of the Manuscript, a Transcript of the Poem and a Study of Its Growth and Significance*. Oxford: Clarendon Press, 1963.

Bindman, David. *The Complete Graphic Works of William Blake*. London: Thames and Hudson, 1978.

Blake, William. *Blake's "America: A Prophecy" and "Europe: A Prophecy."* New York: Dover Publications, 1983.

———. *The Book of Urizen*. Edited and with a commentary by Kay Parkhurst Easson and Roger R. Easson. London: Thames and Hudson, 1979.

———. *The Complete Poems*. Edited by W. H. Stevenson. 2d ed. London: Longman Group, 1989.

———. *Complete Writings*. Edited by Geoffery Keynes. London: Oxford University Press, 1972.

———. *The Illuminated Blake*. Annotated by David V. Erdman. London: Oxford University Press, 1975.

———. *Milton*. Edited and with a commentary by K. P. Easson and R. R. Easson. London: Thames and Hudson, 1979.

———. *The Notebook of William Blake*. A photographic and typographic facsimile edited by David V. Erdman with the assistance of Donald K. Moore. Oxford: Clarendon Press, 1973.

Blamires, Harry. *Milton's Creation: A Guide through "Paradise Lost."* London: Methuen, 1971.

Bloom, Harold. *Blake's Apocalypse: A Study in Poetic Argument*. Garden City, N.Y.: Doubleday, 1965.

———. *Kabbalah and Criticism*. New York: Seabury Press, 1975.

———. *The Visionary Company*. Revised and enlarged edition. Ithaca, N.Y.: Cornell University Press, 1971.

Boehme ["Behmen"], Jacob. *The Aurora*. Translated by John Sparrow. London: John Watkins, 1960.

———. *The 'Key' of Jacob Boehme, with an Illustration of the Deep Principles of Jacob Behmen by D. A. Freher*. Translated by William Law, with an introductory essay by Adam McLean. Grand Rapids, Mich.: Phanes Press, 1991.

————. *The Signature of All Things.* Translated by John Ellistone, with an introduction by Clifford Bax. Cambridge: James Clarke, 1969.

————. *The Works of Jacob Behmen.* Edited by G. Ward and T. Langcake. 4 vols. London: M. Richardson, 1764–81.

Breasted, Barbara. "*Comus* and the Castlehaven Scandal." *Milton Studies* 3 (1971): 201–24.

Bryant, Jacob. *A New System, or an Analysis of Ancient Mythology.* 3 vols. London: Payne, Elmsley, White and Walter, 1774–76.

Burke, Edmund. *Reflections on the French Revolution.* Edited by W. Alison Philips. Cambridge: Cambridge University Press, 1929.

Butlin, Martin. *The Paintings and Drawings of William Blake.* 2 vols. New Haven: Yale University Press, 1981.

Chaucer, Geoffery. *Complete Works.* Edited by W. W. Skeat. London: Oxford University Press, 1912.

Chayes, Irene H. "The Marginal Design on *Jerusalem* 12." *Blake Studies* 7 (1974): 51–77.

Coleridge, Samuel Taylor. *Biographia Literaria.* Edited by George Watson. London: J. M. Dent, 1975.

Cowper, William. *Poetical Works.* Edited by H. S. Milford. 4th ed. Revised by Norma Russell. London: Oxford University Press, 1967.

Curran, Stuart. "Blake and the Gnostic Hyle: A Double Negative." *Blake Studies* 4 (1972): 117–33.

Damon, S. Foster. "Blake and Milton." In *The Divine Vision: Studies in the Poetry and Art of William Blake,* edited by Vivian de Sola Pinto. London: Victor Gollancz, 1957.

————. *A Blake Dictionary.* London: Thames and Hudson, 1965.

Damrosch, Leopold, Jr. *Symbol and Truth in Blake's Myth.* Princeton, N.J.: Princeton University Press, 1980.

De Luca, V. A. "Proper Names in the Structural Design of Blake's Myth-Making." *Blake Studies* 8 (1978): 5–22.

de Sola Pinto, Vivian, ed. *The Divine Vision: Studies in the Poetry and Art of William Blake.* London: Victor Gollancz, 1957.

de Tervarent, Guy. "Attributs et symboles dans l'art profane 1450–1600." *Travaux d'humanisme et renaissance* 29 (1958): 304–5.

Donne, John. *The Complete English Poems.* Edited by A. J. Smith. Harmondsworth: Penguin Books, 1971.

Dunbar, Pamela. *William Blake's Illustrations to the Poetry of Milton.* Oxford: Clarendon Press, 1980.

Erdman, David V. *Blake: Prophet against Empire.* 3d ed. Princeton, N.J.: Princeton University Press, 1977.

————, ed. *Blake and His Bibles.* West Cornwall, Conn.: Locust Hill Press, 1990.

Erdman, David, and John E. Grant, eds. *Blake's Visionary Forms Dramatic.* Princeton, N.J.: Princeton University Press, 1970.

Erdman, David, and Cettina Tramontano Magno, eds. *Blake's The Four Zoas: A Photographic Facsimile of the Manuscript with Commentary on the Illustrations.* Lewisburg, Pa.: Bucknell University Press, 1987.

Essick, Robert N. "*Preludium:* Meditations on a Fiery Pegasus." In *Blake in His Time,* edited by Robert N. Essick and Donald Pearce, pp. 1–10. Bloomington: Indiana University Press, 1978.

————. *William Blake and the Language of Adam.* Oxford: Clarendon Press, 1989.

Essick, Robert N., and Donald Pearce, eds. *Blake in His Time.* Bloomington: Indiana University Press, 1978.

Fisch, Harold. "Blake's Miltonic Moment." In *William Blake: Essays for S. Foster Damon,* edited by Alvin Rosenfeld, pp. 36–56. Providence, R.I.: Brown University Press, 1969.

Fisher, Peter. "Blake and the Druids." *Journal of English and Germanic Philology* 58 (1959): 589–612.

————. *The Valley of Vision: Blake as Prophet and Revolutionary.* Toronto: University of Toronto Press, 1961.

Fox, Susan. "The Female as Metaphor in William Blake's Poetry." *Critical Inquiry* 3 (1976–77): 507–19.

————. *Poetic Form in Blake's "Milton."* Princeton, N.J.: Princeton University Press, 1976.

Franson, John Karl, ed. *Milton Reconsidered: Essays in Honor of Arthur E. Barker.* Salzburg: Institüt für Englische Sprache und Literatür, 1976.

Freed, Eugenie R. "'Sunclad Chastity' and Blake's 'Maiden Queens': *Comus, Thel,* and 'The Angel,'" *Blake / An Illustrated Quarterly* 25 (1991–92): 104–16.

French, J. Milton, comp. and ed. *The Life Records of John Milton.* 5 vols. New Brunswick, N.J.: Rutgers University Press, 1948–58.

Frye, Northrop. *Fearful Symmetry.* Princeton, N.J.: Princeton University Press, 1947.

———. "Notes for a Commentary on *Milton*." In *The Divine Vision . . .* , edited by Vivian de Sola Pinto, pp. 99–137. London: Victor Gollancz, 1957.

———. *Spiritus Mundi: Essays on Literature, Myth and Society.* Bloomington, Ind.: Fitzhenry & Whiteside, 1976.

Fuller, David. *Blake's Heroic Argument* London: Croom Helm, 1988.

Gardner, Helen, ed. *The Metaphysical Poets.* Harmondsworth: Penguin Books, 1972.

Gardner, Stanley. *Blake.* London: Evans Brothers, 1968.

George, Diana Hume. "'Is She Also the Divine Image?': Feminine Form in the Art of William Blake." *Centennial Review* 22 (1979): 129–40.

George, M. D. *London Life in the 18th Century.* Harmondsworth: Penguin Books, 1966.

Gleckner, Robert E. *Blake and Spenser.* Baltimore: Johns Hopkins University Press, 1985.

Grant, John E. "The Female Awakening at the End of Blake's *Milton*." In *Milton Reconsidered: Essays in Honor of Arthur E. Barker,* edited by John Karl Franson, pp. 78–99. Salzburg: Institüt für Englische Sprache und Literatür, 1976.

Grimes, Ronald L. *The Divine Imagination: William Blake's Major Prophetic Visions.* Metuchen, N.J.: Scarecrow Press, 1972.

Harper, George Mills. *The Neoplatonism of William Blake.* Chapel Hill: University of North Carolina Press, 1961.

———. "The Odyssey of the Soul in Blake's *Jerusalem*." *Blake Studies* 5 (1974): 65–80.

Hayley, William. *The Life of Milton.* 2d ed. London: Cadell & Davies, 1796; rprt. with an introduction by J. A. Wittreich, Jr. Gainesville, Fla.: Scholars' Facsimiles and Reprints, 1970.

The Holy Bible. King James Version. 1611. New York: American Bible Society, 1962.

The Holy Scriptures of the Old Testament, Hebrew and English. London: British & Foreign Bible Society, 1963.

Horn, William Dennis. "Blake's Revisionism: Gnostic Interpretation and Critical Methodology." In *Blake and the Argument of Method,* edited by Dan Miller, Mark Bracher, and Donald Ault, pp. 72–98. Durham, N.C.: Duke University Press, 1987.

Johnson, Mary Lynn. "'Separating what has been Mixed': A Suggestion for a Perspective on *Milton*." *Blake Studies* 6 (1973): 11–17.

Jung, C. J. *An Account of the Transference Phenomena Based on the Illustrations to the "Rosarium Philosophorum."* In *Collected Works,* edited by Herbert Read, Michael Fordham, and Gerhard Adler, 16:203–340. Bollingen Series 20. New York: Pantheon, 1954.

Kauvar, Elaine. "Los's Messenger to Eden: Blake's Wild Thyme." *Blake Newsletter* 10 (1976): 82–84.

Keynes, Geoffrey, and E. Wolf 2nd, *William Blake's Illuminated Books: A Census,* New York: 1953.

Klonsky, Milton. *William Blake: The Seer and His Visions.* London: Orbis Publishing, 1977.

Koyré, Alexandre. *La Philosophie de Jacob Boehme.* Paris: J. Vrin, 1929.

Lincoln, Andrew. "*The Four Zoas:* The Text of Pages 5, 6, & 7, Night the First." *Blake / An Illustrated Quarterly* 12 (1978): 91–95.

Margoliouth, H. M., ed. *Vala, Blake's Numbered Text.* Oxford: Clarendon Press, 1951.

Marks, Mollyanne. "Self-sacrifice: Theme and Image in *Jerusalem*." *Blake Studies* 7 (1974): 27–50.

Marlowe, Christopher. *Dr. Faustus.* Edited by Roma Gill. London: Ernest Benn, 1965.

Mellor, Anne K. "Blake's Portrayal of Women." *Blake / An Illustrated Quarterly* 16 (1982–83): 148–55.

The Metaphysical Poets. Selected and edited by Helen Gardner. Hardmondsworth: Penguin Books, 1972.

Miller, Dan, Mark Bracher, and Donald Ault, eds. *Blake and the Argument of Method.* Durham, N.C.: Duke University Press, 1987.

Milton, John. *The Poems of John Milton.* Edited by John Carey and Alistair Fowler. London: Longmans, Green, 1968.

———. *Selected Prose.* Edited by C. A. Patrides. Harmondsworth: Penguin Books, 1974.

Mitchell, W. J. T. "Style and Iconography in the Illustrations of Blake's *Milton*." *Blake Studies* 6 (1973): 47–71.

Murray, E. B. "*Jerusalem* Reversed." *Blake Studies* 7 (1974): 11–25.

Nelms, Ben F. "'Exemplars of Memory and of Intellect': *Jerusalem,* Plates 96–100." *Blake Studies* 5 (1974): 81–91.

Nurmi, Martin K. *William Blake.* London: Hutchinson, 1975.

Ostriker, Alicia. "Desire Gratified and Ungratified: William Blake and Sexuality." *Blake / An Illustrated Quarterly* 16 (1982–83): 156–65.

Otway, Thomas. *Complete Works*. Edited by J. C. Ghosh. Oxford: Clarendon Press, 1932.

The Oxford Dictionary of Quotations. 2d ed. London: Oxford University Press, 1953.

The Oxford English Dictionary. Oxford: Clarendon Press, 1933.

Paley, Morton D. *The Continuing City: William Blake's "Jerusalem."* Oxford: Clarendon Press, 1983.

———. *Energy and the Imagination*. Oxford: Clarendon Press, 1970.

Palgrave, Francis T., ed. *The Golden Treasury*. London: Oxford University Press, 1941.

Pearce, Donald. "Natural Religion and the Plight of Thel." *Blake Studies* 8 (1979): 23–35.

Pierce, John B. "The Shifting Characterization of Tharmas and Enion in Pages 3–7 of Blake's *Vala or The Four Zoas*." *Blake / An Illustrated Quarterly* 22 (1988–89): 93–102.

Piercy, Marge. *A Woman on the Edge of Time*. New York: Alfred Knopf, 1976.

Priestley, Joseph. *The Theological and Miscellaneous Works of Joseph Priestley,* ed. John T. Rutt. London: Smallfield, 1817–32.

Raine, Kathleen. "Berkeley, Blake and the New Age." In *Blake and the New Age,* 151–79. London: George Allen & Unwin, 1979.

———. *Blake and the New Age*. London: George Allen & Unwin, 1979.

———. *Blake and Tradition*. Bollingen Series 35.11. 2 vols. Princeton, N.J.: Princeton University Press, 1968.

———. *William Blake*. London: Thames and Hudson, 1970.

Reiman, Donald H. and Christina Shuttleworth Krause. "The Derivation and Meaning of 'Ololon.'" *Blake / An Illustrated Quarterly* 16 (1982): 82–85.

Rose, Edward J. "Blake's Hand: Symbol and Design in *Jerusalem*." *Texas Studies in Literature and Language* 6 (1954): 47–58.

———. "Blake's Metaphorical States." *Blake Studies* 4 (1971): 9–31.

Rosenfeld, Alvin H. ed. *William Blake: Essays for S. Foster Damon*. Providence, R.I.: Brown University Press, 1969.

Rossky, W. "Imagination in the English Renaissance: Psychology and Poetic." *Studies in the Renaissance* 5 (1958): 49–53.

Rowlands, Henry. *Mona Antiqua Restaurata: An Archaeological Discourse on the Antiquities, Natural and Historical, of the ISLE OF ANGLESEY, the Ancient Seat of the British Druids*. 2d ed. London, 1766.

Sandler, Florence. "The Iconoclastic Enterprise: Blake's Critique of 'Milton's Religion.'" *Blake Studies* 5 (1972): 13–57.

Scholem, Gershom G. *Kabbalah*. Jerusalem: Keter Publishing Publishing House, 1988.

———. *On the Kabbalah and Its Symbolism*. Translated by Ralph Mannheim. New York: Schocken Books, 1969.

Schorer, Mark. *William Blake: The Politics of Vision*. New York: Henry Holt, 1946; rprt. New York: Knopf, 1959.

Shakespeare, William. *The Complete Works*. Edited by Peter Alexander. London: Collins, 1951.

Singer, June. *The Unholy Bible: Blake, Jung and the Collective Unconscious*. Boston: Sigo Press, 1986.

Spector, Sheila A. "Blake as an Eighteenth-Century Hebraist." In *Blake and His Bibles,* edited by David V. Erdman, pp. 179–229. West Cornwall, Conn.: Locust Hill Press, 1990.

———. "Kabbalistic Sources—Blake's and His Critics.'" *Blake / An Illustrated Quarterly* 17 (1983–84): 84–101.

———. "The Reasons for Urizen." *Blake / An Illustrated Quarterly* 21 (1988): 147–49.

Spenser, Edmund. *The Faerie Queene*. Edited by A. C. Hamilton. London: Longman Group, 1977.

———. *Poetical Works*. Edited by J. C. Smith and E. de Selincourt. London: Oxford University Press, 1970.

Swedenborg, Emmanuel. *Divine Love and Wisdom*. Anonymous translation. Amsterdam, 1763; rprt., London: Swedenborg Society, 1987.

———. *Divine Love and Wisdom*. Translated by Clifford Harley and Doris Harley. London: Swedenborg Society, 1969.

———. *Heaven and Its Wonders and Hell*. Translated by J. C. Ager. Revised by Doris Harley. London: Swedenborg Society, 1958.

———. *The New Jerusalem and Its Heavenly Doctrine*. Translated by E. C. Mongredien. Revised by Doris Harley. London: Swedenborg Society, 1972.

———. *The Wisdom of Angels Concerning Divine Providence*. Anonymous translation. London, 1790.

Tarr, Rodger L. ";The Eagle' versus 'The Mole': The Wisdom of Virginity in *Comus* and *The Book of Thel*." *Blake Studies* 3 (1971): 187–94.

Tayler, Irene. "Blake's *Comus* Designs." *Blake Studies* 4 (1972): 45–80.

Taylor, Dena Bain. "The Visual Context of 'Joseph of Arimathea among the Rocks of Albion,'" *Blake / An Illustrated Quarterly* 20 (1986): 47–48.

Tolley, Michael J. "*Europe*: 'To those ychain'd in Sleep.'" In *Blake's Visionary Forms Dramatic,* edited by David Erdman and John E. Grant, pp. 115–45. Princeton, N.J.: Princeton University Press, 1970.

Vaughan, Thomas. *Lumen de Lumine, or a New Magical Light,* ed. Arthur Edward Waite. London: 1651; rpr. London: Watkins, 1910.

Wagenknecht David. *Blake's Night: William Blake and the Idea of Pastoral.* Cambridge, Mass.: Belknap Press of Harvard University Press, 1973.

Webster, Brenda S. "Blake, Women and Sexuality." In *Blake and the Argument of Method,* edited by Dan Miller, Mark Bracher, and Donald Ault, 204–24. Durham, N.C. Duke University Press, 1987.

Werner, Bette Charlotte. *Blake's Vision of the Poetry of Milton.* Lewisburg, Pa.: Bucknell University Press, 1986.

Wicksteed, Joseph. *William Blake's "Jerusalem."* London: Trianon Press, 1954.

Wilkie, Brian, and Mary Lynn Johnson. *Blake's Four Zoas: The Design of a Dream.* Cambridge, Mass.: Harvard University Press, 1978.

Winkler, Gershon. *The Golem of Prague.* New York: Judaica Press, 1980.

Witke, Joanna. "*Jerusalem*: A Synoptic Poem." *Comparative Literature* 22 (1970): 265–78.

———. *William Blake's Epic: Imagination Unbound.* London: Croom Helm, 1986.

Wittreich, Joseph Anthony, Jr. *Angel of Apocalypse: Blake's Idea of Milton.* Madison: University of Wisconsin Press, 1975.

———. "Painted Prophecies: The Tradition of Blake's Illuminated Books." In *Blake in His Time,* edited by Robert N. Essick and Donald Pearce, pp. 101–15. Bloomington: Indiana University Press, 1978.

———. "'Sublime Allegory': Blake's Epic Manifesto and the Milton Tradition." *Blake Studies* 4 (1972): 15–44.

———. "William Blake: Illustrator-Interpreter of *Paradise Regained*." In *Calm of Mind . . .,* edited by J. A. Wittreich, Jr., pp. 93–132. Cleveland: Press of Case Western Reserve University, 1971.

———, ed. *Calm of Mind: Tercentenary Essays on "Paradise Regained" and "Samson Agonistes" in Honor of John S. Diekhoff.* Cleveland: Press of Case Western Reserve University, 1971.

Wordsworth, William. *The Poetical Works,* ed. Ernest De Selincourt, rev. Helen Darbishire. 5 vols. Oxford: Oxford University Press, 1952–59.

Wyatt, David M. "The Woman Jerusalem: *Pictura* versus *Poesis*." *Blake Studies* 7 (1975): 105–24.

Index

Titles of books are indicated by *italics*. Illustrations in black and white are indicated by page numbers in **bold type.** Color illustrations are indicated by the words *color plate* in italics.

Blake's works are listed by their titles, except for those in his *Notebook,* which appear under his name, as do references to his Letters. Milton's works are listed by their titles.